hi *Trionfali fatti nelle Reali & feliciffime nozze del Ser.mo Prencipe di Mant.a*
tura di Gabriele Bertazzolo Ingegnero, delle Alt. Ser.me di Mant.a l'anno i 60

Federico Follino, *Compendio delle sontuose feste fatte l'anno M.DC.VIII nella*
antua, 1608)

The
Monteverdi Companion

Portrait of Monteverdi in his later years by Bernardo Strozzi (1581–1644)

THE MONTEVERDI COMPANION

edited by

DENIS ARNOLD

and

NIGEL FORTUNE

W. W. NORTON & COMPANY INC

New York

First American Edition 1968
Printed in Great Britain

The Contributors

DENIS ARNOLD
Senior Lecturer in Music, University of Hull

NIGEL FORTUNE
Senior Lecturer in Music, University of
Birmingham

CLAUDE V. PALISCA
Professor of Music, Yale University

JEROME ROCHE
Lecturer in Music, University of Durham

DENIS STEVENS
Professor of Music, Columbia University,
New York;
President and Artistic Director, Accademia
Monteverdiana

ROBERT DONINGTON
Professor of Music, University of Iowa

JANET E. BEAT
Lecturer in Music, Worcester College of Education

Contents

Illustrations

Acknowledgments

We are grateful to Mr Cecil Clough, Mr D. G. Rees and Mr J. A. Gatt-Rutter for help and advice over knotty problems in the translating of the letters; and to the Conservatorio G. B. Martini, Bologna, for help in sending microfilms. We thank Mr O. W. Neighbour and the Victoria and Albert Museum, London, for help with the plates.

We are indebted to the following for permission to reproduce the material indicated: the Director of the Tiroler Landesmuseum Ferdinandeum (frontispiece); the Director of the Archivio di Stato, Mantua (plate 1); the Trustees of the Victoria and Albert Museum (plate 6); Universal Edition (musical examples taken from the complete edition of Monteverdi's works edited by G. Francesco Malipiero); and Schocken Books Inc., New York (the quotation from Bernard Berenson on p. 99).

DENIS ARNOLD
NIGEL FORTUNE

Preface

This book is not meant to be a comprehensive account of Monteverdi's life and works. What it sets out to do is to study certain aspects of his music and environment which have been insufficiently stressed in most of the existing books about him and to offer fresh views about some of his more familiar works. Monteverdi is still too often thought of as a revolutionary who single-handed overthrew the principles governing the composition of music for generations past, to become — in the words of the sub-title of one of the best books about him — the 'creator of modern music'. It is, on the contrary, one of the main aims of several chapters in the present book to relate his achievement to the music and ideas of his elders and contemporaries, to illustrate how much he learned from them, and to show how gradual, in the case of the madrigals, for example, was the infiltration into his music of new procedures and principles. In this way, we hope that we have been able to add something new to the store of knowledge of music in Monteverdi's time.

We have prefaced the chapters with an account of Monteverdi's life, as seen in the most direct way, through his letters. A comprehensive English edition of these is long overdue, and indeed is in active preparation. In the meantime, the translation of some forty letters (about a third of the total) should be valuable on its own account and is certainly necessary for the illumination of the essays which follow. The commentary which links the letters attempts to elucidate some of the obscurities in Monteverdian biography; if much still remains to be done in the archives of Mantua and Venice, detail of this kind seems to us very necessary if a definitive life of Monteverdi is eventually to be written.

Preface

Finally, we have attempted to provide a more comprehensive Monteverdi bibliography than has hitherto appeared. The excellent bibliography of Leo Schrade is, of course, now nearly twenty years out of date, and the need for a guide to the multifarious editions of the music which are currently available has been expressed to the editors by many musicians. While an evaluation of these would demand by itself an extended essay, we hope that a simple elucidation of the facts will be of some help to those wishing to perform Monteverdi's music.

DENIS ARNOLD
NIGEL FORTUNE

I

The Man as seen through his Letters

———

DENIS ARNOLD and NIGEL FORTUNE

The Man as seen through his Letters

INTRODUCTION

It is rare for a composer before the later eighteenth century to leave behind any substantial evidence of his life and character. Monteverdi is happily an exception. At least 120 of his letters survive, in addition to the formal documents that normally form the raw material for the biography of a musician of that time. Moreover, many of these letters are fascinating. Some were written in heat to a former employer whom he considered to have been unappreciative of his merits; some were written under stress when his elder son was thrown into prison; others are business letters in which he shows a shrewd and practical approach to his art. Between them they provide a vivid picture of the man.

The vast majority of the letters were printed by Gian Francesco Malipiero in his *Claudio Monteverdi* (Milan, 1929). Since then, just enough new material has come to light to make the modern scholar suspect that a systematic search in Italian archives would yield still more invaluable documents. Such a search must necessarily be time-consuming, but until it has been undertaken it will be impossible to publish a definitive edition or definitive translation of his letters. In view of the fact that this search may be undertaken in connection with the new edition of Monteverdi's works it has seemed best to avoid duplicating future research by attempting such a task at this time.

Instead we have decided to base the translations that follow on Malipiero's edition. From this we have chosen some forty letters in which the composer's ideas, methods and approach to composition and other musical matters are clearly revealed; in addition we have included one or two others which are of human or sociological interest (e.g. No. 7). Except for a few extracts in books on the composer, this is the first attempt to provide a version of Monteverdi's letters for the English reader. It must be said that Malipiero's text leaves much to be desired. There are some obvious mistakes, as can be seen, for example, by a comparison of his two printings of the letter that we have translated as No. 11, which contain one discrepancy serious and misleading enough to make one suspect comparable errors in places where the text seems to be corrupt. It must also be said that Monteverdi is not always clear himself and that professional Italian scholars have found his meaning to be frequently ambiguous. However, since Malipiero's edition can be consulted by any interested scholar, we have not felt it necessary to indicate the various possible meanings at such places and have tried to convey what seems to us to be Monteverdi's likeliest intentions; in one or two instances, though, we have added explanatory footnotes. Our decision on this problem has occasionally involved us in a rather free translation — but not, we hope, in the paraphrases that can be found in certain books on the composer that attempt the same task.

All of Monteverdi's letters begin and (especially) end with elaborate formal compliments, since he was almost invariably writing to his patrons and social superiors. To read these elegant but empty phrases in one letter might be amusing; to repeat them in forty would be tedious in the extreme. We have therefore omitted them, though we have always retained the formal, rather stilted references to 'His Highness' and 'Your Excellency' and similar expressions with which his correspondence is peppered. The dates, and the places from which the letters were written, generally occur at the end; to make the sequence of events clearer we have placed them at the head of the letters in modernized form. The paragraphing is normally ours. We have also linked the letters with a commentary; anything that needs explaining in a letter will normally be found in the commentary preceding it.

Finally, a word about coinage, which is frequently referred to. Values varied widely in the Italy of Monteverdi's day. It is not really practicable to offer modern equivalents. The ducat was relatively constant and probably equalled six *lire*, four *soldi*; a *lira* was worth twenty *soldi*, and the *soldo* twelve *denari*. The *scudo* was a debased gold coin on average worth about five *lire*.

The Letters

Monteverdi's first surviving letter dates from as late as his thirty-fifth year, when he had already been more than ten years in the service of the court of the Gonzagas at Mantua, had published six volumes of music of various kinds and, as this letter shows, had also composed masses and motets which he had not published. Duke Vincenzo I, the recipient of the first two letters in the present selection, had clearly not considered Monteverdi's claims to direct his entire musical establishment as strong enough on Giaches de Wert's death, which took place in 1596 at about the time of Monteverdi's twenty-ninth birthday. The post went to Benedetto Pallavicino, an interesting minor composer, who was almost certainly more experienced; although Monteverdi was clearly upset at being passed over, the Duke's decision is perfectly understandable. By 1601 Monteverdi was in a stronger position to succeed to the coveted post, which in fact he did within a few months of the date of this letter.

The other two composers mentioned in this letter were prominent at the Mantuan court: Francesco Rovigo (d. 1597); and Alessandro Striggio (c. 1535–87), the father of the recipient of many of Monteverdi's letters and an instrumentalist and composer of church music and madrigals who also for a time served the Medici in Florence.

1 (*Malipiero 1, p. 127*) To The Duke of Mantua, at Canisa

Mantua, 28 November 1601

On the occasion of Pallavicino's recent death I hasten to appeal personally to Your Highness's goodwill and to apply for his position of director of music, which was once held also by Signor Giaches [de Wert]. For did I not do so the envy of others might, through words rather than music, work against me to my cost by tarnishing the good opinion that Your Highness has of me.

They might suggest that my ability was somewhat in doubt or that I thought a little too much of myself and was therefore ambitiously waiting for a post for which, as a humble servant, I should be applying with particular humility and affection. Likewise, if I did not seek an opportunity of serving Your Highness further, you would have every right to complain that I was a negligent servant and that moreover I had no eye for favourable opportunities if I did not seek readier means of submitting more of my motets and masses to your excellent musical judgment. Finally, the world has seen how zealously I have served Your Highness and how considerate you have been to me after the death of the famous Signor Striggio, then after that of the excellent Signor Giaches, thirdly after that of the excellent Signor Franceschino [Rovigo] and lastly after that of the capable Master Benedetto Pallavicino. So if I failed to seek — not because of my merit but of the faithful and particular devotion that I have always given in Your Highness's service — the place now vacant in the chapel, and if after all this I did not ask for it humbly and very insistently, people would rightly call me negligent.

For all the foregoing reasons, therefore, and especially because, to my good fortune (which your kindness could increase), you have never disdained to hear my feeble compositions, I humbly apply to become director of music in your chamber and chapel. If your goodness and graciousness make me worthy of it I shall receive it with that humility becoming a modest servant when he is favoured and gratified by a great prince such as Your Highness...

Although Monteverdi did not publish any music between 1592 and 1603 the following letter suggests that he must frequently have been occupied in this period with the composition of occasional music, as he is known to have been throughout the rest of his career. A great deal of it, including the ballet here referred to, has been lost. This letter is also the first to reveal that preoccupation with his health which is a feature of so many of his subsequent letters.

2 (*Malipiero 3, p. 131*)   To The Duke of Mantua

Cremona, December 1604

Ten days ago the courier brought a letter from Your Highness commanding me to compose two *entrées*, one for stars following the moon, the other for shepherds following Endymion; and likewise two ballets, one just for the stars, the other for the stars and shepherds together. And so with an ardent desire to obey and execute promptly Your Highness's commands (as I have always done and always will do until I die), I set to work first of all on the music for the stars. But your instructions did not say how many dancers there are to be. I wanted to alternate the dances, since it seems to me that this would have been original, attractive and agreeable. Thus, to begin with, all the instruments would play a short, lively air, danced likewise by all the stars. Then suddenly the five *viole da braccio* would start up a different air, while the other instruments remained silent; this would be danced by only two stars while the others rested. After this *pas de deux* all the instruments and stars would repeat the first air. I would continue with this arrangement until all the stars had danced, two by two. But as I have not been told the total number, which it is vital for me to know (subject to Your Highness's approval of an alternating type of invention such as I have described), I have put this work to one side until I do know it. To find out about it I have written to Master Giovanni Battista the dancing-master, and he can let me know the exact number through my brother.

In the mean time I have composed the ballet for shepherds and stars, which I am now sending to Your Highness. I have written it, My Lord, with that accustomed passion, and lively desire to further it, that has always been mine and always will be, although at present I lack the energy to work as assiduously as I have in the past. For I still feel tired and weak from recent overwork, and, though I am a little better, neither through medicine, nor going on a diet nor even putting my work on one side have I regained my usual strength. I nevertheless hope in the Lord to recover completely (God willing), and I beseech Your Highness now that for the love of God you never again give me so much to do at one time nor allow me so short a time to do it; otherwise I shall have an unexpectedly short life instead of being able to serve Your Highness longer and to help my poor sons. And so, My Lord, if Your Highness feels that you have on this occasion been served by me neither so well nor so quickly as perhaps you expected and as I desired (as I always have), do not blame my will nor my spirit, since both of them will always be very pleased to undertake whatever Your Highness may choose to command them...

On 10 September 1607 Monteverdi's wife Claudia died, leaving him to bring up two sons. During the winter of 1607–8 he was given little time to dwell on his misery, however, since he had to provide music for the elaborate festivities planned for the early summer of 1608 to mark the marriage of Prince Francesco, heir to the Gonzaga succession, to the Infanta Margherita of Savoy. This music included *Arianna* and *Il Ballo dell'Ingrate*; he had to write both of these major works against time, a fact he remembered for many years. His preoccupation with his health is now reinforced by what was to become almost an obsession about his pay and what he obviously considered to be the shabby treatment accorded him by the Gonzagas. It is interesting to find that he was given an income in money, for it had been the custom at Mantua, in the past at least, to supplement pay with offerings in kind. This can be seen from a pay-sheet in the Gonzaga Archives (Busta 395) drawn up at an unknown date during Wert's time as *maestro di cappella* and which includes the following payments (the significance of the actual amounts is not known):

	Bread	Rolls	Veal	Beef	Fish	Salt	Oil	Candles	Bacon	Cooking cheese	Money
Wert	2–4	—	2	2	4	2	2	2	—	—	45.0.0
Pallavicino	1–2	—	2	—	2	—	—	2	—	—	12.12.0
Marinoni	2–4	—	4	—	4	2	—	2	—	—	13.19.0

The 'usual provisions' that Monteverdi says Orazio della Viola received were no doubt of this nature.

To stress his unfortunate plight Monteverdi had also gone to the trouble of investigating the incomes of other composers — not only two who had worked at Mantua (Rovigo and the singer-composer Ippolito Fiorino) but also four famous ones who had not. He also rather airily runs down Marco da Gagliano's contribution to the wedding festivities: the eminent Florentine did after all compose a ballet and one of the *intermezzi* for a play by Giovanni Battista Guarini, *Idropica,* and earlier in the year had helped to produce in Mantua his opera *Dafne,* which seems to have been imported to some extent to ensure the performance there of at least one opera that year in case Monteverdi did not finish *Arianna* in time.

Follino was court chronicler and friend of Monteverdi. The recipient of the letter, Annibale Chieppo (Chieppio), was one of the principal administrators at court.

3 (*Malipiero 6, p. 135*) To Annibale Chieppo, Counsellor at the Mantuan Court

Cremona, 2 December 1608

Today, the last day of November, I have received a letter from Your Excellency from which I learn that His Highness commands me to return to Mantua as soon as possible, excellent Signor Chieppo, in order to work on an attractive new commission. I must say, though, that if I do not have a rest from working at music for the theatre my life will surely be short. For from my recent hard labours I have developed a bad head, and itching all over my body which burns so fiercely that neither by applying cauteries and taking medicines, nor by blood-letting and other drastic remedies, have I got more than slightly better. My father attributes my bad head to overwork, and the itching to the Mantuan air, which does not suit me, and suspects that the air alone will soon be the death of me.

Now, Your Excellency, consider what would be the effect of the further work that His Highness has thus commanded if I am to receive thanks and favours from His Highness's kindness and goodness. I must tell Your Excellency that my experience of Mantua during nineteen successive years has led me to regard it not as friendly but as unfriendly. For while I was pleased and honoured to be able to serve His Highness the Duke in Hungary I was displeased at incurring such great expense that our poor household still feels the effects of that journey. I was also called upon to serve His Highness in Flanders, but that journey was no more rewarding, since Signora Claudia, who stayed at Cremona, had to bear our household expenses, including a servant and a maid, at a time when she had only 47 *lire* a month from His Highness plus some money my father gave me afterwards. This gave me an opportunity to get the Duke to increase the allowance of twelve-and-a-half Mantuan *scudi* to 25 *scudi* a month, but even this had its black side in that the Duke later decided to send word by Federico Follino that out of this increase it was intended that I pay expenses to Signor Campagnolo, who was then still a boy. Because I did not want any trouble I agreed to set aside five *scudi* a month for this purpose; I was therefore left with twenty.

I was favoured when the Duke asked me last year for music for the marriage celebrations, but again it was not a very happy occasion, for I had to work almost impossibly hard, and I suffered as well from the cold, the livery and my servile position; I almost did not have enough to eat, with the loss of the allowance to Signora Claudia, and I contracted a serious illness. I was never favoured by His Highness with any public acknowledgment, but Your Excellency well knows that servants appreciate marks of favour, both to their honour and to their advantage, from great princes, particularly in front of strangers. Though they made me have a new livery from His Highness to wear at the time of the marriage celebrations this also had drawbacks, for it was made of a mixture of silk and floss-silk, and it did not include an overcoat, fine stockings, a sword-belt and silk lining for the cloak; and I had to spend on it twenty of my own Mantuan *scudi*. If His Highness has shown me favours from time to time there has been the disadvantage that whenever he has spoken to me it has been to make me work and never to make me a little happier or better-off. And if, finally (to cut a long story short), His Highness has favoured me in giving me to believe that I should receive a fee of 100 Mantuan *scudi* for acting as master of ceremonies in the piazza,[1] it was a mark of disfavour that when the wedding was

[1] This is a possible interpretation, relating to the wedding celebrations already mentioned, of the unclear original, 'sopra al capitaniato della piazza'.

over the 100 *scudi* had shrunk to 70, with the loss of the fee for the commission and of my income for these past months. It was almost as if they thought that 100 *scudi* was too much. Added to the twenty *scudi* that I have at present, that makes about 22 *ducatoni* a month, which, had I received them, I would have used to provide for my poor sons.

Orazio della Viola would have had to work very hard to earn an income of 500 *scudi* a year without the usual provisions[1] if he had had only what I have had each month; Luca Marenzio likewise would have had to work extremely hard, and Philippe de Monte too, and Palestrina, who left his sons an income of more than 1,000 *scudi*; Luzzaschi and Fiorino would have had to work very hard to achieve an income of 300 *scudi* each and leave something to their sons; finally, to mention no more examples, Franceschino Rovigo would have had to work very hard for his income of 700 *scudi* if he had had only what I have had. This income is barely enough to keep a servant and clothe him, let alone two sons as well, as I have. So, Your Excellency, if I must draw conclusions from the facts I will say that I never receive thanks nor favours at Mantua but will hope rather that I have come to the end of my ill-fortune. I know very well that His Highness the Duke is very well disposed towards me, and I know that he is a most liberal prince, but I am too hard done by at Mantua, as Your Excellency will see from this account. I know very well that on the death of Signora Claudia His Highness intended to leave me her pension. But when I got to Mantua he suddenly changed his mind, and thus to my misfortune this was not done. As a result I have up to now lost more than 200 *scudi,* and every day I go on losing them. So he resolved, as I have said above, to give me 25 *scudi* a month. Then lo! he suddenly changed his mind, to my misfortune, and reduced it by five. So, Your Excellency, you can see plainly that being at Mantua does me no good at all.

Do you wish, Your Excellency, for anything clearer: to give 200 *scudi* to Master Marco da Gagliano, who can be said to have done nothing, and nothing to me, who did all that I did? Knowing

[1] Cf. *supra*, p. 25.

this and how ill and unfortunate I am at Mantua, I beg you, most excellent Signor Chieppo, for the love of God, to help me obtain a favourable release from His Highness, for I know that this would be of great benefit to me. In his letter asking me to return from Cremona to Mantua last year to work on the marriage celebrations, Signor Don Federico Follino promised me what Your Excellency can read for yourself, since I am enclosing his letter; and then in the end nothing has been done, or rather what I have had is 1,500 lines of text to set to music. Dear sir, help me to a favourable release, for this seems to be the best possible thing for me: it will give me changes of air, work and fortune, and, heaven knows, I could not do worse than to stay poor as I am at Mantua. Wishing as I do for nothing but a favourable release from His Highness's service, I will do anything to obtain it.

I can assure Your Excellency that wherever I may be I shall beg favours of His Highness on your behalf and shall always remember you in my humble prayers to God: I could do no less, considering the favours and benefits I have so often received from the most excellent Signor Chieppo. You may be sure that I never think about such things without feeling ashamed at being in so miserable a state when I have received them. But even if my body is too weak, let me at least unite my mind and voice as I appeal to your boundless good nature and remain for ever obliged to Your Excellency...

Interrupted only by No. 6, there follows in the present selection a long series of letters addressed to Alessandro Striggio: he was the son of the composer mentioned in the first letter; the poet of, among other things, *Orfeo*; a prominent official at the Gonzagas' court and later (1622–1628) its Secretary; and a man of whom Monteverdi was clearly very fond and to whom in all probability he felt he could, if need be, write more frankly and spontaneously than he could to other personages at court.

The music mentioned in the first paragraph of Letter No. 4 cannot be identified. Like other letters the last paragraph of this one reveals that Monteverdi was required from time to time to report on potential recruits to the Mantuan musical staff. We have seen already that

Monteverdi was obsessed with the idea that he was paid too little: this paragraph also seems to show a parallel concern, almost comic in its directness, lest others inferior in status and accomplishment to himself be paid too much.

4 (*Malipiero 7, p. 139*) To Alessandro Stricci [Striggio], Counsellor at the Mantuan Court

Cremona, 24 August 1609

Yesterday, the 23rd, I received a letter from Your Excellency together with some words to set to music at His Highness's request. I shall get down to them as soon as I can, and when I have finished I will let Your Excellency know, or else bring the music to Mantua myself, because I want to come back to work shortly. I have decided to set them in the first place for a solo voice, and then if His Highness asks me to rework this aria for five voices I shall do so. I do not think there is anything more to say.

I hope, Your Excellency, that tomorrow, the 25th, my brother will receive copies of *Orfeo* straight from the printer, who will send them to him by the Venice courier due tomorrow. As soon as he receives them he will have one bound and send it to Your Excellency for the Prince. When you give it to him I beseech Your Excellency to accompany it with words that will signify my great desire to show him how very devoted and humble a servant I am and that I give little to His Highness (who deserves much) through ill-fortune and not through lack of affection.

I should also like to take this opportunity of letting His Highness know that I have spoken to those cornett- and trombone-players, as he asked me to, and they tell me they will come and serve His Highness on two conditions. One is that they would like His Highness to provide them with letters of introduction to the Count of Fontes or to the appropriate person, so that they can be paid certain wages due to them since the Count of Fontes went to Milan; I ought to tell Your Excellency that the wages are due to them for playing in the castle at Cremona. The other condition is that the father and two sons who play all wind instruments would like twelve *scudi* a month each. I am utterly against this and told them His Highness would offer up to eight. I think they would be satisfied with that, though they have said neither 'yes' nor 'no'. Because they are less proficient than these three, I think the other two should have lower wages. They play pretty well together and in a lively manner, both dance music and chamber music, because they practise every day. I will await your reply and will do what His Highness orders and no more. With this I will end...

In the next letter we see Monteverdi writing one of his reports, this time at much greater length and in a particularly lively manner. Giovanni Gastoldi (*c.* 1550–1622) had recently left Mantua, where he had been in charge of church music, to become *maestro di cappella* at Milan Cathedral, and Sirena was clearly being considered as his successor. In the event Sirena (1571/2 — after 1626) appears never to have served the Gonzagas after all but did rise to become *maestro di cappella* of Cremona Cathedral. Except for an isolated motet, he published nothing until 1626, when he brought out a collection of church music no doubt including some of the music to which Monteverdi here refers. It is typical of Monteverdi's insecurity at Mantua and of his suspicious character that he should have feared that Sirena's appointment might endanger his own position as director of *all* the music at Mantua, even though one would imagine that this was scarcely in the Duke's mind at this time.

5 (*Malipiero 8, p. 140*)　To Alessandro Striggio

Cremona, 10 September 1609

On the 9th I had a letter from Your Excellency enjoining me not to confirm the appointments of those wind-players without further instructions but to keep them hoping. This is what I have done and would have done without receiving further instructions; however, since I have received them, I shall be able to act more confidently. I told them three days ago: 'If the captain or governor of the castle knew you wanted to leave he would give you permission'. To this they replied that not only would he not give them permission but would put every obstacle in the way of their leaving. 'And if it came to the point, how would you leave?' They replied: 'We would go without saying anything'. I did not discuss the matter further. Your Excellency now knows the difficulties attending their departure.

On the 4th I also had a letter from His Highness the Prince written from Madorno. In it he mentions a certain Galeazzo Sirena, a composer and organist, and asks me if he would care to enter His Highness's service and for what salary, and would I tell His Highness whether he is capable and intelligent. I do in fact know this Galeazzo very well: indeed he comes to see me every day, so I know him intimately. As soon as I had this request I put it to him, and he replied unhesitatingly that it is not to his taste to go off and serve princes: he wants to settle in Milan as choirmaster at the Scala, and some of the Milanese singers have promised to make this position available for him. He says he would then be able to teach music for the civic authorities, compose for the convents, and make guitars and harpsichords for sale: thus he would hope to get rich quickly. To this I replied that I hoped he would think a little about what I had said and that if he did not want to enter His Highness's service at least he should let me know what excuse I should offer; I have seen him several times since but still have got nothing out of him. I have thought it best to tell Your Excellency the position so that you can inform His Highness. I want to wait until Galeazzo comes to a decision before writing to His Highness, but I am afraid that because of the delay His Highness will think me negligent in carrying out his orders.

I ought therefore to tell Your Excellency that Galeazzo is a poor man of thirty-seven, with a wife and children, a father who is a workman in the carriage and chair trade, and a mother who is much worse off, spinning in the mill all day long. He has an all-round talent, and when he applies himself does not do badly. He set about making a psaltery and a chitarrone and made a very good job of them; the same goes for a harpsichord and many other examples of his handiwork. He is certainly an able musician and he knows it; he is anxious that every product of his talent should be of the best, and he will be the first to praise them if others are slow to do so. Of his music I have heard only the following: parts of two eight-part masses — the *Kyrie* and *Gloria* of one, and the whole of the other except the *Sanctus* and *Agnus*, which he had still to compose; a *Credo* from another for four voices; a twelve-part *Dixit*; and some four-part *canzoni da sonare* for viols or wind instruments. These last are very well composed for the medium and show some originality. But though the masses and the *Dixit* sound well they are difficult to sing, since the parts are full of both canons and rests that overtire and annoy the singers. I am sure he would adapt himself to His Highness's demands, though I have not heard any stage music by him and do not wish to give the impression that he is experienced in this medium; however, I would expect him to succeed in it without much trouble. He has spent his life in the sphere of sacred music and has gladly put in plenty of hard work to master it.

Knowing him as a poor man who has a mind to be very rich and not being sure that he would entirely satisfy His Highness, I said to him: 'Because I know you wish to be well paid and because His Highness must know on whom he would be spending his money and it would not be difficult for me to invite you, why not come to Mantua on probation for three months and show what you can do? I will see that you are given a room, your keep and a little money besides, and thus you will be able to negotiate your contract.' To this he replied that he did not want to. I went on: 'You have published nothing, so there is no way of judging your ability; you neither wish to come on probation nor have you ever written music for the theatre: how then are we to decide about you with nothing to go on?' As Your Excellency will have realized, he has little tact, nor has he the ability to make himself liked by singers; although they respect him the singers here in Cremona do not like singing under him, and he freely speaks ill of strangers. His organ-playing is all right from the point of view of counterpoint, but he lacks manual dexterity and is unable to tackle *tirate* and *gruppi* and other ornaments. He admits to being unskilled, though he plays the organ at S. Agostino here in Cremona; but he does this because he is poor.

He asked me after two or three days what I would say to his coming to serve His Highness if His Highness wanted him as his *maestro di cappella* or in some other post. I said I did not know what His Highness had in mind. So, Signor Striggio, I thought I would write Your Excellency a few words about the matter, since I have an open mind about it. His Highness is an employer who does what he pleases and appears best. But if he accepts either him or anyone else as *maestro di cappella* — supposing he wishes to give him this title, which is something I do not know about — what in God's name would happen to me if His Highness the Duke were to die? And if he does appoint a *maestro di cappella* what does he want me to do now — leave Mantua? I should be obliged if Your Excellency would let me know, with that excellent skill that I know you to be more capable of commanding than I am of expressing, if such is His Highness's intention, so that I may know what to do.

Forgive me if I have written at too great length, but the blame lies with my ignorance, which has kept me from learning brevity ...

Cardinal Ferdinando Gonzaga, now 24, was Vincenzo I's second son and a future Duke. He was a good example of the more civilized prince of the period, passionately interested in the arts and — as we see from the following letter to him — a dilettante practitioner of at least one of them.

The contralto Adriana Basile, now aged about 30, was one of the most famous singers of her day; she was in the service of the Gonzagas from 1610 to 1616 and after 1623. The other singer named here cannot be identified for certain.

This is one of several letters in which Monteverdi shows his eager concern for his sons' advancement and well-being.

6 (*Malipiero 13, p. 151*) TO CARDINAL FERDINANDO GONZAGA

Mantua, 22 June 1611

I have just received Your Excellency's very kind letter together with your two beautiful madrigals. I have read and reread the letter, sung the madrigals over and over again and kissed all three time and again, all with extreme gratification: for I am sensible of the great kindness that Your Excellency shows towards a humble servant like me, who deserves nothing.

Every Friday evening we make music in the Hall of Mirrors. Signora Adriana [Basile] comes to sing in ensemble music and invests it with such power and striking beauty as to delight the senses and to turn the room almost into a new theatre. I am sure that before we come to the end of the festival of concerts His Highness the Duke will have to stand guard at the entrance: for I swear to Your Excellency that this last Friday there were in the audience not only Their Highnesses the Duke and Duchess, Signora Donna Isabella of San Martino, the Marquess and Marchioness of Solferino and knights and ladies from all parts of the court but also more than a hundred other people from the city. On another such splendid occasion I shall make the house-hold musicians play the chitarroni to the accompaniment of the wooden organ — a delightful sound. Signora Adriana and Don Giovanni Battista will sing the very beautiful madrigal *Ah, che morir mi sento* to these instruments, the other madrigal to the organ alone. Tomorrow I shall go and give the two pieces to Signora Adriana, and I know how much she will like them. I do not want to tell her the composer's name until she has sung them. I shall describe for Your Excellency the success of the whole affair.

I shall not fail to attend to the needs of Franceschino, my son and Your Excellency's most humble servant, and teach him three virtuous things: first, to serve God ardently and fearfully; second, the art of writing; and third, a little music: indeed he seems so far to have done very well at *trilli* and *gorgie*. I hope therefore that by means of Your Excellency's patronage he may obtain through God and His Holiness the grace I humbly pray for every day.

I do not know, excellent sir, if I would be too bold in beseech-ing you — now that the bishopric of Novara is vacant, with its income of 8,000 *scudi* — to be good enough to intercede in connection with the pension for my son that should pay him a dozen [*ducatoni?*], which must be worth at least 100 golden *scudi*. If I am in fact too forward in mentioning this, forgive me for the love of God, but if I could thus be favoured I should feel such peace of mind as if I had come by all the gold in the world. Dear sir, help me if possible through your boundless grace, acting, in doing me this favour, more in accord with your infinite kindness than with my merits; for I know full well that there is nothing in me that does not spring from your infinite goodness...

The next letter is the only one we have included entirely for non-musical reasons. Monteverdi's vivid, if slightly muddled, account of his distressing experience seemed, however, too good to be omitted. (And after all we are able to deduce from it, in passing, that he was a tall man!)

7 (*Malipiero 14, p. 152*) TO ALESSANDRO STRIGGIO
Venice, 12 October 1613

I am writing to tell Your Excellency how, while I was in the company of the Mantua courier on my way to Venice, we were robbed unawares of all we had by three ruffians at Sanguanato (or rather, to be precise, two miles from there).

This is what happened. Two of them suddenly came out of a field giving on to the main road. One of them had brown hair and not much beard and was of medium height. He had a long musket with the trigger cocked. The other one came up to me and scared me with his musket. The third got hold of the bridle, and the horses let themselves be led into the field without any resistance; I immediately dismounted, and as I did so he made me kneel down and demanded my purse. One of the other two dealt with the courier and demanded the bags. When the courier had got them down from the carriage and opened them one by one the ruffian took what he wanted, and the courier readily gave him everything; I was still kept on my knees by the one with the musket. Thus they took what they wanted.

The third robber, holding a dagger, had been acting as look-out and still did so, keeping anyone from coming off the road. When they had turned out all the stuff the one who was going through the courier's things came up to me and told me to take all my clothes off so that he could see if I had any other money. But I swore that I had not, and he went over to my maidservant for the same purpose. But she so helped her cause with all manner of prayers and entreaties that he left her alone. Then he turned to the bags and their contents and made a bundle of the best. Looking for something to cover them with he found my brand new, long serge cloak that I had had made at Cremona and said to the courier: 'Give me that cloak'. Seeing that it was too long, the robber said: 'Give me another'. So he took my son's, but he found it too short, and the courier said: 'Gentlemen, that belongs to that poor innocent little boy; give it him back'. And he agreed and found the boy's suit and did the same with that. With many entreaties the courier also asked for the maidservant's things and he handed them over to him. They made a big bundle of the rest, took them on their backs and carried them off.

Then we went on and arrived at an inn. The morning after, we reported the incident at Sanguanato and we set off and reached Este. I was feeling very upset. We took a boat for Padua, which was stuck on a sandbank all the Thursday night and nearly all day Friday, nobody caring whether we moved. We got going at last at eight o'clock in the evening in heavy rain and wind, in an open boat and with no one to row at the stern but our courier, who made a good job of it; and we got to Padua, though it was nearly one in the morning before we did so. On the Saturday morning we rose early to leave for Venice, but it was two hours before we did so. While we waited at Padua the courier put his arm in a sling; he said this was because of what happened to him in that episode of the cloaks when he was robbed. I knew that nothing of the courier's was touched or even searched, and I was sceptical. This action of the courier's aroused suspicions in all who were with us and who previously had seen nothing wrong with him at all. So somebody in the Padua boat said to him: 'What's the meaning of this, brother?' and would have liked to say more (though no doubt in jest), but the courier broke off the conversation. With the courier laughing and joking in the boat we thus arrived at Venice at midnight on the Saturday. He stayed there not more than two hours before leaving again for Mantua. The other Mantuan courier was there with me and said he was sorry to hear I harboured suspicions about the previous courier, but I told him I suspected nothing and took him for an honest man. Yet it is true that he put his arm in a sling on the Saturday morning simply because of what had happened on the previous Wednesday evening; moreover, nobody had touched him, and he did all that rowing[1] on the Friday.

I now inform Your Excellency that I entertained no suspicions of this man and that if any such thoughts had entered my head I should have told Your Excellency straightaway. I admit that that action of the courier in putting his arm in a sling gave one to think; and I leave it to Your Excellency's judicious opinion to decide if there is anything in it. As for me, I think nothing and look for nothing except through the hand of God. I certify, Excellent sir, that I was robbed of more than a hundred Venetian ducats in money and effects. I was pleased to receive from the Lord President when I was in Mantua my salary for six months, and I shall be due for some more in three months.

I have told the Lord President all about my misfortune, and although he is kindness itself I should be extremely grateful if you would be good enough to have a word with him on my behalf, for I am very greatly in need . . .

Monteverdi had been happily settled in Venice for more than two years as director of music at St. Mark's by the time he wrote the next letter, but he continued to accept commissions from the Mantuan court, which could no longer boast a composer of distinction and which indeed was entering politically and artistically upon a period of gradual decline. Vincenzo I had died in February 1612; his successor, Francesco II, died of smallpox only ten months later and was succeeded by his younger brother, Ferdinando II (the recipient of Letter No. 6), who had of course resigned his cardinalate.

It is impossible to identify the first ballet mentioned in this letter. *Tirsi e Clori,* to a text by Striggio himself, was produced at court in 1616 and printed three years later as the last work in the seventh book of madrigals; the actual *ballo* following the lovers' dialogue is in five parts and not eight as might be imagined from Monteverdi's account.

[1] Monteverdi clearly writes 'all day Friday' ('tutto il venere'), which conflicts with his remark above that the boat was stuck on a sandbank for most of the Friday. This account is in fact less than clear in one or two other respects; e.g. two couriers must be involved, though he does not clearly distinguish between them; we have tried to make his intentions clearer.

8 *(Malipiero 19, p. 161)*   To Alessandro Striggio

Venice, 21 November 1615

His Highness of Mantua's most excellent Resident in Venice has given me these last few days letters from Your Excellency telling me of His Highness of Mantua's request that I compose a ballet. The commission does not specify any particular differences from similar works in six, eight or nine movements commanded by His Highness Duke Vincenzo of blessed memory. He used also to specify some narrative interest, and I would try and devise for it the most suitable music and tempi I could. I think a six-movement work will likewise please His Highness now.

For a long time I have tried to finish the enclosed work [*Tirsi e Clori*], which lacked two sections: in fact I began it some months ago with the intention of presenting it to His Highness in the summer, when I expected to be in Mantua on some private business. I am sending it now via the Resident to Your Excellency so that you can present it to His Highness. I thought it a good idea too to send Your Excellency a letter saying that if His Highness wishes to change any of the airs or would like additions, whether slow and grave, or fuller and without imitative counterpoint, he should not worry about the existing words, which could easily be changed. But at least the ones I am sending will serve to show the nature of the metre and of the vocal line. If His Highness desires extensive changes I beg you to speak for me and to say that if he will be so good as to repeat the commission I, as his most devoted servant and desirous of acquiring his favour, will not fail to satisfy him.

If by fortunate chance the present version is to his liking I should think it would be best if the performers were deployed like a half moon, with a chitarrone and a harpsichord at the corners playing the continuo parts, one for Cloris, one for Thyrsis. These two should be holding chitarroni and should form a consort with the other two instruments as they sing and play them. It would be better still if Cloris had a harp instead of a chitarrone. When the point is reached at which the dancing begins, after their dialogue, other voices should join in to make a total of eight, together with eight *viole da braccio*, a *contrabasso* and a spinet in support; it would be nice if there were also two small lutes. The ballet should be danced in the measure appropriate to the nature of the airs.

Without upsetting the singers and players and with the dancing-master's ingenuity I hope it will not be displeasing to His Highness if sung in this way. It would be best if you could see the singers and players in it for an hour before His Highness sees it. The present opportunity has been unusually pleasant for me, for not only have I been able to show myself prompt to obey His Highness's wishes, which I so ardently desire to do, it serves to recall my time as Your Excellency's trusted servant; and I trust you will therefore consider me worthy of further commissions ...

The next few letters centre round the marriage in 1617 of Ferdinando II Gonzaga to Caterina de'Medici and the music Monteverdi was writing for the attendant celebrations. The music was for the series of *intermezzi, Le Nozze di Tetide,* by Scipione Agnelli, that were to be performed out of doors between the acts of a play; at first, however, Monteverdi seems to have thought that the text was that of a true opera. Even when he discovered its real function (Letter No. 11) he seems to have been little more enthusiastic about it than he was at first, and it was not long before he abandoned the music, none of which has survived. In Letter No. 9 in particular, which has often been quoted, he makes absolutely clear how important it was to him, as to so many great opera-composers, to be given opportunities for developing 'living' characters and for delineating human passions.

Francesco Rasi, who lived at the Mantuan court for some twenty years, was a good composer of monodies, a poet, a harpsichordist and a lutenist, but especially famous in his day as a tenor; he created important roles in several early operas. 'Signor Don Francesco' was perhaps the Francesco Gonzaga, a minor member of the ruling family, who published some canzonets and arias in 1619. Cardinal Montalto was passionately addicted to the arts, especially music, and was one of the leading patrons of the time.

9 (*Malipiero 22, p. 165*) TO ALESSANDRO STRIGGIO
Venice, 9 December 1616
I was delighted when Signor Carlo de'Torri gave me your letter together with the book containing the *favola marittima Le Nozze di Tetide.* Your Excellency tells me that you have sent me this so

that I can read it through carefully and then give you my opinion of it as a text for me to set to music for His Highness's forthcoming marriage. Excellent sir, I must first of all say that, as one who desires only to be of some small service to His Highness, I always apply myself promptly to whatever His Highness may see fit to command me and without fail will always be honoured to receive everything that he may command.

If His Highness approved this text then it should be beautiful and attractive to me. But you add that I should let you know my own views, and I am ready to obey Your Excellency's orders respectfully and promptly, if you will bear in mind that these views are of no importance; for I am a person who counts for little, and I am always ready to honour every honourable person, in particular the poet of the present work, whose name I do not know. Bearing in mind that poetry is not my profession, I will first of all say, since thus you ask me, and with all due respect, that music is an art that wants to be mistress over the 'air' and not just over the water. In other words, in my language, the *concerti* described in such a text are all base and earthbound — a very serious obstacle to beautiful music. Moreover, the musical sounds will be provided by the coarsest wind instruments on the stage; these will be so placed as to be heard by all and will be joined by other instruments behind the scenes. I leave judgment on this error to your refined, impeccable taste: but because of it three chitarroni would be needed instead of one, three harps instead of one, and so on; instead of singing elegantly the singer would have to force his tone. In addition, the proper imitation of the text should depend in my view on wind instruments rather than on the more refined strings. I am sure that the sounds appropriate to the tritons and other sea creatures should be entrusted to trombones and cornetts rather than to citterns, harpsichords and harps, since this is a maritime performance and thus takes place outside the city. And did not Plato teach that 'cithara debet esse in civitate, et thibia in agris'?[1] So the sounds and instruments will

---

[1] 'The kithara should be played in the city, the aulos in the country.' The reference is to a passage in *The Republic*, I, also translated in Oliver Strunk, *Source Readings in Music History* (London, 1952), p. 6.

be either elegant and inappropriate or appropriate and inelegant.

Moreover, I see that the characters are winds, *amoretti, zeffiretti* and sirens, so that many sopranos will be needed; and also that the winds — the west winds and the north winds — have to sing. How, dear sir, since winds do not speak, shall I be able to imitate their speech? And how, by such means, shall I be able to move the passions? Ariadne moved the audience because she was a woman, and Orpheus did the same because he was a man and not a wind. Musical sounds can imitate sounds — the rushing of winds, the bleating of sheep, the neighing of horses, and so on — without the aid of words; but they cannot imitate the speech of winds, since it is non-existent. The dances too, which for such a tale are few and far between, lack the movement of dances.

In sum, and due to my no little ignorance, I find that this tale does not move me at all and is even difficult to understand; nor do I feel that it can naturally inspire me to a moving climax. Ariadne inspired in me a true lament, and Orpheus a true prayer, but I do not know what this will inspire in me: what does Your Excellency really wish the role of music to be in this piece?

However, I shall accept it all with due respect, and honour what His Highness commands and desires, since he is without question my master. And when His Highness orders that I set it to music I shall bear in mind that the majority of the singing parts are deities. So I should like to hear them sung really expressively. I think the three sisters — Signora Adriana [Basile] and the other two — could sing them and also compose them, likewise Signor Rasi[1] his part, and Signor Don Francesco [Gonzaga?] his, and one could mention many others: thus we would be following Cardinal Montalto, who wrote a comedy in which every performer composed the music of his own part. If this tale were one which led up, like *Arianna* and *Orfeo*, to a single climax, certainly it should be composed by a single hand — also, that is, if it suggested sung speech and not, like the present libretto, spoken song. Even from this point of view I consider each part of it to be too long — from the speech of the sirens onwards and in certain other places.

Forgive me, dear sir, if I have said too much, not to denigrate

[1] 'Rasco' in the original; but it seems certain that Francesco Rasi is meant.

anything but out of a desire to obey your instructions and so that Your Excellency may ponder my thoughts if I were commanded to set the libretto to music . . .

10 (*Malipiero 23, p. 168*)   To Alessandro Striggio
Venice, 29 December 1616

Forgive me, Your Excellency, if I have not sought with my letters to know Your Excellency's reply to the letter I sent you three weeks ago, in reply to that kind letter of yours which was accompanied by the *favola marittima Le Nozze di Tetide,* in order to find out from you what my instructions were in connection with it; for Your Excellency wrote that in the first place I was to tell you what I thought of it.

I am slow in writing because of my work on the mass for Christmas Eve: I have had to spend the whole of December, almost without a break, composing and copying it. Now, praise be, I am free, and everything has passed off very well, so I once more ask Your Excellency to be good enough to inform me of His Highness's wishes. Since all my work for Christmas Eve and Christmas Day is behind me and I have for a while nothing to do for St. Mark's, I shall start work on that tale [*Le Nozze di Tetide*] if you tell me to do so and will even accept any new commission from Your Excellency.

I have taken up the libretto again and considered it more closely and attentively. As far as I can see, there are parts for many sopranos and many tenors and very little dialogue — and that little to be recitative and not sung as attractive ensembles. As for sung choruses, the only one is for the Argonauts in the ship; and this will be very beautiful and forthright; it will be for six voices and six instruments. Then there are the west winds and north winds: I do not know how these are to sing, though I know they can whistle and blow — indeed Virgil, speaking of winds, uses the verb 'sibilare', whose very sound resembles wind. There are two other choruses, one for nereids, the other for tritons, but these should, I think, be treated as concerted pieces with wind instruments: if they are, Your Excellency can imagine what delight it will afford the senses. So that Your Excellency too may be alive to the truth of all this, I am sending on the enclosed sheet the list of scenes, as they stand, in this tale, and perhaps you will be so kind as to tell me what you think.

The whole thing, however, will be admirable if it depends on the judgment of His Highness, to whom I readily bow and show myself his most humble servant. I shall therefore await Your Excellency's reply in order to know what you are pleased to command me...

11 (*Malipiero 25, p. 170*)[1]   To Alessandro Striggio

Venice, 6 January 1617

The very welcome letter I have just received from Your Excellency, together with the sheet listing for me the characters appearing in the tale of Thetis, has made it quite clear to me what I have to do to fall in with Your Excellency's wishes, which I know will also be His Highness's. I desire with all my heart to produce something that will gratify them.

When, excellent sir, I wrote my first letter in reply to your first one I confess that the text that you sent me, which had no title beyond *Le Nozze di Tetide: favola marittima,* seemed to be something that should be sung and represented in music as *Arianna* was. Now, however, that I know from Your Excellency's recent letter that it is to serve as *intermezzi* to the main comedy, what I first thought to be rather a monotonous piece I now on the contrary consider both fitting and distinguished. In my view, though, it lacks at the very end, after the final line,

Torni sereno il ciel, tranquillo il mare,

a canzonet in praise of the princely bridal pair; the harmony of this piece might be heard in heaven and on the earth, as depicted on the stage. To this music noble dancers could dance a noble dance — a noble conclusion to the whole noble conception. Moreover, it would surely be much more fitting if one could adapt to the dance rhythms the words that the nereids will be singing at the same time as the accomplished dancers are dancing their graceful steps.

I am not altogether happy about the three songs sung by the three sirens, for if all three have to sing separately the audience

[1] Malipiero also prints this letter, with the wrong date, as No. 11, p. 147.

will find the work too long and too unvaried, since there will need to be inserted a symphony between them, as well as *tirate* to sustain the declamation, and *trilli*: this will produce a certain monotony. So to make it all more varied I would suggest that the first two madrigals should be sung alternately by one and two voices respectively and the third by all three voices together. The opening of the part of Venus, which comes after Peleus's lament and is the first time one hears music embellished with *tirate* and *trilli,* would be best, I should have thought, if boldly sung, perhaps by Signora Adriana [Basile] and by her two sisters in the guise of an echo, since the text includes the line

E sfavillin d' amor gli scogli e l'onde.[1]

But first the audience's minds should be prepared by a symphony played by instruments in the middle of the stage; for after his lament Peleus has these two lines:

Ma qual per l' aria sento
Celeste soavissimo concento![2]

I think Signora Adriana should have time to change her costume, or at any rate one of the three[3] ladies should.

It now looks as if I have 150 — perhaps more — lines to set, and I think that by next week at the latest, God willing, I shall have done all the solos — those, that is, that are to be recitatives — and then I shall get on with the expressive aria-like pieces.

May it please God that I succeed in my intentions, since I desire earnestly to produce something to His Highness's taste, and that the result will serve as proof of my capacities in the eyes of His Highness, whom I so much love and admire and to whom, as his humble servant, in whatever condition and place, I shall always devote them . . .

The poet Ottavio Rinuccini (1562–1621) is best remembered as the librettist of several of the earliest operas, including *Arianna.*

[1] 'And let the rocks and the waves tell of love.'
[2] 'But what sweet, divine music I hear on the breeze!'
[3] Monteverdi writes 'tre altre' ('other three'), though he has mentioned a total of only three ladies previously in this letter.

12 (*Malipiero 27, p. 173*)   To Alessandro Striggio

Venice, 20 January 1617

Your Excellency informs me that a marriage has been arranged between His Highness and the house of Tuscany [Caterina de' Medici], that as a consequence I shall definitely have to compose something for this Easter and that you will therefore send me a new libretto to set. If my desire thus to serve His Highness, the son of the Duke of Mantua my former master, does not keep me in Venice I shall certainly go to Florence. I have had an extremely cordial invitation from Signor Ottavio Rinuccini, who tells me that the joyful occasion of His Highness the Duke of Mantua's marriage is a good opportunity for me to go there. He says that I shall be seen not only by all the Florentine nobility but by the Grand Duke himself and that in addition to the present marriage with the Duke of Mantua they hope for others, which I should like to see, for he more or less tells me that I would be asked to compose something. He says the marriage with His Highness of Mantua has been vociferously welcomed by the whole of Florence. May Our Lord grant that affairs will thus always go well with His Highness the Duke of Mantua and all his territories: with all my heart I desire that that Serene House may eternally prosper, and for this I will pray to God.

I shall, then, await Your Excellency's instructions, reminding you that

> Il presto con il bene
> Insieme non conviene

— in other words, if you are slow to tell me, no one should complain if I do less than may be expected of me in the time available ...

The next four letters make it quite plain that a fresh commission from Mantua, to write music for *Andromeda,* a libretto by the ducal Secretary, Ercole Marigliani, was no more congenial to Monteverdi than *Le Nozze di Tetide* had been; once again, nothing survives. He received the text early in 1618 and must have done very little about it: it was certainly indefensible of him to try two years later (Letter No. 15) to wriggle out of completing the music on the grounds that there was far too little time to do so before the proposed performances in the 1620 Carnival season. In the other three letters in this group he offers his work in Venice and his health (twice) as excuses for delay, though it is certainly true that Ascension Day was one of the grandest occasions in the Venetian calendar: the Doge and the Signory went out in their barge, the *Bucintoro*, to marry Venice to the sea, and extended services were held in which music played a prominent part. The reference to *Arianna* in No. 15 tells us how much work might be put into the preparation of an opera at that time, though Monteverdi exaggerates somewhat when he speaks of 'five months' strenuous rehearsal', since the opera was finished in February 1608 and performed on 28 May.

Vincenzo Gonzaga was Ferdinando II's younger brother, Vincenzo I's fourth and last child.

The other work mentioned in Letters Nos. 15 and 16, *Apollo,* with a text by Striggio himself, is also lost; it seems to have been a sort of dramatic cantata.

13 (*Malipiero 30, p. 176*) To Alessandro Striggio

Venice, 21 April 1618

As I have been so busy in St. Mark's during Holy Week and over Easter I have been unable before now to send Your Excellency the music for the *Andromeda* libretto. I do not know whether it will be to your liking; I do know, though, that I have written it out of a single-minded desire to serve Your Excellency with all my heart, for I crave the favour of Your Excellency, whose devoted servant I remain. I pray, therefore, that if my music is defective you will feel yourself to be rewarded instead by the riches of my devoted goodwill.

I have received by the last post further lines from the same tale of Andromeda, but I do not know whether, with Ascension Day approaching, I shall be able to do as much as Your Excellency commands me and as I wish. For next Thursday is the festival of the Holy Cross, when the Holy Blood is exhibited, and it falls to me to prepare a *messa concertata* and motets for the whole day, since the Holy Blood will be displayed all day long on an altar set up high in the middle of St. Mark's. Then I have to rehearse a particular cantata in praise of His Highness [The Doge of Venice], which is sung annually in the *Bucintoro* while he goes with all the

Signory to marry the sea on Ascension Day, and also rehearse a mass and solemn vespers which are sung in St. Mark's at that time. So, excellent sir, though I fear I shall not accomplish all that I would wish I shall try and do all I can so that I can show in a practical way how devotedly I serve you. I shall be very glad to know who will be singing the part of the Messenger, so that I can decide how to write most appropriately for his voice, and whether one or two are to sing the part, since there are two messengers, the one bringing sad, the other joyful tidings. I should also like to know how many singers there will be in the women's chorus so that I can compose their music for four voices or more or fewer, as appropriate...

14 (*Malipiero 31, p. 178*)   To Alessandro Striggio
Venice, 21 July 1618

By this post I am sending Your Excellency the rest of the music for the 'joyful' messenger, which was missing from what I sent you before. I hope it will make a good impression, for it is the product of a mind bent on ministering to Your Excellency's wishes. I would have done more had I not been kept from working by a slight headache caused by the heat that suddenly followed the recent rains. I should have delayed sending it to Your Excellency until the next post so as to have time to improve it, but since I imagine that in your eyes lateness is a worse fault than lack of musical ideas I have decided to send it now and to content myself with being admired for service that is prompt but second-rate rather than good but slow: I know too how important it is for a singer to have time to study his part in advance.

I shall now get on with setting the remaining lines so that before too long you can hear the complete score and have time to ask me to recompose according to your instructions anything that you do not like. I shall be sending Your Excellency by the next post the canzonet sung by the chorus of fishermen beginning 'Se valor di forti braccia', but I should be very glad to know how many voices to compose it for, which instruments are to accompany it, and whether it is to be preceded by any symphony for instruments, and if so which, so that I may score it appropriately.

For the same reason I should be very pleased to know if the canzonet 'Il fulgore onde risplendono', for the chorus of maidens, will be sung and danced, which instruments are to play it and how many voices are to sing it. I also hope to write quickly the 'sad' messenger's song 'Sarà mai ver che veggia' and send it to Your Excellency . . .

15 (*Malipiero 37, p. 185*)   TO ALESSANDRO STRIGGIO
Venice, 9 January 1620

I am sending Your Excellency the lament from my *Apollo*. By the next post I shall be sending the first part of the work up to where the enclosed piece begins, since I have nearly finished it already and only a little quick revision remains to be done. Where Love begins to sing I think it would be a good idea if Your Excellency were to add three more lines in the same metre and with the same general sense so that I can repeat the same aria. I hope this contrasting touch of gaiety will not make an unfortunate effect following Apollo's doleful expression of his feelings. I shall also show how the nature of the music changes in accordance with the words.

I would have sent Your Excellency the enclosed song by the last mail had not Signor Marigliani in a letter addressed to me asked me at the very urgent request of Signor Don Vincenzo [Gonzaga] to finish the music for the play *Andromeda* by Signor Marigliani himself, which I had already begun, so that it could be presented before His Highness during the coming Carnival on his return from Casale. But just as I shall have to compose it badly through having to finish it in a hurry so also do I believe it will be badly sung and badly played because of the very short time available: I am amazed that Signor Marigliani is willing to engage in so dubious an enterprise. There would not even have been enough time if they had started to rehearse the piece — let alone learn it — before Christmas. Now what does Your Excellency think should be done, since there are still more than 400 lines to be set to music? I can envisage only bad singing, bad playing and bad musical ensemble. These are not things that can be done in such a hurry — you know that *Arianna* needed five months' strenuous rehearsal after the cast had learned their parts by heart.

If you were agreeable I should like Your Excellency to ask His Highness if he will make do with Your Excellency's ballet: I am sure it would be enough to make the occasion a success since so short a work would fit in with the short time available. I could then complete *Andromeda* at my leisure, and there would be sufficient time for it to be learned and successfully performed; I could also give more careful thought to your ballet. If I were to serve Signor Don Vincenzo and Your Excellency in any other way over so short a period I am sure I should have to send you more unworthy than worthwhile music, and not without reason; for it should be remembered that my service as a church musician has removed me somewhat from the sphere of stage music, with which I used to be familiar. If I have to write a lot in a short time I shall be reduced to note-spinning instead of composing music appropriate to the text.

I am, however, extremely anxious to give of my best to His Highness, Your Excellency and Signor Marigliani, and so I beg Your Excellency to arrange matters to the satisfaction of us all; otherwise I shall do what I can with all my heart. Please do let me know if you like the enclosed music, and if not I will do all I can to satisfy you ... And do please let me know what form the ballet will eventually take ...

16 (*Malipiero 39, p. 188*)   To Alessandro Striggio

Venice, 1 February 1620

I have received Your Excellency's very kind letter; I understand the reason for the delay and what you want me to do. I have given up work [on *Apollo*] until now, as I thought this is what you would wish me to do, but now that you have told me that the piece is to be performed I can assure you that by the next mail you will receive from me the whole of that part of the score that you lack — or if not the whole of it, only very little will remain for me to compose. If the text is finished it only remains for you to tell me what more I have to do and whether the piece is to be danced and sung. If Your Excellency will send me the words I will try and devise appropriate music in whatever metre you have chosen; even if the metre is constant all through the text I shall vary the tempo from time to time.

Certain gentlemen here have heard Apollo's lament and admired its conception, both words and music; it was given after an hour of concerted music that is regularly heard these days in the house of a certain gentleman of the Casa Bembi before an audience consisting of the most important ladies and gentlemen. These people think that the next thing should be for this beautiful piece of Your Excellency's to appear on a stage; so if I am to compose some ballet music perhaps Your Excellency would send me as soon as possible the lines to be set, whereupon I will add some invention of my own so that people may enjoy such a beautiful work as Your Excellency's.

I thought of going to Mantua to present Her Highness with the books I have had printed and dedicated to her [i.e. the seventh book of madrigals]; this seems a good way of trying to obtain what I have desired and worked for — the modest pension that His Highness Duke Vincenzo of blessed memory was pleased to grant me. But I remembered that Signor Marigliani's comedy should have fallen on my shoulders; and knowing that with the passage of time that feeble branch has come to bear so large a fruit that it is impossible for it to do so without breaking, I did not want to come so soon to sustain this impossible burden lest I in my low state of health also break. Haste is inimical to such a project, which even with plenty of time is no small matter to bring to a successful conclusion; I have therefore decided to stay here, though I am sorry, because this is not in my best interests. But in order not to destroy any interest you may possibly have in me I hasten to assure you that the work Your Excellency has asked me to do has been welcome to me, since I have already savoured how very agreeable it has been, and if it had been possible I should have esteemed it a privilege to be able to serve you, as it will always be whenever you are pleased to command me . . .

The next letter is one of the longest and most passionate that Monteverdi wrote — a sustained denunciation of the humiliating treatment repeatedly meted out in the past to a great artist who was aware and proud of his gifts, who no doubt knew that in his compositions he had served his former masters better than they had deserved and who with enthusiastic scorn holds up to them the enlightened example of his present employers. Again, as in Letter No. 3, he invokes the salaries of others — on the one hand his eminent Venetian predecessors, on the other performers contemporary with him at Mantua through whose example he voices the traditional protest of the creative artist against the preferential treatment so often accorded the interpretative artist. Sante Orlandi, whom he also mentions, was his mediocre successor in Mantua, whose death had created the vacancy the Gonzagas were now trying unsuccessfully to persuade Monteverdi to fill.

17 (*Malipiero 46, p. 198*)   To Alessandro Striggio
Venice, 13 March 1620

I am replying to the second point in Your Excellency's letter, which I have found time to reply to by the present post. So in the first place I must tell Your Excellency that the singular honour His Highness has done me in making me this exceptionally gracious offer to return to his service has touched me and pleased me so much that I cannot find words to express my gratitude. The years of my youth that I spent in that Most Serene service have implanted in my heart such strong feelings of devotion, goodwill and reverence towards that Most Serene house that I shall pray to God on its behalf as long as I live, and desire that it may enjoy the greatest prosperity that a devoted servant could hope and wish for. And certainly if I had thoughts only for myself Your Excellency could rest assured that I should feel bound to return if I could minister to His Highness's commands without taking other matters into consideration.

But there are two factors — one relating to this Most Serene Republic, the other to my sons — that cause me to have second thoughts: perhaps you will allow me to say a little more about these two matters, for I know that I can count on Your Excellency's kindness and that wisdom and brotherly love are among your greatest qualities. I shall therefore ask Your Excellency to bear in mind that this Most Serene Republic, which has never given a salary of more than 200 ducats to any of my predecessors

1 Page of Monteverdi's letter of 13 March 1620 to Alessandro Striggio

— whether Adrian [Willaert], Cipriano [de Rore], Zarlino or any other — gives me 400, a favour that I must not lightly set aside without taking it carefully into account; since, Excellent sir, this Most Serene Signory does not make innovations without careful thought I must regard this particular act of grace very favourably indeed. Nor, having done this, have they ever had second thoughts: indeed they have honoured me further, in that they will accept no singer into the *cappella* without first hearing the opinion of the *maestro di cappella,* neither will they accept any reports on the singers except that of the *maestro di cappella,* nor accept organists or *vice-maestro* without the opinion and report of the *maestro di cappella.* There is no gentleman who does not esteem and honour me, and when I go and perform, whether church music or chamber music, I swear to Your Excellency that the whole city runs to listen. My position is the more agreeable also because the whole *cappella* is under temporary appointment except the *maestro di cappella*: indeed it is up to him to appoint and dismiss the singers and to grant leave of absence or not; and if he does not go into the *cappella* no one will say anything about it. His position is assured until he dies and is not affected by the death of the procurators or of the prince, provided that he gives loyal and devoted service and not the opposite. If he does not go and collect his salary at the right time it is brought to his house. This is his basic income. There are also useful additional earnings outside St. Mark's: I have been begged again and again by the wardens of the schools and earn 200 ducats a year, for anyone who wants the *maestro di cappella* to make music for them will pay 30, even 40 or as many as 50 ducats for two vespers and a mass and afterwards will also thank him very warmly.

Now, Your Excellency, weigh against this in the balance of your fine judgment what you have offered me in His Highness's name and see whether there are any genuine grounds for my moving or not. In the first place, Your Excellency, kindly consider the damage I would do to my reputation with these excellent gentlemen here and with His Highness [the Doge] himself if I decided to exchange my present income, assured for life, for that offered by the Mantuan treasury, which ceases with the prince's death or his least displeasure; if I were to give up more than 450 ducats (in Mantuan currency), which is what I receive from the Venetian treasury, in order to accept 300 in Mantua like Signor Sante [Orlandi], what would not these gentlemen say about me, and with reason? It is true that on behalf of His Highness you add a further 150 *scudi* from land that would be my freehold. But to this I reply that His Highness cannot give me what is mine: there would not be 150 but rather 50, since His Highness already owes me the 100; so he should not take into account what I have earned in the past by great toil and sweat, There would therefore be 350 ducats altogether; here I earn 450. and 200 more on the side.

So Your Excellency can see that people would undoubtedly speak very ill of me, especially as there are others — though I should not say so — who have hitherto been much more liberally rewarded than I have: Adriana [Basile], a brother of hers, [Francesco] Campagnolo, Don Bassano. How ashamed I should feel beside them to see them rewarded better than me! Compare Venice! Your Excellency should also remember that His Highness made me a better offer, verbally through Signor Campagnolo, when I was staying in the latter's house after Signor Sante's death: this was a salary of 300 *scudi* from land, 200 of which were to be mine up to my death and 100 as a gift as payment of my annual rent. Then when I said I did not wish to have anything to do with the treasury he offered me a pension of 200 more, which came altogether to 600 Mantuan ducats. Now His Highness would like me to settle for so much less, as well as going to the treasurer every day to beg him to give me what is mine! As God sees me, I have never in my life suffered greater humiliation of the spirit than when, almost for the love of God, I had to go and beg the treasurer for what was mine. I would rather go from door to door than submit again to such indignity. (I beg Your Excellency to forgive me if I speak freely and to be so kind, on this occasion, and for the love I bear you as your devoted servant, as to listen to me at least with your boundless humanity if not on behalf of your servant's singular merits.)

When the excellent procurator Signor Landi, together with

the other excellent gentlemen, wished to increase my salary by 100 ducats he spoke as follows: 'Excellent colleagues, he who desires an honourable servant must grant him an honourable contract'. So if the Duke wishes me to come and live honourably it is only right that he should treat me likewise; if not I beg him not to bother me, since, as Your Excellency well knows, I have acted honourably.

I have said nothing of my sons. Yet Your Excellency, who is also the father of a family, knows very well how zealous a father has to be in desiring that honour, for himself and for the household depending upon him, which by the laws of nature he feels to be their due.

My conclusion, excellent sir, is this. Taking everything into consideration, Claudio, who has already in the past completely submitted himself to His Highness's wishes and commands, cannot honourably move unless for the better and thus feel entirely justified in leaving the service of these excellent gentlemen; for he has been so honoured and favoured by them as no longer to be laughed at by those of little merit who have earned much nor blamed by the world and by his sons. His Highness has the opportunity, now that the illustrious Bishop of Mantua has passed to a better life, of satisfying Monteverdi with a pension and a little more land without exposing him to the repugnant practices of an unreliable treasury: in short, a pension of 400 Mantuan *scudi* and 300 from land would be little to His Highness, and to Claudio a truly generous settlement. Perhaps Claudio is asking the impossible? He asks in fact for less than Adriana, and possibly one Settimia, used to get; he asks for what he is getting now. The only other difference I can see is that I would attain sufficient security to enable me to do my duty and leave at least something to my sons. If I were to leave something provided by the Most Serene house of Gonzaga it would be to their eternal honour, for they would have helped a long-serving employee and would not surely be despised for it by other princes. And if this seems too much to His Highness let him do me the honour of assigning me a little land so that I may have a little capital, since the 400 ducats I am getting now are in effect a pension. Moreover, if His Highness pays his servant well he will find that I will get up in the middle of the night the more expeditiously to carry out his orders.

Please forgive me, Your Excellency, if I have written at too great length. It only remains for me to thank Your Excellency with all my heart for the exceptional favour you did me in presenting my madrigals [i.e. Book VII] to Her Highness; I am sure that, since they were handed over by no less a person than Your Excellency, they will have been the more gratefully received...

In the next letter Monteverdi again uses his duties in Venice as an excuse for delaying work for the Mantuan court. However, there is evidence that the Procurators of St. Mark's did not like their *maestro di cappella* to be away for a long period, and Holy Week was traditionally a time for elaborate ceremonial music. The performance of *Arianna* was probably contemplated in connection with the celebrations on the occasion of the election of the Duke to be Holy Roman Emperor.

18 (*Malipiero 47, p. 203*)   To Alessandro Striggio
Venice, 17 March 1620

I am writing this (since at this time Signor Don Vincenzo of Mantua is bringing it to Mantua) to inform you that I have received a letter of Your Excellency from Signor Bergamaschino, which as before commands me in the name of His Highness to have *Arianna* copied. Since I despatched it to Your Excellency, and gave it to the courier some time ago, I hope that Your Excellency will receive it without fail within eight or ten days. I would have written by the last post if Signor Bergamaschino had given the letter to me at the time of the courier's arrival. I have also heard that His Highness has asked you to instruct me to come to Mantua for eight or ten days, making sure that I should not be away from Their Excellencies of Venice any longer, so that in any case I should be back in time for the duties of my office concerned with Holy Week. I shall do all in my power to obey the commands of His Highness, but, to tell the truth, there are people who arouse the suspicions of the Signory, in a slanderous way. Besides which there is the Dean of St. Mark's, for whose oratory every Wednesday, Friday and Sunday I provide the music, to which half the gentry come. If I talk of taking a long leave, they jump on me. Nevertheless, if it is possible to delay my visit until after the first three festival days at Easter, I should be able to arrange it all so that I should find myself at liberty to obey you. If, however, this is not possible, I will do whatever Your Excellency shall command, hoping that in your wisdom you will not ask me to do anything that is not in my best interests. I have written in reply to the second point of Your Excellency's letter by the last post; I shall therefore await to hear what your instructions are, praying for the love of God to keep me in your favour, in which I hope I shall not be disappointed, for I know that it is full of infinite humanity and generosity . . .

Monteverdi had dedicated his seventh madrigal book to the Duchess of Mantua in December 1619 (cf. also Letter No. 16), hoping no doubt to remind the Gonzaga household that his pension from them had been awarded in perpetuity and recently had not been paid promptly. Following the custom of the time, he had probably received some tangible recognition for his dedication, hence the thanks in the next letter.

19 (*Malipiero 51, p. 207*)   TO ALESSANDRO STRIGGIO
Venice, 4 April 1620

I do not know whether it would have been advisable or not to have written the present letter directly to Her Highness to thank her for the especial favour she has been so kind as to accord me, due to Your Excellency's influence; together with it I am sending her by the courier that beautiful necklace. I should be grateful if Your Excellency would cast your eye over it, and if you think it would be a good idea, may I beg Your Excellency to have a clasp put on it, and to present it to her. If you think this is not a good idea I beg you to act with tact on my behalf, thanking Her Highness on my account with all possible affection.

I ask Your Excellency also to perform the same office towards His Highness the Duke, my especial patron as prime mover in this act of grace.

I am sending Your Highness the remainder of *Arianna*. If I had had more time I would have revised it more thoroughly, and it would perhaps have been therefore greatly improved. I shall not let a day go by without composing some stage music of this kind, the more willingly if you would be so gracious as to let me have some of your beautiful poems, so that I can show you how much I wish to remain in Your Excellency's favour and how much I wish to retain your good opinion...

The abandonment of the performance of *Arianna* was apparently made practical by the composition of *Adone* by Peri (which has also been lost). For some years now the Gonzagas had turned to Florentines for the composers of their festival music, a link strengthened by the marriage of the Grand Duke Cosimo of Tuscany to Ferdinando's sister. In the end, *Adone* was also abandoned, and a ballet, which Domenico de Paoli[1] surmises may have been Monteverdi's *Tirsi e Clori,* was performed.

20 (*Malipiero 53, p. 210*) TO ALESSANDRO STRIGGO

Venice, 10 May 1620

The infinite favours I receive every moment from the generous hand of Your Excellency, and which increase every day, are such that I, conscious of my obligation to the noble favour of Your Excellency, wish I could do something worthy of my feelings so that I could be more worthy of Your Excellency's commands. But such is my fortune that I must be tormented by receiving such kindness from your favour and not to deserve it. I have received such a gracious reply to my letter from the infinite bounty of Her Highness that even against my will this singular act of grace alone would make me her perpetual servant, if I knew no better; but I am not so ignorant of the truth, which is that the major part of my credit in the favour of Her Highness is born from Your Excellency's singular protection. Therefore I must remain not less obliged to Your Excellency in recognizing your favour than to His Highness. I hope to lean even more on the grace of both His Highness and Your Excellency in the future than I have in the past, trusting to be made worthy of that little

[1] *Claudio Monteverdi* (Milan, 1945), p. 234.

store of it to which I may aspire by favour if not by merit, from the liberal hand of His Highness the Duke of Mantua, formerly my ever kind and fair master. And I dare to hope that once more before I die I may be able to enjoy that grace which the kindness of Duke Vincenzo of blessed memory granted me.

His Highness the Duke made the right decision not to stage both *Arianna* and the other composition of Signor Jacopo Peri [*Zazzerino*] in such a short time, for truly haste is damaging in these affairs: the sense of hearing is too fine and too delicate, the more so in an audience which includes a great prince and people of his standing. And Her Highness has shown great wisdom in deciding not to have the ballet, since it is enough in itself to have a noble subject for some such festivals, although on other occasions it does not work. So this could give the opportunity to Signor Peri to show himself worthy of His Highness's grace. He has all the qualities about which you wrote to me, and not only that: his sweet and honest example will give a greater incentive for others to do things to win themselves favour; for without knowing the way one cannot arrive at one's goal. But I can assure you that it is the affection Your Excellency is showing me which binds me, more than bonds of service.

It is more to help the needs of my sons than myself that makes me so bold as to accept your most kind offer made spontaneously in your exceptionally gracious letter; namely that my father-in-law should be seen by His Highness so that he can prove that the bill that he has this moment in his hands should be settled. Blame this boldness on my need and your kind nature, for the one makes me bold, the other daring, and it is not just my own boldness, since I knew well how much this has inconvenienced you. So my father-in-law will come to you, and please forgive any inconvenience...

Monteverdi kept in touch with the Mantuan court in the succeeding years, partly because of various commissions, partly because his son Massimiliano went to study at Bologna, and Monteverdi wanted the Duchess to use her influence in finding him a place in the college of Cardinal Montalto, in the hope of keeping him away from the 'licentious, free life of students'. But his letters of this period tell us comparatively little of either his music or his day-to-day living. The next letter shows him in typically practical negotiations about singers. Monteverdi had strong links with Ferrara at this time through his deputy in St. Mark's, Alessandro Grandi, who had been *maestro di cappella* to the academy (or religious confraternity) of the Spirito Santo until 1617.

21 (*Malipiero 78, p. 237*) To The Duke of Mantua
Venice, 2 March 1624

I am writing to offer Your Highness the most heartfelt thanks of which I am capable, for the great honour which you have been so kind as to pay me; for I have been honoured by your commands, which I shall always value as sent to me by God as the greatest honour and fortune that anyone could receive. Although at the present time, Your Highness, there is no suitable person here in Venice, I heard [of one] by chance through a father of the order of St. Stephen in Venice (who is a singer in St. Mark's) who ten days ago told me that he has a brother in the service of His Grace the Archbishop of Salzburg, a young castrato with a good enough voice, capable of suitable *gorgie* and *trilli*; who, since there is nobody in the service of the Archbishop who can improve him in those qualities, would like to come to Venice if there was something in it for him. I told him to send him to Venice and that I would not fail to be of service to him in dealing with employers and giving him advice. Just this morning in chapel, before I received Your Excellency's commands, the father told me that he has written to tell him to come. Now that I know how much trouble I must take to suit Your Highness I shall be diligent in obtaining better information, and if the time becomes suitable I shall not neglect to speed the matter so that I can show with deeds as well as my most eager spirit how much I desire to be Your Highness's servant. And not just in this matter: I shall never fail to follow up elsewhere any other opportunities of which I will at once inform Your Excellency. I believe that Signor Campagnolo, as one who was once in the same service, could perhaps give Your Highness some information.

During the past few days I have heard that there is a singer in

Ferrara who was in the service of the gentlemen of the Spirito Santo, who has a good enough voice and good manners and who has given more than usual satisfaction. Since His Highness the Prince of Modena is beginning, as he does, to delight in music, will not do without it and takes trouble to find musicians, I do not for this reason entirely believe those who have told me about this singer in Ferrara; but I did not wish to refrain from mentioning this to Your Highness, so that, God willing, you may be served as I desire ...

The following letters offer a fascinating account of the birth of an opera, almost as revealing as Mozart's letters about *Idomeneo* or the correspondence of Strauss and Hofmannsthal. Our only regret must be that the opera itself has been lost so that we cannot always see what Monteverdi's solutions to the various problems were. Even so the references to the rapid changes of mood, the lullaby (if the music while Licoris is sleeping took this form), and the realism of the music for the various situations remind us of the later operas, especially *L'Incoronazione di Poppea*, where he clearly exploited to the full the experience he had gained in *La Finta Pazza Licori*. It is interesting that, although Monteverdi complains of the shortness of time when writing about the Duke's suggestion for a libretto, in fact a work which he had had the chance to think about was completed very quickly.

It is not known who all the singers were for the festival, which was probably to celebrate the accession of Vincenzo II to the dukedom. The Mantuan Jacomo Rapallini was in the service of St. Mark's, where he had been appointed as a singer on 10 December 1622 at a salary of 80 ducats. This was an average but not outstanding stipend, so that Rapallini may not have been an exceptional performer. The Florentine celebrations mentioned were for the wedding of Margherita de'Medici to Odoardo Farnese, Duke of Parma. As will be seen from subsequent letters, this took place after considerable delays.

22 (*Malipiero 89, p. 249*) TO ALESSANDRO STRIGGIO
Venice, 1 May 1627

Your Excellency will excuse me for my delay in replying to your most kind and valued letter. I had no time then, both because of the delay in receiving the letter and because as it happened it was the Vigil of St. Mark, a day on which I was extremely busy with the music. So please, Your Excellency, accept this present letter to make up for the omission in the last post, and, to enhance this present one, know that I could certainly never receive more grace from my good fortune than to be made worthy of His Highness; so I shall pray to God that He will give me the strength to be able, with greater effect than I have hitherto been capable of, to show myself worthy of such conspicuous favours, giving ever grateful and infinite thanks to Your Excellency for the great honour I have received.

I wish, however, to beg and ask Your Excellency that, if His Highness is pleased that I should set to music the play which he has commissioned me to do, he should take two things into account: the one that I might be allowed to have time to compose it, the other that it should be written in an excellent hand. For otherwise it would be quite an effort and not much to my taste, indeed it would be a very great trial to set verses to music in the slipshod way that I should do given that short time; and it was the shortness of time that brought me almost to death's door in writing *Arianna*. I know that it could be done quickly, but for it to be done both quickly and well is just not possible. If, therefore, there were time, and also if I had the libretto (or part of it) made by your most noble talent, rest assured that I should feel an infinite joy, because I know how much comfort and satisfaction, Your Excellency, it would bring me. If the task were to provide *intermezzi* for a big play, it would neither be so tiring nor so long; but as for a play sung throughout that attempts to say as much in a small space of time as an epic poem does, believe me, Your Excellency, it cannot be done without falling into one of two errors — to do it badly or to make one ill.

I have, however, set many verses of Tasso . . . the one where Armida begins *O tu che porte/parte teco di me, parte ne lassi*,[1] and all the following lament and her anger, together with Rinaldo's reply that perhaps would not be displeasing; and I have set the fight between Tancred and Clorinda. I have also been thinking about a little work of Signor Giulio Strozzi, which is very beauti-

---

[1] *Gerusalemme liberata*, XVI, 40. In the next line Monteverdi has 'Ruggiero' for 'Rinaldo'.

ful and curious and from which some four hundred lines could be taken. It is called *Licori finta pazza inamorata d'Aminta*. In it Licoris, after doing a thousand comical things, brings about her marriage with Amyntas by the art of deception. These and similar things can serve as short episodes, which put amongst other music should make their effect, and I know it would not be displeasing to Your Excellency. If after that it is necessary to have some music of this kind in church at vespers and mass, I believe that I should have something to His Highness's liking ...

23 (*Malipiero 90, p. 251*) TO ALESSANDRO STRIGGIO

Venice, 7 May 1627

I am sending Your Excellency *La Finta Pazza Licori* of Signor Strozzi, as you, in your kindness, have asked. It has not been set to music as yet, nor been printed nor ever played on the stage, since the author gave me the present copy into my own hands as soon as he had finished it. If Signor Giulio is given to know that it would be to the taste of His Highness, then, with the deepest affection and to some effect, he will arrange it in three acts or as it will please His Highness, for he desires beyond measure to have me set it to music, enjoying the sight of his admirable creation clothed in my unworthy notes. Truly, in the beauty of both the verse and the plot, I have found it a subject both excellent and easy to set, so that if the story is to your liking, do not be put off by its present form, for I know that the author would certainly arrange it to your complete satisfaction in a very short time. The plot does not seem to me to be at all bad, nor the way it develops. It is true that the part of Licoris, because of its varied nature must not be given to a woman who is unable to play the role of both man and woman using lively gestures and expressing distinctive emotions. For as the acting of this feigned madness must be based only on what is happening in the present, without thought of either the past or the future consequences, so must the acting come from the single word rather than the sense of the phrase. When, therefore, war is mentioned, the acting must imitate war; when one speaks of peace, it must imitate peace; when the word 'death' is spoken, it must imitate death and so on. And because the transformations and the acting of them happen in the shortest space of time, the person who takes the principal part, which demands both humour and compassion, must be a woman who can lay aside everything except the appearance of the word that she is saying. I believe, in spite of these difficulties, that Signorina Margherita will be excellent.

But to show the more effectively my affection towards you, I am sending you *Narciso*, the work of Signor Ottavio Rinuccini, even though I know for certain that the work would involve me in a greater effort. This has not been printed, nor set to music, nor has it ever been given on the stage. This gentleman when he was alive (that he is now in heaven I pray most fervently) was not only kind enough to give me a copy of it but to ask me that I should set it, since he was very fond of this work. I have made several attempts, and I have turned it over in my mind a good deal, but, to confess the truth to Your Excellency, it does not appear to me that it would be as great a success as I would like. For it would need a great many sopranos to take the parts of the many nymphs, and many tenors for the many shepherds, and it has little variety. And in addition it has a tragic and sad ending. However, I did not wish to omit sending it to Your Excellency, so that your taste can be arbiter. I have no copy of either of them other than these which I am sending to Your Excellency, so when you have read them completely I should be grateful if you would return the originals to me so that I can use them if it is in my interest to do so; and you know that they are valuable to me . . .

P.S. To tell Your Excellency who would be suitable for bass. Considering the taste of His Highness, and the need for the excellent parts for women sopranos, I can only report from hearsay. However, I have heard from a distance that there is a bass (whom I do not know myself) who works in Milan at the cathedral. Here, for chamber music there is nobody better than Rapallini of Mantua, called Don Jacomo. He is a priest but is a baritone rather than a bass. For the rest, his diction is good, he is not bad at *trilli* and *gorgie,* and he sings confidently. I shall wait, however, to see if there is a better one, and here again I offer my regards to Your Excellency.

24 (*Malipiero 91, p. 254*)   To Alessandro Striggio

Venice, 22 May 1627

I was very sorry to hear from your most kind and courteous letter that Your Excellency is suffering from gout, which has been causing you pain. Nature, by this means, wants to pass on the catarrh the better to the feet, hands, the extremities of the body, so that the other, more important parts may enjoy good health. I therefore pray to the Lord that this will mean many years of strength and happiness, and not only that you will be preserved in health but that the affliction which plagues your extremities will leave them. I hope that by now you are better so that this letter will find you out of bed and feeling well; and that Our Lord will grant this and give it to you is my deepest desire, and I pray for this with real affection.

I have received from the courier not only Your Excellency's most gracious letter, but also the copies of both *Narciso* and *La Finta Pazza Licori*. I have also received your opinion and commands concerning *La Finta Pazza Licori*, and truly I agree with Your Excellency that this woman who feigns madness [*finta pazza*] will be a great success on the stage, being novel, varied and delightful. Now that I know your views, I shall not fail (when Signor Giulio Strozzi comes back from Florence in three or four days' time), I shall not fail, I say, to discuss it with him, and you will see that he will enrich the piece with still more variety, and with new and diverse scenes to fit in with my ideas; likewise I shall see if he can add new scenes with more characters in them so that the 'mad girl' does not appear so often; and see also that each time she comes on the stage she always has new gestures and changes of music to match these gestures. I shall tell Your Excellency in great detail about all this. In my view the work is excellent in two or three places, but in two others it seems to me that it could be improved, not so much in the actual verse but in the originality of ideas. In another place it seems to me that it would be better for Amyntas's speech to fit in while she is asleep, for I would like him to speak not loudly enough to wake her. The necessity for him speaking *sotto voce* will afford me the opportunity to compose new music differing from what has gone before; and also the dance which is inserted in the middle ties me down both in its particular content and as a contrast. And as I have said, I will give you a detailed account later.

I have not as yet been able to talk with Signor Jacomo Rapallini, who has been in Padua for a couple of days. Before that, however, I did have a few words with him, and he told me that he felt himself to be ever the most humble servant and subject of His Highness and that he would be honoured to receive His Highness's orders, hoping that His Highness would be kind enough to arrange it so that he was able, by means of some ecclesiastical benefice, to enjoy a secure living as long as he lives. Here, the Doge's chapel pays him 80 ducats, he is at liberty to say masses, and he has 40 ducats from the Procurator Foscarini for being his chaplain (for which he has only to say mass without doing anything else). It is true that when this gentleman dies the stipend dies with him. He adds another 100 ducats to his income by singing on religious festivals in the city. His secure income is that from the chapel of St. Mark, and from the daily masses, which can amount to some 60 ducats; as long as he keeps well, he has the occasional fee around the city, and that is all.

I shall not fail to think about the matters that Your Excellency has commanded. I have so far given quite a lot of thought to the changes in the libretto, and soon I hope to send you something for Signorina Margherita as principal singer; but I should like to know the exact register of her voice, what her highest and lowest notes are. And here, giving my most humble reverence to Your Excellency, I pray for your every happiness.

25 (*Malipiero 92, p. 256*) TO ALESSANDRO STRIGGIO

Venice, 24 May 1627

Signor Giulio Strozzi has not yet come back from Florence. I await his return eagerly, for with all my heart I want to do everything Your Excellency has asked of me concerning *La Finta Pazza Licori*. I should have written at length to you if I had not been expecting the author to make substantial improvements. According to the last letter from him he must certainly be in Venice within two or three days, please God, and I hope that he will alter the play satisfactorily, so that Your Excellency will be content with it. I have already digested it so thoroughly that I know that I could set it to music in the shortest possible time; but my aim is that every time the mad girl comes on the stage she should always introduce some new delights with new variations. And in three places she will have new variants in which I hope to make a great effect. The first one, when the camp is being set up and sounds and noises will be heard behind the scene in imitation of the words, should be rather successful. Another is when she pretends to be dead; and the third is when she pretends to be asleep, at which moment music suggesting sleep must be used. But in certain other places, where the words cannot give rise to appropriate gestures or sounds or other obvious kinds of imitation, I fear that the surrounding passages will fall flat. For such effect I am awaiting Signor Strozzi, on whose arrival I shall immediately inform Your Excellency.

I hope that you will receive the news, by the grace of Our Lord, when you are rid of the pain from the gout and are no longer in bed, for pleasure ill assorts with pain. I pray and shall continue to pray with all my heart, nevertheless, that Our Lord will grant Your Excellency a return to complete health; and I also pray and shall continue to pray to be worthy of your commission. . . . When you are so kind as to tell me what to do about Signor Rapallini, I shall do it with all possible tact.

26 (*Malipiero 93, p. 257*) To Alessandro Striggio
Venice, 5 June 1627

Three days ago Signor Giulio Strozzi returned to Venice, and after I asked him most insistently that he should do me the honour to allow me to think of using *La Finta Pazza Licori* for the occasion of the royal celebrations, he freely agreed. He confessed that the work had not been brought to the pitch of perfection inherent in its conception. He also said that he is writing a piece in dialogue for a musical serenade which a certain Signor Mocenigo, my patron, has been arranging, but I, seeing that differences of a substantial nature would be needed, do not want to set this to music. Telling me that he would like to serve His

Highness, the Duke of Mantua, by giving the piece on a special occasion, and knowing that besides Signorina Margherita there were also two other virtuoso singers, he says that he will rearrange it so that each of the other singers in His Highness's service will be heard an equal amount. He also confesses that the part of Licoris will have to be extended and that therefore she will not appear in every scene; and her songs will add new ideas and actions to the plot. I hope that with the convenience of having this excellent poet near to help me (for he is my dear friend and patron) that I shall produce something that will be displeasing neither to His Highness nor Your Excellency, for I desire truly with all my heart to obey your commands. If what I have said pleases Your Excellency, instruct me accordingly, and I shall begin work.

I shall not deal with Signor Rapallini unless I receive fresh letters from Your Excellency asking me to do so. I trust now that your strength is increasing after the gout and that Our Lord will preserve you in the best of health and happiness ...

P.S. I heard from Signor Giulio Strozzi, on his arrival from Florence, that His Highness there wanted to send me a theatrical piece for me to set to music. But since Signor Gagliano has been chosen for this, it seems that His Highness will be happy with the present arrangement, and Signor Giulio adds that they are preparing some magnificent things, although he does not know for what occasion.

27 (*Malipiero 94, p. 259*)   To ALESSANDRO STRIGGIO

Venice, 13 June 1627

It is already six days ago that I gave *La Finta Pazza Licori* to Signor Giulio Strozzi, who promised me he would alter it at once to suit your taste, and today, Saturday, I went over to his house to see the changes he has made so that I could give some details of them to Your Excellency, and at the same time to have the piece to hand, so that I could begin to send it in its musical form to Your Excellency. I found that he had gone to Padua for two or three days for the festival of St. Anthony which is celebrated tomorrow, so I cannot tell you about it earlier than the next ordinary post.

I know for certain, however, that he is retouching it with great eagerness and adding things that he wants, so that the other women singers will have them in their parts, as I told you in my other letter.

There is here in Venice at the moment a certain young man from Bologna. He is about 24 years old and dresses *alla longa*.[1] He composes a little and professes to sing baritone parts in chamber music. I have heard him sing a motet in church with various embellishments and a pleasing manner, with an honest *trillo*. The voice is pleasant enough but not too deep, and he projects the words very well. His voice will become a pleasing tenor, and he is most secure in singing. He has an offer of employment from a certain Tarroni, who directs music in Poland, but he would prefer to stay in St. Mark's so that he could remain in Venice. He does not know that I am telling Your Excellency about him, and as God shall be my judge, and as I am His Highness's most humble servant, I think Your Excellency would do well to accept him; but I have not committed myself in any way, knowing how things are. If Your Excellency also does not give me the sign, it will not matter much because, as I have said to Your Excellency, he has no idea of my opinion...

28 (*Malipiero 95, p. 260*) To Alessandro Striggio
Venice, 20 June 1627

I shall tell Your Excellency by the next post the results of the negotiations with the bass singers with which you have been pleased to entrust me, since I have not as yet had time to meet and talk tactfully to those whom you have commissioned me to see, for I am doing the job personally and not through anyone else. I must ask Your Excellency, however, as I hinted in another letter, to take into consideration that Rapallini has, I believe, 80 ducats from the church, 60 or 70 from masses, and 40 for being chaplain to one of the Procurators, not including the occasional fees for singing in the city at various musical events. The young man from Bologna now in Venice has no secure income but obtains the odd fee from singing in church. He does not say

[1] The significance of this term is not known.

masses; he is a young man of good height, who, however, dresses *alla longa*, sings with a more pleasant voice than Rapallini — and more securely since he composes a bit — and makes his words well understood. He sings ornaments freely enough and has something of a *trillo*. True, he has not a very deep voice, but in both theatre and chamber music, however, he would not be displeasing to His Highness (at least, I hope this is so). This young man came to Venice with letters of recommendation that he be employed in his different capacities, but among the others was one straight from Signor Rossi, the Resident at the court of His Imperial Majesty. It seems to me that it would be a good thing if you would commit the negotiations to the said Signor Rossi, since these singers could not then say that I misled them; and I believe that Your Excellency will agree with me in this.

Signor Giulio Strozzi has returned from Padua, and although he has been there he has still not forgotten to improve his *La Finta Pazza Licori*, which he has arranged in five acts; and in about four days he will give me either the whole thing finished or at least two or three acts so that I can begin; and at the outside by Saturday I hope to send some of it to Your Excellency with the music underneath. I hope that you will see things that will appeal to you greatly, for Signor Giulio is a worthy man and gladly fits in with my ideas with great kindness, which makes it rather easier for me to set it to music . . .

29 (*Malipiero 96, p. 262*) To Alessandro Striggio

Venice, 3 July 1627

I received the first act of *La Finta Pazza Licori* from Signor Giulio Strozzi eight days ago, and I got on with the work every day until suddenly, three evenings ago, I began to suffer from a catarrhal infection in the region of my right eye which was most painful and which was accompanied by such a feeling of lassitude that I thought I should never get over it. But, praised be God, it has already begun to get a little better, and today it has allowed me to write this to Your Excellency, which I could not have done yesterday or the day before. I hope to send you by the next post a beautiful part of the act that is already done, and I shall send with it a copy of the words of the complete act so that you may judge it by reading it.

The young bass has petitioned the Procurators [of St. Mark's] to release him, and I believe you will be better informed about these negotiations by the person to whom Your Excellency wrote, for I know he has dined with these gentlemen [the Procurators] at least twice . . .

30 (*Malipiero 97, p. 262*) TO ALESSANDRO STRIGGIO
Venice, 10 July 1627

I am sending Your Excellency the first act of *La Finta Pazza Licori* of Signor Giulio Strozzi, as you commanded me. I would like to have sent the original itself so that Your Excellency could see not only the verses but the plot and the characters of the tale in the author's own hand. Two of the middle acts are completed, and the author will give me these tomorrow or the day after. He says that the feigned madness will begin in the third act, and as soon as I have this I will send them on to you. There will be a dance in each act, each one different from the others and all in a fantastic vein. I beg Your Excellency to be so kind as to return each act as soon as you have read it, since I was not able to make another copy owing to the eye complaint about which I told you in my last letter. Praise be to God this has now almost cleared up.

Signor Giulio has told me that in each act new events will emerge, so that I believe it will certainly be a great success. It remains only for Signorina Margherita to become a brave soldier and for her to master the appropriate gestures completely, now bold, now timid, without fear or restraint. For I am inclined to have her bold in imitation of the music, actions and changes of time [*tempi*] which are done offstage.[1] And I believe that this will not displease Your Excellency since there will be sudden changes between the strong, noisy music and the sweet soft sounds that will make the meaning of the libretto absolutely clear.

I will not say anything else about the part for the young bass, since I am awaiting Your Excellency's reply. That gentleman,

---

[1] The original Italian of this passage is obscure.

however, told me that he [the young man] had made an exorbitant demand for 500 Mantuan *scudi*. I told him that he should inform that young man that they consider him well paid with twenty *scudi* for the month when His Highness had wanted him to come, since he would not have been able to obtain any extra fees here. And I believe that he will already have told you everything ...

31 (*Malipiero 98, p. 264*) To Alessandro Striggio

Venice, 24 July 1627

I beg Your Excellency to forgive me for not replying to your kind and generous letter by the last post. On the day of the post, last Saturday, I was extremely busy with two tasks: one, some chamber music for the Prince of Nuremberg (who was staying incognito in the house of the English ambassador) which lasted from five to eight o'clock; and immediately after this, at the insistent demands of friends, I had to go to the Carmine church for the First Vespers of the Holy Mother of that order, and I remained there, busy, until almost one in the morning.

Now I can write to let Your Excellency know the impression I have received, since seeing your views contained in your letter, from the first act of the 'Spartan Licoris' of Signor Giulio Strozzi. I now have all of this to hand from Signor Giulio, full of excellent improvements. I am now writing it out at home, since copies of neither the whole nor the parts are available. I have already done almost all the first act and would have been able to do more had it not been for the eye trouble of which I told Your Excellency and if I had not had to write some church music. I shall get on with it in the immediate future, and if you would like to read it all when I have copied it I will send it to Your Excellency, so that you can read it through; and you will see that Signorina Margherita will have a great deal to do. I see how much Your Excellency has proposed to give to the young bass, and it appears to me that he has decided to come at His Highness's commands. Really the fee seems to me to be somewhat above his merits, for if it is true that he sings securely, he sings a trifle lugubriously, and his ornaments are not sufficiently articulated, as he fails most of the time to join the chest to the throat voice; and since the throat voice is not joined to that of the chest, the ornaments become crude, hard and displeasing. If the chest voice is not joined to that of the throat, the *gorgie* become quite offensive and ill-defined. But when both are functioning properly, the *gorgie* become sweet and well articulated, and this is the most natural way. Although he is not a member of the chapel he does earn something here and there, for festivals both large and not so large are frequent in this city, especially at this time. He likes to feel that he has a little money coming into his purse, as it does in the blessed liberty [of this city]. I cannot give you any other reason. The young man is rather quiet, modest and unassuming . . .

The fate of *La Finta Pazza Licori* is unknown. It was probably never performed owing to the continuous illness of the Duke of Mantua, who died in 1628; and the ensuing quarrels over the succession eventually erupted into a major war in which Mantua itself was sacked by the Imperial troops. Meanwhile, the festivities for the wedding of the new Duke of Parma began to be considered. Although Monteverdi had received no commission from the bride's household at Florence, he was now engaged to compose music for the activities at Parma itself. These celebrations, which involved the building of the Farnese theatre, have been described in some detail by Stuart Reiner in his excellent article 'Preparations in Parma, 1618, 1627–28'.[1] An additional letter (dated 18 September 1627) in the correspondence has recently been discovered and published.[2] In view of the complications caused by the various delays in the wedding arrangements, we shall refer the reader to these publications for the details. Here it may be said that the *intermezzi* and *torneo* must have been an added incentive for Monteverdi to explore the warlike style of writing of the *stile concitato*.

32 (*Malipiero 102, p. 267*)　To Alessandro Striggio
Venice, 10 September 1627

I am sending Your Excellency the remaining part of *La Finta Pazza Licori*. I did not send it by the last post as I was unable to give it to the copyist by the time the courier left. I have fully

[1] *Music Review*, XXV (1964), p. 273.
[2] Cf. Albi Rosenthal, 'A hitherto unpublished letter of Claudio Monteverdi', *Essays presented to Egon Wellesz*, ed. J. A. Westrup (Oxford, 1966), p. 103.

understood how much Your Excellency has been pleased to tell me, and even without this I would have kept the matter to myself, there being things which if talked about here could have also caused me some embarrassment in my present position. For there are odd goings-on amongst our crowd of singers, and it would be necessary for this reason for me to know how to handle the situation, and the more so when it is commanded of your innate graciousness. The Marquis Bentivoglio, my master for many years past, wrote to me a month ago, asking if I would set to music some verses of His Excellency to be used in a certain noble play that will be given at the marriage of a prince, and would act as *intermezzi* (the play not being sung throughout). As he has been my especial patron, I said that I would do everything possible to obey His Excellency's commands. He replied thanking me deeply and told me that it was a work to be performed at the wedding of the Duke of Parma. I replied that I would do whatever he liked to command me. I wrote immediately to that Prince and had a reply that I must set to work on this commission. Therefore he sent me at once the first *intermezzo*, and I have already done almost half; and I shall do the job easily since it consists almost entirely of solo work. I feel especially honoured that Their Highnesses should have given me this commission, having heard that there were six or seven who tried to obtain the job, yet without any move on my part these gentlemen were so good as to prefer me. Such has been the affair.

Next, with regard to the paragraph which contains the good wishes of His Highness, Duke Vincenzo, my singular master, to whom I shall always bear a special respect at all times, wherever he may be, having received many favours from his boundless goodness; and I shall say that His Highness will always be my master and my patron. Having no doubts of the favour of His Highness, and being certain in the knowledge that he would not consent to ruin me, or to cause me unhappiness, now that I find myself in a secure way of living and thus able to accept or not accept commissions at will — for such is the security, not only of the *maestro di cappella*, but also of the singers who are never asked to do something that they would not be able to do in the time — I shall say that I find myself very unfortunate, do believe me, Your Excellency, to have the bad luck to be so played about with; to be told nine times out of ten that there is no money in the Treasury to pay me that pension which His Highness was pleased to grant me. I would be left thus without any provision in case of illness or death. It would be enough to give peace to my soul to have a canonry at Cremona, together with land of my own without any further recourse to the Treasury. And the Cardinal of Cremona himself would grant this canonry if Her Imperial Highness would so command the Governor of Milan. This canonry could give me some 300 *scudi* in that currency. Certainly, with this sinecure added to my own land, I would be sure that, having worked as long as I am able, I would pass my last days honourably and in the sight of God. With the other situation I should always be in doubt whether, as I have said to Your Excellency, I should be made part of a solemn game to my discomfort. And I would hope for this security, since I am not so young as I was. To this end of gaining the said canonry before these overtures were killed by His Majesty, I was going to pass through Mantua and ask for letters of recommendation from His Highness to Her Imperial Majesty, at the same time presenting him with some of my compositions, in the hope of being favoured with the said canonry. The Prince of Poland has busied himself with this matter, but, unfortunately for me, for various reasons I did not want to present his letters. I am not rich, but equally neither am I poor; but here I live with the security of my salary until my death, and with the even greater security of having my pay every two months at set times without fail; and if it is late for any reason, they send it to my house. Next, I can go into the chapel [of St. Mark's] whenever I want, since there is an assistant director with the title of *vice-maestro di cappella*. I am not required to teach anyone, and the city is most beautiful; and if I want to exert myself just a little I can earn 200 ducats in additional fees. This is my condition. None the less, the Duke will be ever my master and I shall be his servant most certainly and humbly in every place and state . . .

33 (*Malipiero 103, p. 270*) To The Marquis Enzio
Bentivoglio

Venice, 10 September 1627

Yesterday, the 9th, I received from the courier a package of Your
Excellency's in which there was an *intermezzo* and a letter from
Your Excellency, full of infinite kindness and honour towards
my poor person, together with a paragraph of a letter of Her
Highness the Duchess of Parma written to Your Excellency, in
which she graciously commands me, through Your Excellency,
to set to music something that Your Excellency will command
me. I have scarcely had time to read the *intermezzo* through twice
before writing, since the courier leaves today. I have seen, however, how beautiful it really is, so that I am attracted most strongly
to such a fine work. And although there has been little time, this
has not been entirely wasted because I have already begun work,
some evidence of which I will show Your Excellency next
Wednesday. For I have already seen that four kinds of music will
be those best suited to setting the *intermezzo*; one which goes from
the beginning and continues until the start of the anger of Venus
and Diana before their quarrel; the next, from the beginning of
their anger until the finish of the quarrel; the third when Pluto
enters to establish order and calm, during which Diana begins to
fall in love with Endymion; and the fourth and last, from the
beginning of their love until the end. But believe me, Your
Excellency, without your sensitive help there will be places that
would give me not a little trouble, about which I will give Your
Excellency more detailed information on Wednesday. For now, I
will do no more than give thanks to God that He has been gracious
enough to make me receive such a distinguished commission
from such distinguished gentlemen and patrons, praying that He
will make me worthy in mind and spirit, with both of which I
certainly will seek to serve my patrons with every power that I
can muster . . .

Monteverdi went to Parma to finish off his music for the wedding
celebrations and stayed there for some time, much to the disgust of the
Procurators of St. Mark's, who wrote him a stern letter requiring him

to be home for the Christmas festival. A letter from one of his fellow-musicians at Parma[1] tells us that it was Monteverdi's habit to compose only in the mornings and evenings, and to rest in the afternoons. It also hints that he was something of a chatterbox and confirms the impression that he was a difficult man with whom to have dealings.

We have included the following letters less because of their information on Monteverdi's music — all the works mentioned in this phase of the correspondence have been lost — than to show his reaction to a disastrous accident. His son Massimiliano was now a man of 23 and presumably still a medical student at Bologna.

34 (*Malipiero 111, p. 279*)   TO ALESSANDRO STRIGGIO

Venice, 18 December 1627

I received two of Your Excellency's letters at Parma, in one of which you commanded me to compose *Armida*, since this was to His Highness's liking, and also that I should come to Mantua; and in the other, I was commanded to find a really fine castrato soprano. I did not reply to either letter because I was expecting daily to be going back to Venice and to write from there. Now that I find myself in Venice I gave *Armida* to be re-copied immediately three days ago, and I shall send it to Your Excellency by the next post. Concerning the castrato, in Parma the best of them is considered to be Signor Gregorio, who is in the service of His Excellency Cardinal Borghese and who, after a great deal of effort, could, I believe, come [to Mantua]. There is also Signor Antonio Grimano, but there is no hope of having him. There are two others from Rome. One sings in St. Peter's and does not seem to me to be very good since his voice suffers from catarrh, being none too clear, hard in *gorgie* and not having much of a *trillo*. There is also a boy of some eleven years, who seems to me to have a pleasing voice, capable of *gorgie* and *trilli*, but who pronounces everything in a rather stupid way. If Your Excellency would like it, I will approach these two; but I believe that nothing can be done about the others. I have, however, left it so that I could speak with them, and if it pleases God on my return (which will be in the next two or three months) I shall give

[1] Cf. Reiner, op. cit., p. 301

Your Excellency better information, for I was late receiving your most kind letters.

About my visit to Mantua, I shall have to excuse myself at present since, by my honour, I cannot come. My son Massimiliano has been in the prison of the Holy Office for the past three months for the offence of reading a book which he did not know was forbidden: he was accused by the owner of the book, who was himself imprisoned. My son was deceived by the owner, who told him that the book contained only medical matters and astrology, and as soon as he was imprisoned by the Father Inquisitor he wrote to me that I would have to deposit a pledge of 100 ducats so that he could be released before the trial was held. Signor Ercole Marigliani, the councillor, offered voluntarily to help my son, and knowing his kindness I asked him to use his influence so that the Father Inquisitor would accept my security, backed by the annual pension paid me by my master His Highness the Prince. Two months having passed in which I have received no reply from either the Father Inquisitor or Signor Marigliani, I beg with humble reverence to be favoured with the protection of Your Excellency, in using your influence with Signor Marigliani to help Massimiliano in this matter. And if, in his interest, he does not wish to accept this security, I shall be quite prepared to deposit 100 ducats to secure his release; and this I would have done already if I had had a reply from Signor Marigliani. In the hope that Your Excellency will help my son, you may be sure I shall pray to Our Lord for your health this holy Christmastide and New Year...

35 (*Malipiero 112, p. 281*)   TO ALESSANDRO STRIGGIO
Venice, 9 January 1628

I shall be grateful if Your Excellency would forgive me because the last post did not bring you immediately a reply to your most kind and courteous letter. The reason was that the person who collected the letter did not give it in before the post departed. I write now, not having had an earlier opportunity, to give Your Excellency my deepest thanks for the great favour you so spontaneously did me in the matter of that poor unfortunate, Massimiliano my son, to obtain his release from prison. This is so great a favour that I do not know how I shall ever be able to return the smallest part of it, and it puts me under the obligation of always praying to God for the continued happiness of both you and all those in Your Excellency's family. The favour which I now ask with all my heart for you to support with your great authority is this: that you should simply work upon the Father Inquisitor so that Massimiliano be allowed to go home, by virtue of the pledge which the Father has asked from me. I do not desire anything else from Your Excellency, since I have taken a necklace worth 100 ducats to Signor Barbieri, the rich jeweller who lives here in Venice and is both my countryman and my dear friend of many years past. He will write by the present post to Signor Zavarella, who looks after the customs of His Highness the Duke of Mantua and is also a very close friend of Signor Barbieri. He will come to Your Excellency to offer the said pledge personally. I do not intend to inconvenience you in any other way than to ask the Father Inquisitor to let Massimiliano go home. If I have presumed too much on Your Excellency's kindness, blame the great need which I have of your favour, and blame your great humanity and graciousness, which have given rise to my presumption.

I have just heard with extreme sorrow of the death of His Highness Duke Vincenzo, whom God has called to heaven; the more so since, deeply though I have respected all my patrons, I particularly had friendly feelings towards His Highness, both because of the spontaneous goodwill with which he was moved to remember my humble person in showing his liking for my poor compositions, and because I hoped that by his kindness I might have the capital that provides my pension or remittance [corisponsione] of 100 *scudi*. And I hoped to obtain such a privilege more easily so that I could put a little money on one side and thus add something to that which I had earned by my work in the service of Their Highnesses of Parma. But my fate, which has always been fickle rather than happy, has deigned to give me this great mortification. Please God that I have not lost both my patron and that small amount of property which God has given me after so much hard work. I pray and beg with all my heart that the present Duke may live in peace and happiness, which I am quite certain he deserves, since he comes from that Most Noble House. I do not believe nor shall I ever believe that I would have been successful if I had not been able to lean on Your Excellency's favour, to which I hope I shall confidently be able to turn when I am in need of help. Dear Sir, console me with a word about this matter which is so vital to me . . .

P.S. I said above that Signor Zavarella would come to Your Excellency to offer the pledge but now must add that it will be Signor Giovanni Ambrogio Spiga, the jeweller to His Highness, who will do this instead. For the love of God, forgive me for causing you such inconvenience . . .

Having been back to Venice for Christmas, Monteverdi returned to finish his Parma commission. In the end, Duke Odoardo's marriage was postponed until the end of the year, which explains Monteverdi's remarks about the delay, and when the music was eventually given the open-air performance suffered from inclement weather.

36 (*Malipiero 114, p. 285*) TO ALESSANDRO STRIGGIO

Parma, 4 February 1628

The news which Marquis Enzio Bentivoglio (who has passed through Mantua and has now arrived at Parma) gave me, that Your Excellency has just been made a marquis by the present Duke, is delightful and pleasing to me. The infinite duty which I owe and shall continue to owe as long as I live, and the long and continued love that you have so kindly given me, by showing me your special and extraordinary grace continually during my long period of service, make me ever desirous to be made worthy to be known through your grace to be your true servant . . .

How sorry I was to receive Your Excellency's command to send *Armida* to you again after I arrived in Parma, for I left *Armida* in Venice, God be my judge! I did not send it to Your Excellency this Christmas, never thinking that you would want to use it for this carnival after the death of His Highness Duke Vincenzo (now in heaven). This mistake of mine has caused me great pain, as Your Excellency would know if you could see into my heart. *Armida* is at the moment, however, in the hands of Signor Mocenigo, my most friendly and dearest patron. By this post, which today leaves for Venice, I am writing urgently to this gentleman to ask him to send a copy and to give it to Signor Jacomo Rapallini of Mantua, who is much indebted to Your Excellency. He is a singer in St. Mark's and a dear friend of mine, and I am now writing to him pressingly to tell him that he should obtain this from Signor Mocenigo (his master and much loved by him) and to send it without delay to Your Excellency. Knowing the gentleman to be politeness itself and that Signor Rapallini wants to become known as one of Your Excellency's servants, I have no doubt that it will be sent to Your Excellency as quickly as possible.

Here in Parma, in the piazza, they are rehearsing the music I have composed. Their Highnesses, believing that their wedding was going to be much earlier than it has turned out, and having made such attempts to bring to Parma singers from Rome and Modena and instrumentalists from Piacenza and elsewhere, have seen how well it fills their needs and how successful it is; and in the secure hope that at the time everything could be arranged in a few days, they think that we shall all go home until there is definite news of the event. Some say that it could be this May, others that it will be September. There will be two beautiful festival productions. One is a spoken play with *intermezzi* set to music — and these *intermezzi* will each be at least 300 lines long; all kinds of emotions are expressed in these works, which have been written by Signor Don Ascanio Pii, son-in-law of Marquis Enzio, the most exalted and gifted knight. The other will be a *torneo* in which four squadrons of knights will take part, and the master of ceremonies will be the Duke himself. The words of this *torneo* have been written by Signor Achillini and consist of more than 1,000 lines, suitable for a *torneo* but not in the least for setting to music, so it has given me a lot to do. Now they are rehearsing the music for this *torneo*, and where I have not been able to find variety of mood I have sought to create variety by the methods of playing it, and I hope it will please.

I have asked Signor Barbieri, the rich jeweller of Venice, to obtain money to rid Your Excellency of the pledge you have made in respect of Massimiliano; and to this effect, I left with him a necklace worth 100 ducats. I am waiting for a reply, and Your Excellency will forgive the delay...

37 (*Malipiero 115, p. 287*) To ALESSANDRO STRIGGIO
Venice, 1 July 1628

Forced by an event which depressed me deeply, and trusting in the ultimate kindness of Your Excellency, I am writing to ask you that you will honour me in reading these few words and will help me by your favour. This I ask with all my heart. This is what has happened. After believing that my son Massimiliano had been released from his misfortune, both because of the pledge and for various other reasons, a fortnight ago he wrote to me saying that he must return to prison because his trial, concerning the matter of his reading a forbidden book, had not yet come up. I do not know why this is so, for, as you know, it is not my fault. Now about this I begged Signor Marigliani, my master, to arrange for permission for my son to come back to me, which permission, by his good offices, he obtained; and after gaining the information about the facts and discussing them with the Father Inquisitor of Padua, they have certified that my son is in no way guilty and did not deserve to be in prison at all. Now, anxious that they should not imprison him in spite of Signor Marigliani's certificate, I am writing to beg Your Excellency to arrange this with Signor Marigliani. I pray for the love of God that you will want to help me in this, considering not only that my son has not been guilty of anything serious, but also that he is from Mantua and has entered the College of the Medici, and is Your Excellency's servant...

Massimiliano was eventually released. After this incident Monteverdi's known correspondence becomes much more sparse: the reason for this is that the War of the Mantuan Succession destroyed the wealth of the Gonzaga court, and henceforth there were no commissions for Monteverdi. In Venice the great plague of 1630 carried off perhaps half the population, and although Monteverdi and his son Francesco survived, artistic activity there took some time to recover. A new incentive for opera composition came from the opening of the Venetian opera houses in the later 1630's, but as his librettists were presumably nearby, no correspondence was needed, and no letters concerning his late dramatic works are extant. But there are two letters written in the last decade of Monteverdi's life which throw some light on his views on composition. It is not known to whom these letters were sent, although they were clearly directed to someone interested in what were by now old-fashioned 'academic' principles, a fact which has made Prunières surmise that he may have been Giovanni Battista Doni. Since we lack the other side of this correspondence, it is difficult at times to know exactly what Monteverdi means, and the references to a 'new instrument' are mysterious. Perhaps it was an imitation of some Greek instrument, perhaps an *archicembalo*-type experimental harpsichord to try out various methods of tuning. Be this as it may, these final two letters reveal a great deal about Monteverdi's attitudes and help to explain why he persisted with such things as the *stile concitato*.

38 (*Malipiero 118, p. 291*)

Venice, 22 October 1633

I received a most kind letter from Bishop Cervaro, my master and dear patron, at Padua, to which there was another attached, addressed to me from Your Reverence. It was rich in the fruits of honour and full of such great praise for my weak person that I remained almost dazed by it; but considering that from a plant so virtuous and kind, as is the person of Your Reverence, no other fruit than of a similar nature can be born, I am silent, taking this praise not at its face value, but rather as a sign of Your Reverence's rare worth. Knowing myself to be a green plant of a nature that can only bring forth leaves and flowers lacking scent, please be so kind as to accept from me a reply to the praise of your most noble letter, and the knowledge that I feel myself deeply honoured by this letter received by your most humble servant.

Monsignor the Vicar of St. Mark's, having favoured me with a description of Your Excellency's noble qualities and singular worth, told me that you have written a book about music. I replied that I too was writing one, but because of my weakness I fear it may never be finished. Since that gentleman is a servant of His Grace the Bishop of Padua, I believe that Your Reverence may have heard of my writing through these channels; however, I do not know, since I am not aware of what is generally known. But as Your Reverence has been so kind as to honour me thus, may I ask Your Reverence as a favour to look at the remainder of this letter.

You should know, therefore, that while it is true that I am writing it is only with great effort. Years ago events made me do so, but it was natural for me to draw back. Not that I meant to promise to the world something that I was unable to do (owing to my weakness), yet I promised to print a demonstration meant for a certain theoretician of the Prima Prattica that there were other considerations about music, unknown to him, which I called the Seconda Prattica. But I was forced to this because he had chosen to print an attack on one of my madrigals, some of the harmonic progressions of which he considered from the point of view of the Prima Prattica, that is the ordinary rules that were taught in counterpoint to a youth who was beginning to learn note-against-note, not taking into account the melodic factors. But on hearing about the reply which my brother printed in my defence, he quietened down so much that after this he not only declined to continue the argument but actually took up his pen in praise, beginning to like and respect me. The public promise thus remained a promise. Yet though it is hard for me, I intend to pay my debt. I ask you therefore to excuse me for my temerity.

The title of the book will be this: Melody, or the Second Musical Practice. By 'second' I mean the modern ideas; by 'first' the old usage. I am dividing the book into three parts, corresponding to the three parts of Melody. In the first, I deal with word-setting [oratione]; in the second with harmony; in the third with rhythm. I believe that this book will not be without its usefulness in the world, since I found in practice that when I was composing the lament of Ariadne, not finding any book but Plato which opened up to me the way of imitation of nature, nor one which told me that I ought to be an imitator of nature — and he [Plato] shed so dim a light that I was scarcely able to see, in my ignorance, what he showed me — I found, I say, what hard work is necessary to do even what little I did in this matter of 'imitation'. I hope therefore that it will not displease but will in the end be a success. I shall be content to be praised for offering a few new ideas rather than many conventional ones. And for this new presumption I must ask forgiveness.

It has given me great consolation to hear that a new instrument has been re-discovered in our times. God knows how much I pray for the continued happiness of the clever person who invented this — in fact, Your Reverence. Truly I have pondered a great deal about the reason for this discovery, on which I say that where the Greeks based their discoveries on so many differences[1] as they have done, there were not only many of those that we use today, but also many that have been lost. Among the theorists of our days who have professed to know the whole of our art, not one has shown this to the world. I hope, however, to say something about this in my book that will not be displeasing.

Taking account of these considerations of which I am speaking, it would be a good idea if Your Reverence would do me the favour you promised in your kindness, to send me at a convenient time a copy of your kind letter about these erudite and new matters; and I beg of you to fulfil this gracious promise ...

39 (*Malipiero 119, p. 294*)

Venice, 2 February 1634

I have received two letters from Your Reverence. One arrived before Christmas, at a time when I was very busy writing the midnight mass, which, according to the traditions of this city, is a mass composed afresh each year by the *maestro di cappella*. The other came a fortnight ago by the courier, when I was not in good health owing to a catarrhal discharge which began to affect my left eye just after Christmas, so that I have passed long days in which I was unable not only to write but also to read. I am still

---

[1] The meaning of this word in this context is obscure and makes the passage difficult to understand without knowing what his correspondent has said. Perhaps the 'differences' refer to various divisions of the octave.

not completely recovered and am in some pain. For these two reasons I ask Your Reverence to excuse the delay in writing.

I read your most kind and gracious first letter only a fortnight ago, learning from it your admirable views, all worthy of my close consideration, and for which I offer my deepest thanks. I have not seen them before. It was Galilei who dealt with the practice of the ancients twenty years ago.[1] I enjoyed reading your letter and examining that part in which the differences in practical notation between the ancients and ourselves are shown. I am not going to go on to try and understand them, for I am sure that they would be no more to me than obscure signs (not to put it more strongly), since the practical methods of the ancients are wholly beyond recall. In view of this I have turned my studies in another direction, basing them on the fundamentals of the best philosophers who examined the nature of things; and because, according to my reading, I hold that they search for the affections by means of reason and to satisfy the laws of nature, I am writing on practical matters and am attempting to show that really one has to follow only the present rules to achieve the aforementioned satisfactions. For this reason I have put the name 'Second Practice' at the head of my book and hope to make it all clear. So that it will not be attacked and that everyone will think well of it, I have in my writings kept away from the methods of the Greeks and their words and musical signs, keeping to the voices and the notation that we use today in our musical practice; for it is my intention to show how far I have been able to draw the thinking of those philosophers into the service of good art and not to follow the manner of the First Practice, which takes only the music into account.

Would it please God that I could be near you, so that, with Your Reverence's singular kindness, wisdom and advice, we could discuss everything personally and you could hear all I have to say about the ordering of the principles and the divisions of the various parts of my book. But distance makes this impossible. I have an obligation to visit the Holy House at Loreto, to thank the Holy

[1] The precise meaning of this passage is obscure, and in any case Vincenzo Galilei died in 1591.

Virgin for Her kindness during the plague year in Venice. I hope in the Lord to manage this soon, on which occasion I shall come on to Rome, if the Lord grants me grace, so that I can not only enjoy both the sight and noble sound of your most noble instrument but also have the honour of your most learned conversation.

I have seen a drawing of this instrument on a piece of paper which you sent me. This was meant to satisfy my curiosity, but on the contrary it has made it grow. In your second letter you ask me to make the attempt with Scapino to send Your Reverence drawings of the many extraordinary instruments that he plays but although I would like to serve you very much in this matter, I have been unable to help you, for he is performing in Modena, not in Venice. I am very sorry about this. However, I have been quite busy persuading certain friends at least to describe what they can remember. So they gave me the present little drawing, which I am sending now to Your Reverence. I have not seen the instruments myself, but from the little information that I am sending it seems to me that they are new in shape but not in sound, since all of them resemble the sounds of the instruments that we use.

One that I saw in Mantua thirty years ago was made and played by a certain Arab who came from Turkey, and this man was in residence at the court of His Highness of Mantua, my master. This instrument was a cittern about the same size as ours, strung with the same strings and played in the same way, with the difference that the cover was half of wood from the part nearest the neck and covered with vellum on the underneath part. This was well executed and glued together. The strings of the cittern were attached to pegs, but pegs on the underside, and they were supported by the grooving which was put in the middle of the said vellum, and the player's little finger made the vellum vibrate while he was playing the harmonies. These harmonies came out in the form of a tremolo, which gave a pleasing effect. I have never heard anything more novel which was to my liking. I shall keep on the lookout, and if anyone shows me anything that might be to your liking I shall not fail to send you a sketch of it immediately . . .

II

The Musical
Environment

DENIS ARNOLD

Monteverdi and his Teachers

Some, perhaps many, composers seem to know little of other men's music; and that little is often a curious selection of our heritage, chosen to help the individual solve his problems of technique and style, without much thought of its intrinsic worth. It is rare for a Mozart to find inspiration in the work of Johann Sebastian Bach, or a Haydn to receive a renewed impetus from Mozart. The chosen guide is just as probably a Sarti or Wagenseil, who serves the somewhat narrow purpose of the composer just as well.

Monteverdi, by contrast, was extremely well informed. Scattered throughout his letters, prefaces, and the documents relating to his life, there are references to no fewer than three dozen composers. Some are men he may have known personally. Of the list of composers mentioned in the preface of the *Scherzi Musicali* of 1607 as involved in the development of the new manner which Monteverdi called the *seconda prattica*, all had been at courts neighbouring that of the Gonzagas: Luzzaschi and Gesualdo at Ferrara, where Cipriano de Rore had also worked; Bardi, Alfonso Fontanella, Cavalieri and the other members of the Camerata academy at Florence. Marc'Antonio Ingegneri had been his teacher at Cremona, Giaches de Wert was for some time his immediate superior at Mantua. Such is the common acquaintance of musicians. But the list of *prima prattica* composers is a different matter. Ockeghem, Josquin, Pierre de la Rue, Mouton, Crequillon, Clemens non Papa, Gombert and Willaert were part of the distant past. They had little to offer any musician of the early seventeenth century and least of all to the 'modern' composer of up-to-date madrigals and dramatic entertainments.

The impeccable taste of Monteverdi's choice from musical

history arouses our suspicions. His taste in contemporaries was mixed enough. Mingling with the admittedly great masters are minor, even insignificant composers whose names were soon to perish and whose music today has little interest. The old Netherlanders were without exception great composers, quoted as authorities by all the writers of treatises to display their learning. Could Monteverdi have copied their names from some august theoretician without really knowing their work by anything except reputation? To this the reply must surely affirm Monteverdi's honesty. The motets and masses of Gombert and most of the others were in the library of the Duke's chapel at Mantua for his study. His parody mass *In illo tempore* shows that he had a thorough grasp of the old manner, and the fact that the Roman publisher Masotti invited him to edit Arcadelt's ever-popular madrigals for four voices in 1627 suggests that he was known to have an interest in the music of the early sixteenth century. Remembering that Monteverdi possessed a copy of Zarlino's *Istitutioni harmoniche*[1] and was acquainted with Bottrigari's theoretical writings, we can build up the picture of a man thoroughly versed in his art, interested in its many branches, and one of the first historically minded composers.

Great composers rarely owe much to their teachers, but Monteverdi's breadth and astonishing technical competency from a very early age surely indicate that his Cremonese master, Ingegneri, was a man of extraordinary ability. Not that he was an outstanding worldly success. The cathedral *maestro di cappella* was never as fashionable or as well paid as the court composer or virtuoso; and Cremona was no great centre of music-making or high society. Ingegneri was not particularly successful in his published works either. He was clearly a reasonably fluent composer of secular music, who could produce eight books of madrigals during the twenty years of his maturity. Yet scarcely a dozen of his pieces were included in the popular anthologies in his lifetime, a sign that he was not in the main stream of North Italian music. Only one of his madrigal books (significantly an early collection) achieved the distinction of being reprinted more than

[1] See Gustave Reese, *Music in the Renaissance* (London, 1954), plate IV.

once, and this at a time when a single collection by Marenzio usually went through half-a-dozen Italian editions before being taken up by the foreign presses, and even an anthology of pieces by a group of Mantuan mediocrities achieved a reprinting, so fashionable was the genre.[1]

Ingegneri was as competent as any of the composers of the 1570's and 80's — a great deal more so than many — but there is a simple explanation for his neglect. Tastes changed rapidly in his lifetime. Andrea Gabrieli's light touch transformed the semi-serious madrigal form from a 'learned' style, based essentially on extended melodic lines, to one based on easily memorable tags and short phrases. For those demanding more earnest essays in the modern manner, Marenzio managed to bring the resources of clear-cut harmony and dramatic chromaticism to the form, without completely disrupting it. Ingegneri remained of a previous generation, not unlike Lassus, who came to his peak of stylistic development in the period just before 1575, and thereafter became something of an anachronism. And like Lassus he is best thought of as belonging to the post-Rore generation, for he undoubtedly took up the basic philosophy of that master without making radical changes. Ingegneri was proud of his indebtedness, for in dedicating his *Primo libro de madrigali a sei voci* to the Duke of Parma in 1586, he thanks him because '. . . the favours and patronage which you as liberally gave in former times to M. Cipriano de Rore of happy memory were favour and patronage to all practitioners of his art; since under your protection and with the opportunity which he received from you, he made such advances that he became an everlasting example and master to all in the craft of perfect composition. But those who more especially and heavily than the others must remain obliged to Your Highness are those who could at that time, when he flourished at your most happy court, be on friendly terms with M. Cipriano, and talked with him, and personally received his tuition. . . .'[2]

[1] *L'Amorosa Caccia de Diversi Eccellentissimi Musici Mantovani Nativi a cinque voci* (Venice, 1588).

[2] For the original Italian, see Emil Vogel, *Bibliothek der gedruckten weltlichen Vocalmusik Italiens* (repr. Hildesheim, 1962), I, p. 330.

There were two basic lessons that were to be learned from Cipriano, and both were well mastered by Ingegneri. The prime importance attached by Rore to the expression of the words infected all the succeeding composers. Some interpreted this as a licence to try extreme experiments; but, like the master himself, Ingegneri found it possible to maintain the musical interest while matching the detail of the verse. A melisma to make the lips part in a smile to express the word 'rise', as in *Quasi vermiglia rosa*:[1]

Ex. 1

(When heaven smiled.....)

or a broken line to express the trembling of the apprehensive lover:

Ex. 2

(I tremble......)

do not essentially interrupt the musical thought of a craftsman-composer. Nor is there any departure from musicality in the second instructive feature of Rore's music, the use of chromaticism, in the way it is applied in the madrigals of Ingegneri. Tonality is not disintegrating but merely widening in the occasional use of D flat and A flat chords in *Hore sacre*,[2] or in the imitations of the chromatic tetrachord of *Ah tu Signor*:[3]

[1] *Il Quinto Libro de Madrigali a cinque voci* (Venice, 1587).
[2] *Il Primo Libro de Madrigali a quattro voci* (Venice, 1578 — not the first edition).
[3] *Il Quarto Libro de Madrigali a cinque voci* (Venice, 1584).

Ex. 3

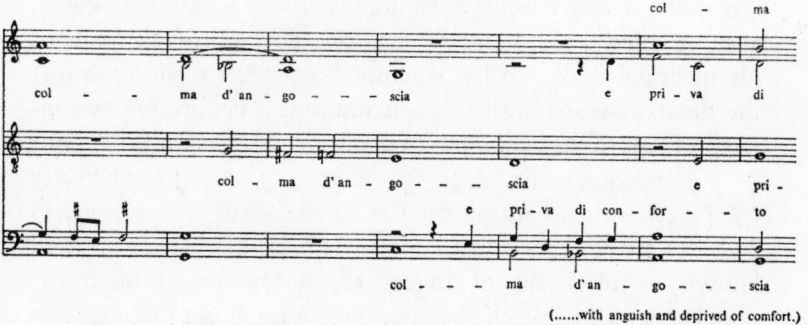

(......with anguish and deprived of comfort.)

And more than anything else Ingegneri is like Rore in that musical form is one of his prime interests. Far from breaking the genre into segments for the better expression of the contrasts of the verse, as Marenzio and later composers were to do, his madrigals show a basic unity of mood. This is achieved by an equally basic unity of texture, and by the working-out of contrapuntal material at sufficient length to make the enigmatic, dramatic changes of the final phase of the madrigal quite unthinkable. Even in his most mature works, written at a time when the 'modern' style was well established, this feeling for the general rather than the particular was kept well to the fore. In *La verginella*,[1] for example, published in the year in which Monteverdi's first madrigals also appeared, the main preoccupation is with pattern. In the very first phrase, the lower parts may enter with different words to prevent too great a length, but four out of the five voices enter with the same musical theme. The second section uses up its words quickly too, in a number of close imitations between the voices; but then the whole section is virtually repeated to give the correct musical proportions. The final paragraph is given a similar treatment so that the musical material is spread over some thirty bars — nearly half the madrigal. Repetition of concluding sections is, of course, quite

[1] *Il Quinto Libro de Madrigali a cinque voci* (Venice, 1587), available in a modern edition edited by Gian Francesco Malipiero, *Adriano Willaert e i suoi discendenti* (Venice, 1963), p. 23.

common in early madrigals (the most famous of all of these, Arcadelt's *Il dolce e bianco cigno*, shows how it was usually done), and Ingegneri uses it no fewer than two dozen times throughout his madrigal books. What is unusual about *La verginella* is that the thematic material of this conclusion is a deliberate development of that of the beginning of the madrigal. The canzona motif ♩ ♩ ♩ becomes first 𝄾 ♩ ♩ ♩, then 𝄾 ♩. ♪ ♩ ♩ and finally ♫ ♫. There is no reason for this in the verse. The musician's desire to shape predominates; and if the *da capo* idea was well known to musicians of Ingegneri's generation through the popularity of the French chanson, there is no doubt that here it is applied with subtlety and skill.

Ingegneri, then, was a worthy master for such a pupil as the young Monteverdi. Yet he was so old-fashioned that, at first sight, he would appear to be the kind of model young men tend to ignore. Certainly so sagacious a critic as Alfred Einstein thought that the older man had little deep effect on his pupil, and a preliminary glance at Monteverdi's *Il primo libro de madrigali* apparently confirms the disparity between the two. A closer examination reveals more similarities, for Monteverdi has many of the solid musical interests of his master. If the contrasts of texture, the pathetic dissonance of the fashionable pastoral madrigal have proved too attractive to ignore, his attention to shape and the adequate development of musical sections is still of paramount importance. Last sections are often repeated *in extenso*. Earlier passages are equally not devoid of thematic links between sections to make for smooth musical development. In *Amor, per tua mercè*, there is even the same use of the chanson motif as in Ingegneri's *La verginella* with the ♩ ♩ ♩ changing first to ♩ ♫ and 𝄾 ♩ ♩ ♩ — although Monteverdi is less sure of himself, and the madrigal scarcely explores the possibilities of either the verse or the contrapuntal tags at all thoroughly. And if there is any doubt about the relationship of master and pupil, a comparison of their settings of the fashionable poem *Ardo sì, ma non t'amo* and its reply, *Ardi e gela*,[1] will remove it. Again at first sight Monteverdi appears much more modern. He prefers the lighter colours

[1] Malipiero (ed.), op. cit., p. 31.

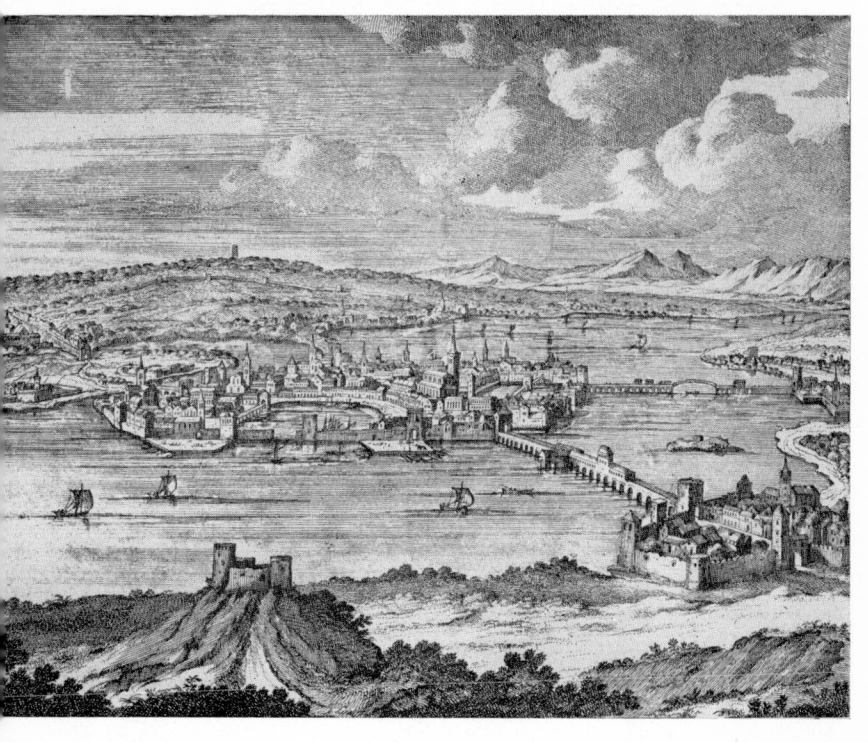

2 A view of Mantua with its lakes, from a 17th-century engraving

provided by the use of the upper voices (the lowest part is written
in the tenor clef), and this feeling for contrasts of colours revealed
in the concertante play of various groupings of them is something
Ingegneri is too old to appreciate. Then the similarities appear.
The opening motifs are virtually identical:

Exx. 4*a* and 4*b*

(I burn, yes, but do not love you......)

Monteverdi covers the ground of the verse more speedily than
does his master, but even so, until the closing section of the
madrigal, when he invents a 'modern' short motif to work out,
his vocal lines are smooth and well developed. He also accepts
the final hint of the older man. Ingegneri binds his two madrigals
together by using the same thematic material. The suggestion
has come from the repetition of the word *sdegno*, and since the
concluding section of the first madrigal has been repeated at
great length, some return of its tag seems natural if the two pieces
are to become an artistic entity. The composer is not unsubtle
about this. The material used may be the same; its treatment is not.
Having displayed it at great length in its exposition, the re-
statement is necessarily more concise. Monteverdi is a shade more
obvious. He not only repeats his concluding section in his first
part, he repeats the concluding section of the second part also;
and as the two are virtually identical, even the least educated of
the noble dilettanti can hardly have failed to notice the device.
Nevertheless, Monteverdi has his own touch of sophistication.
The first madrigal ends with a definitive cadence. The lover is
quite sure that he has said the final word:

I burn with anger and not with love.

The reply startles him:

> *Burn and freeze just as you will ...*

After this, there is no certainty, and the second madrigal ends with an inconclusive cadence, which, however common in the early part of the sixteenth century, by the 1580's is distinctly unusual in the up-to-date madrigal. Equally, when Monteverdi adds yet a third madrigal to the group, a *contrarisposta*, he adds to the air of dissension with a similarly unsure ending. Again we notice his interest in pattern, for having used the *risposta* as a middle section, he opens his third piece with an inversion of the opening theme of *Ardo sì*:

Ex. 5

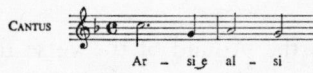

A composer of 23, with four published volumes behind him, does not admit to his pupillage without good reason, and the fact that Monteverdi put 'discepolo del Sig. Marc'Antonio Ingegneri' on the title-page of his *Secondo libro de madrigali* in 1590 proves that he held his master in high regard. Probably the main lesson he had learned from him was that the craft of music was just as important as inspiration or philosophy. In an age when the amateur composer (albeit often the professional performer) was rife, it was a necessary lesson. It went deeply into Monteverdi's mind. To his final years he remained a craftsman when craftsmanship was comparatively little esteemed, at least among the general public. That he later took to the duet rather than the solo song is a symptom of his attitude. The duet requires more craft, less hedonistic melody.[1] And it is no coincidence that in as late a work as *L'Incoronazione di Poppea,* the famous ensemble of Seneca's friends, 'Non morir, Seneca', is a madrigal very similar in both its attitude and technique to the chromatic works of Rore and Ingegneri.

[1] Cf. *infra,* pp. 200–1.

If he had gone directly to Florence from Cremona, it is just possible that the path on which Monteverdi had started would have been diverted into the by-ways of monody and operatic experiment. As it was, by finding his first job in Mantua he ensured for himself a second thoroughly professional master, Giaches de Wert. No documents tell us that he was active in the development of the young man's style, but, as Bernard Berenson has said, '. . . in this [finding out what spirit influenced an artist], the really vital matter, historians with their documents seldom give us any help. It is a matter which we must establish for ourselves by the study of the artist's own works, and by determining their relation to those of his predecessors. . . .'[1] And there can be absolutely no doubt that the 'eccellente Giaches', to quote Monteverdi's earliest known letter, was one of the most influential of his associates. By the time Monteverdi met him, he was probably well in his fifties, a man of great experience and much respected by the musical world. A Netherlander, he had come to Italy in his early twenties and had visited and worked at several courts before becoming *maestro di cappella* to Guglielmo Gonzaga in 1565. He remained in Mantua for the rest of his life, building up the distinguished musical establishment which was to reach its highest point in the last decade of the century. Wert himself died in 1596 and was buried in the ducal chapel of S. Barbara.

It is easy to understand why Monteverdi was deeply affected by him, for Wert was one of the great original madrigal composers of the century. Arriving in Italy at a time when the great vogue for Rore's style was at its height, it is remarkable to find him taking a somewhat different attitude to the problems of secular composition. In a few early works he shows his Northern upbringing. Such a madrigal as *Chi salirà per me madonn'in cielo*,[2] from his *Primo libro de'madrigali a quattro voci* of 1561, is in the old polyphonic tradition, its motifs worked out as skilfully as anyone could wish. Only the thoroughly professional composer

[1] Bernard Berenson, *Rudiments of Connoisseurship* (New York, 1962), p. 25; originally published as *The Study and criticism of Italian art*, second series (London, 1902).

[2] Cf. William Barclay Squire, *Ausgewählte Madrigale,* II (Leipzig, n.d.).

would have thought of the opening of *Quand'io mi volgo*[1] in his second book for five voices (published in the same year), with the inversion of the soprano theme given out simultaneously by the second voice:

Ex. 6

(When I turn back to gaze over the years)

But even at this time, Wert was fully aware of Rore's innovations and was in fact prepared to take them a stage further. His inventiveness in creating musical imagery to catch the detail of the words was from the beginning quite remarkable. There are the usual symbols to express such words as 'alto' ('high') or 'lungo' ('long' or 'slow'); conventional figures such as the sighing rest to precede 'sospiro' or the smiling melisma for 'riso' are the commonplaces of his style. He will invent a natural fanfare motif suggested by *Accend'i cor a l'arme* ('The heart is stirred to take up arms') and expand it into a section remarkably reminiscent of a Monteverdian *madrigale guerriero*:

Ex. 7

(The heart is stirred to take up arms.)

[1] Ed. Carol MacClintock, Giaches de Wert: *Collected Works,* II (American Institute of Musicology, 1962), p. 53.

Still more impressive is his economy of means in this expression of the verbal image. The opening of *Cantai, or piango*[1] (also from the second book of five-voiced madrigals) at first looks conventionally polyphonic with its suggestion of inversion between soprano and tenor. Within half-a-dozen bars it has established the fluctuating emotions of the manic lover. His joy ('cantai') reveals itself in the *note nere*, the fast movement still comparatively new and up-to-date around 1560. His gloom ('piango') brings about a violent contrast, requiring dissonance and slow motion, in the original made the more startling to the singer who sees the page by the use of open 'white' notes in the ligatures:

Ex. 8

(I sang, now I weep.)

So vivid an equation of words and music continues throughout the madrigal. 'Dolcezza' and 'dolce' call forth consonance; 'canto' has a melisma; 'altezza' displays a rising motif; 'amaro' ('bitter') finds expression in an unusual intensity of dissonance.

[1] Ibid, p. 32.

Such mastery of the idiom is remarkable in a man in his mid-twenties.

The mastery was Wert's; the idiom (as far as these characteristics are concerned) was essentially Rore's. Nevertheless, even in *Cantai, or piango* there are signs of another attitude to the problems of setting words. For after the opening section has set the mood (or rather moods), there follows an extended passage in which the audibility of the poem seems the prime concern. Declamation is careful and exact; and the texture is for the most part homophonic. What variety exists comes from the different groupings of voices, not from the interplay of the several voices. Most remarkable of all is the fact that the repetition of the individual phrases of the poem occurs comparatively rarely in this section. An examination of the uppermost part shows extraordinarily little 'laceration of the poetry' (to quote the Camerata's telling phrase). If we quote the poem, underlining each repeated phrase, the result is revealing:

> *Cantai, or piango, e non men di dolcezza*
> *Del pianger prendo che del canto presi,*
> *Ch'a la cagion non a l'effetto intesi*
> *Son i miei sensi vaghi pur d'altezza.*
> *Indi e mansuetudine e durezza*
> *Et atti feri et umili e cortesi*
> *Port' egualmente, nè mi gravan pesi,*
> *Nè l'arme mie punta di sdegni spezza.*

Even more revealing is a comparison with a more or less contemporary madrigal, a typical example of the epoch by Vincenzo Ruffo, published in 1558:

> *L'alto splendor ch'in voi sovente infonde*
> *La fida aurora nell'aprir del giorno*
> *E quel che i monti scalda e i piani e l'onde*
> *Mentre gira felice il ciel adorno*
> *Agguagliar non potrà mai lo splendore*
> *Ch'ognor nel viso di Virginia splende.*[1]

[1] Malipiero (ed.), op. cit., p. 14.

The difference lies less in the quantity of repetition than its relevance to the expression of the basic emotions of the verse. Ruffo repeats the phrases casually, with little thought for their importance, thinking mainly of the musical balance that is needed to work out the various contrapuntal tags. Wert, on the contrary, does this only to keep the traditional expansion of the last lines. His main repetition in the middle section is to show how intensely the lover feels, stressing the emotional words 'mansuetudine e durezza' ('gentleness and harshness'), which are given out in pure homophony. Again the mastery is astonishing, less this time for the composer's youth than for the fact that he was working in a foreign language and with some of its greatest poetry.

And again these features of his idiom are by no means unique to Wert. Another style common in the 1550's has clearly affected his thinking. This is the homophonic declamation of Willaert's *Musica Nova*, published in the very year that these madrigals of Wert appeared — though declamation is perhaps too strong a term for any music by either composer. Rather is it that Wert shares with Willaert the understanding of the importance of clarity and emotional balance in setting words to music. Both were musicians first and last; neither seems to have attempted consciously to work out an academic theory, though such speculation was as popular in their time as in Monteverdi's. In neither is there a hint of amateurism; Monteverdi's lineage is based on the great professional traditions of the composers from the Netherlands.

Unlike Ingegneri, Wert was one of the great successes of his time. By virtue of his post as *maestro di cappella* at Mantua, he was at the top of his profession. He was prolific. He produced a dozen books of madrigals, some canzonets and a considerable body of church music. For years, the principal anthologies contained his music. Yet there is one aspect of his success which needs explanation. His early madrigal-books were reprinted many times. His first book of five-voiced madrigals appeared five times, his second book four times. His later music was apparently not so well received. His eighth book achieved two editions, the ninth and tenth not even that. And whereas Marenzio's madrigals continued in favour well into the seventeenth century, by 1600 Wert's music was already in process of being forgotten.

One reason for this seeming decline in popularity is suggested by the dedication of his *Ottavo libro de madrigali a cinque voci* to the Duke of Ferrara: '... I would have committed a most grave mistake if I had dedicated these compositions of mine to anyone else, since they were for the most part written in Ferrara ... And where in the world could they be better sung than at the court of Your Highness? ... To whom today is not known these marvels of both art and nature, the voices, the grace, the temperament, the memory and the other, rare qualities of the three noble young ladies of Her Highness the Duchess of Ferrara? ...'[1] Not only could they not be sung better than in Ferrara; few courts had the requisite women singers who could cope with their difficulties. Quite a number of the madrigals in this book are thus occasional music for the renowned ensemble of the Este court. Without the art of Lucrezia Bendidio, Tarquinia Molza and Laura Peperara, with their gift for improvisatory decoration, their dexterity of voice and intelligence, these madrigals can hardly have made much effect. The opening of *Usciva homai*, in spite of the bright colours of the upper voices, seems to cry out for virtuoso decoration, not to mention the evenness of tonal quality to make such altitudes bearable:

Ex. 9

(At last, came of the soft, cool womb......)

---

[1] Original in Vogel, op. cit., II, p. 343.

Mantua could perhaps rival the Ferrarese group; few other courts or cities were in this category.

But there were other reasons for Wert's receding fashionability. His development of both the Willaert-ian clarity of words, and the Rore-ian vividness of the musical image eventually became a little eccentric. His declamatory madrigals late in life became very austere. Whereas a piece such as *Aspro cor'e selvaggio* from the first book for five voices had been relatively short and achieved intensity because the variety of vocal grouping could maintain the interest throughout, the madrigal sequence *O Primavera* of Book XI is so extended that it really requires all the resources of the madrigalist to underscore the emotions of Guarini's poem. This is precisely what is lacking in Wert's setting. In spite of some daring chromaticism and the occasional delicious touch of word-painting, it appears shapeless. The recitative-like progress which setting a huge piece of verse in such a limited space entails, allows little contrast of rhythm. Even in lesser works, this is a serious drawback. So often it is the detail which stands out, rather than the overall effect, as in *Quel rossignol*, where an exquisite melodic idea at the beginning peters out before achieving the emotional potential inherent in the verse:

Ex. 10

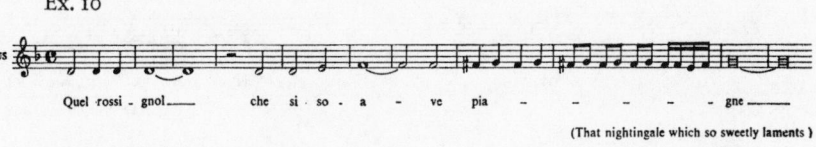

Quel rossi - gnol —— che si so - a - ve pia - - - - - gne ——

(That nightingale which so sweetly laments)

If it is the lack of musical incident which causes the declamatory madrigals to seem a little dull, the unsatisfactory nature of some of the pictorial madrigals is the result of too much. Even in his earliest books there are roughnesses of style which are unusual for the second half of the sixteenth century. A little of this roughness comes from the harmony. Wert obviously had a liking for false relations, which lead him to use even an occasional 'English' cadence — although unlike the English he uses it for direct expression of the verse. But Wert's main asperities concern melody. At the beginning of his career there are some unconventional intervals in the vocal lines of some otherwise unremarkable madrigals. The augmented second is quite common, and no addition of *musica ficta* that is at all satisfactory will eliminate them. Leaps of sixths (not difficult for the professional singer but tricky for the amateur) and of sevenths (not encouraged by the theorists at all) are not unknown.

In Wert's early madrigals such awkwardnesses seem casual (though with his splendidly sure technique he could have avoided it if he had felt so inclined). In his later music, there can be no doubt of his deliberate intent. Having invented a phrase using an unusual interval, he lingers on it throughout the parts until it yields its full intensity. The use of the diminished fourth in *Valle che de' lamenti miei*, to take an example from the ninth book of madrigals, would be of little consequence if it happened just once in the *cantus*; add the *altus* with the same interval, and immediately a false relation occurs, to give still more atmosphere:

Ex. 11

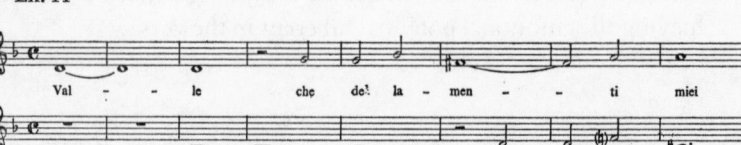

(Valley that of my laments......)

Then Wert adds each voice in turn, all of them using the same melodic trick, until the paragraph has expanded to some thirty bars of slowly moving harmony. There is little actual dissonance, yet the melody has done its work — to create a sombre, smouldering atmosphere. This kind of melody reaches its farthest point in Wert's setting of Petrarch's sonnet *Solo e pensoso*.[1] Again it is impossible to find a single interval which by itself would cause any real trouble to the singer or listener. But follow a downward

[1] *Das Chorwerk*, No. 80, *Vier Madrigale von Mantuaner Komponisten*, ed. Denis Arnold (Wolfenbüttel, 1961), p. 1.

perfect fifth by another perfect fifth (instead of the conventional fourth) and the strangeness of mood immediately imparts itself. Or use a succession of sixths, give them out in parallel motion in three voices, and the effect is very odd:

Ex. 12

(But yet [be] the paths so harsh or so wild)

Finally, to make the bass voice sing the extreme notes of a two-octave range within the space of three bars, in the manner of Purcell's John Gostling, and it becomes clear why Wert's late madrigal-books never sold well.

Why did Wert do this? The romantic biographer would no doubt find the reason in his tragic love-affair with the singer Tarquinia Molza, a match not allowed to a mere musician and 'povero fiammingo'. A more realistic musicologist must search elsewhere — and probably in the lost archives (if indeed they ever existed) of the Accademia degli Intrepidi of Ferrara. For it was in the musical academies of Ferrara that the 'modern' style was forged. It was there that the *archicembalo* was created to try out the chromatic experiments of Vicentino; and was played by Luzzaschi and Gesualdo. It was at Ferrara that the new orchestral sonorities were tried out by Bottrigari and his associates. And it was in Ferrara that the singers existed to try out the various theories concerning the expression of the words, which derived from the Platonic ideas of universal interest to musicians in the later sixteenth century. That such ideas were to lead to monody and opera in the hands of the Florentines need cause no surprise, since the main revolution came from the amateurs who were especially strong in Count Bardi's Camerata. The Ferrarese academies had started earlier and were more firmly orientated musically.

Wert's compromise style seems logically the result of some

such compromise in thinking. So does Monteverdi's. The closeness of their relationship is seen most clearly in the latter's second, third and fourth books of madrigals. At first, as in *Ecco mormorar l'onde*, which resembles Wert's *Vezzosi augelli*[1] so closely, it is the realistic, Tasso-esque elements which attracted him. It was the declamation and the violence of Wert's music that turned him into the style of the *Vattene* madrigal-cycle in which the older man's manner is not fully assimilated; and then into the agonies of the Guarini settings in the fourth book. Here Wert's experiments are finally fulfilled in a volume intended as a homage to Duke Alfonso d'Este, as was Wert's best music. And when, later, Monteverdi went appreciably beyond Wert's acerbities, his style still remains based solidly on the older man's principles. The difference between the Sestina, *Incenerite spoglie*, of Monteverdi's sixth book, published in 1614, and some of the madrigals of Wert's eleventh book, which appeared twenty years earlier, is one of degree, not of kind. The very opening of Monteverdi's cycle indeed could have been written by Wert, as could the pastoral climax of the last section (based on an old-fashioned madrigalian tag); and if this is not true of the dissonance of the fourth section, *Ma te raccoglie*, it is hardly surprising, considering what had happened to the art of music in those intervening years.

From Ingegneri, Monteverdi had learned craftsmanship. From Wert he learned the art of expressing passion, and this was to be just as rare a quality in the early years of the seventeenth century. For although it is usually assumed that the term 'baroque' implies extravagance of feeling, this is certainly not true of most of the composers who flourished in what music historians have liked to call 'the early baroque period'. The Camerata composers, for all their technical novelty, were emotionally restrained in comparison with some of the madrigalists who were working around the turn of the century. The Venetian church musicians who set the style of seventeenth-century church music were monumental rather than passionate in their stately motets. Only those who had learned their art in the later decades of the previous century — Gesualdo and Marco da Gagliano in vocal music,

[1] Ed. Arnold (London, 1961).

Frescobaldi in instrumental music — retained the grand excesses typical of those inbred North Italian courts. They are, in fact, mannerist rather than baroque composers, and Monteverdi is the greatest of them.

DENIS ARNOLD

Monteverdi: some Colleagues and Pupils

ew things could be worse than indifferent mannerism. Extra-vagance of the kind in which Wert and Monteverdi indulged demands genius; anything less seems merely eccentric. So perhaps it is not surprising that only one other of the Mantuan composers seriously attempted to follow this path (though nearby Ferrara had produced a greater crop of strange compositions over the years). Benedetto Pallavicino was a composer of whom Monteverdi apparently did not think very highly,[1] but this is something not unknown with colleagues in any situation — the more especially in the claustrophobic atmosphere of a small court. Added to which, Pallavicino had been promoted to be *maestro di cappella* at Mantua when Monteverdi probably considered himself to be in the running for the job, although admittedly he was still only in his late twenties and should not have expected to gain it over the head of a man of much greater experience. But Pallavicino, having also come from Cremona, was no distinguished foreigner, and young men are apt to consider themselves as special cases, worthy of rapid promotion.

In the event, it is not difficult to understand the Duke's point of view, for long before Monteverdi had appeared on the Mantuan scene Pallavicino had proved himself a perfectly competent composer. By 1593 he had written seven books of madrigals, and from a casual sampling of these it is evident that he was thoroughly up-to-date, without being a revolutionary. The contents of the fourth book for five voices, for example, are not unlike those of Monteverdi's second book. Diatonic and short-breathed phrases

[1] Cf. *supra*, p. 23.

make singing them a not too arduous pleasure. The tendency to repeat sections either exactly or with variations mainly of texture gives an air of easy memorability. The words are expressed by conventional symbols, and if there is no grand passion there is a quiet efficiency which is attractive. The concluding section of *Mentre che qui d'intorno* is typically modern and resembles that of Marenzio's *Dissi a l'amata*, a popular madrigal from a popular book published only a year or two earlier.[1] No wonder Pallavicino was esteemed at Mantua.

Ex. I

(Yes, I languish: and I burn with love at every hour.)

In these earlier works there are few hints of the revolution to come and unexpectedly few signs of any influence of Wert. But, like Marenzio and Monteverdi, Pallavicino was to change greatly in the last decade of the century. His sixth book of madrigals for five voices, published in 1600, is as mannerist as any of Monteverdi's volumes and, in a different way, not unlike the extremist volumes of Gesualdo beginning to appear at this time. Not surprisingly in the work of an older man than Monteverdi, the Wertian characteristics are less strong than in the latter's third

[1] Cf. Denis Arnold, *Marenzio* (London, 1965), p. 11.

book, and perhaps better integrated. Even so, it was Wert who again gave the basis for the advanced style, and most of the traits of his eleventh book of madrigals for five voices reappear in Pallavicino's work. Again there are the signs of an attempt at choral recitative. The whole of the first section of his setting of Guarini's *Era l'anima mia* is written in pure homophony, with the usual elisions to give an exact declamation, and if here the atmosphere is somewhat lost because of this academicism (as a comparison with Monteverdi's superb but distinctly 'un-academic' setting makes clear), in *Deh, dolce anima mia*, the downward sixth leap in the melody is as effective as it is in any of Monteverdi's madrigals:

Ex. 2

(Alas, my sweet spirit......)

This downward sixth is one of the least disturbing of the melodic awkwardnesses which Pallavicino inherited from Wert. Others are more difficult to sing, sometimes because a false relation takes the harmony in an unexpected direction,[1] sometimes the composer wants the interval itself to be a conscious asperity:

Ex. 3

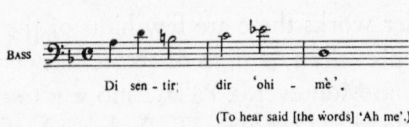

(To hear said [the words] 'Ah me'.)

Such melodic expression is the commonplace of Pallavicino's music just as much as it is of Wert's, although it does not draw attention to itself quite as much as do the similar progressions in Monteverdi's third book. But what is certainly not derived from

[1] Cf. bars 43–4 of *Cruda Amarilli* in *Das Chorwerk*, No. 80, *Vier Madrigale von Mantuaner Komponisten*, ed. Arnold (Wolfenbüttel, 1961), p. 19.

3 The interior of the ducal church of S. Barbara, Mantua

Wert is the harmonic astringency which permeates the contents of Pallavicino's sixth book. In this it is hard to find an exact equivalent in any contemporary madrigalist. Even Monteverdi himself is scarcely as concerned to wring out the last drops of emotion from dissonance. Not only do we find the occasional unprepared discord of the type about which Artusi felt so keenly. When quite conventional suspensions are used they are often strung out to form an almost continuous phrase of dissonant harmony. The following passage from *Lunge da voi* has after its opening scarcely a quarter of its time filled with actual consonances, and its opening, with the tenor's leap of a seventh, is hardly lacking in event:

Ex. 4

(A voice afflicted......)

The opening of *Cruda Amarilli*[1] is not much less pungent, and even the more ordinary madrigals of the book contain short sections of similar harmonic strain. In *Ohimè*, a cadential formula of a most conventional kind becomes far from harmless when it is repeated half-a-dozen times within ten bars, coupled with the occasional suspensions and a bass line which thrives on what can only be considered pedal notes.

There is nothing amateurish in Pallavicino's use of dissonance, and the madrigals which rely extensively on this as a means of expression are worthy of consideration along with those of Monteverdi's magnificent fourth book. Where mannerism

[1] Ibid., p. 19.

becomes dangerous is in the chromatic works, or rather works with chromatic progressions, for, whereas the dissonance is always logically developed, the chromaticism is often haphazard. Pallavicino has a liking for the contrast of major and minor chords closely juxtaposed. Where this does not interfere with the basic tonality, this is an effective device, and in the following example from *Ch'io non t'ami* the use of the minor to deny the major chord at the beginning of the bar adds to the meaning of the verse:

Ex. 5

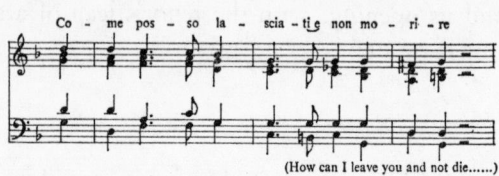

(How can I leave you and not die......)

Elsewhere the chromatic progressions are more eccentric, for they change the basic tonality without giving enough time for the new 'key' (as it must be called) to settle, as in these concluding bars of *Ohimè*:

Ex. 6

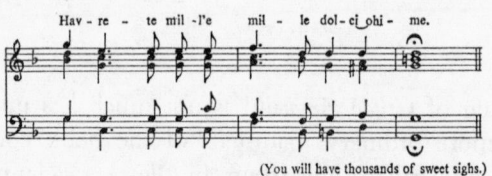

(You will have thousands of sweet sighs.)

Nevertheless, in spite of a number of strange passages which scarcely seem to fit into the overall scheme, there is no doubt that Pallavicino was a worthy colleague for Monteverdi. The nervous discontinuity of his mannerist madrigals reminds us that Gesualdo's improvisatory pieces came out in 1596, and Pallavicino's music (with the later work of Wert and Marenzio and the third book of madrigals of Monteverdi) seems to belong with that interesting by-way of musical history.

It is tempting to see Mantuan music solely in these terms; for the great palace set in the small town lends itself to the romantic fantasy and conjures up gothick gloom. The history of the Gonzagas as a dynasty is no less inspiring of a darkly glowering *Götterdämmerung* atmosphere. But, as far as music is concerned, such a view distorts the truth considerably, for among the composers of the court were excellent purveyors of light, cheerful music. Though Monteverdi seemingly found it hard to compose such music in his earlier Mantuan years, even Pallavicino produced the occasional madrigal meant for delight rather than emotional intensity. In his sixth book, *Hoggi nacqui ben mio* offers undemanding charm; and *Ch'io non t'ami*, for all its close attention to the detail of the words, is a frothy piece written with the bright sonorities of the Three Ladies of Ferrara much in mind. Considering that most of his colleagues had at one time or another written canzonets or balletts, this is hardly surprising, and in fact during the years surrounding Monteverdi's arrival various publications seem to indicate a sudden new interest in light music. Wert, until then a very serious-minded composer, published at the age of around 54 his first book of *Canzonette villanelle*, dedicating them to his patroness the Duchess Leonora Medici-Gonzaga to congratulate her on the birth of the future dukes Francesco and Ferdinando. In the same year of 1589 the principal instrumentalist at the court, Salomone Rossi, produced his first book of canzonets, dedicated to the Duke himself; early the next year the organist at Mantua Cathedral, Lodovico Grossi da Viadana, produced yet another set of canzonets, and, although not a member of the court, Orazio Vecchi, the leading composer of light music at that time, dedicated a book of not too serious madrigals to the Duke of Mantua. Was it the accession of the new Prince Vincenzo which stimulated a new gaiety in Mantua? Or, perhaps more likely, was it Vincenzo's new interest in Agnes de Argotta of Cordoba, who (we may assume) became his mistress in this year?

In any case, Vincenzo was the dedicatee of the most popular volume of light music to be produced in the sixteenth century — Gastoldi's balletts for five voices, which first came out in 1581, to be followed by no fewer than twenty reprints and new editions, published in Venice, Antwerp, Amsterdam, Paris and Nuremberg;

and with this, we have not mentioned the 'parodies' (to use a polite term for what was really 'pirating' in one or two cases) with which Thomas Morley commandeered the English market for the product in 1595. After a year, Gastoldi produced a set of canzonets for three voices; in 1594 some more balletts, this time for three voices; and in the following year a second set of canzonets. All these volumes went through a number of editions, and if they were not quite as popular as his first light-music volume, there can be no doubt that the director of music in the Ducal Chapel of S. Barbara was, however, inappropriately, known throughout the world as a composer of truly popular songs.

'Songs', perhaps, is the wrong word; 'dances' would almost certainly be better. For while it is difficult to think of some of Morley's imitations of Gastoldi as anything but madrigals with fa-la refrains (an attempt at dancing to 'Fire, fire' would be amusing, to say the least) the originals are so artless and naïve that they can hardly stand as 'pure' music. While such a predecessor of the genre as Baldissare Donato's *Chi la gagliarda*[1] places the dance rhythms in an interesting polyphonic context to make it rewarding for everyone to sing, Gastoldi is too regular, too homophonic and a shade too diatonic to be really interesting to performer or listener. But for dancing his pieces are perfect, and we realize the truth of the title-page of the volume: 'Dances for five voices with their verses, for singing, playing and dancing'. The 'verses' are clearly an afterthought. Dancing is the main *raison d'être*.

It seems perverse to connect these trifles with Monteverdi until we realize that he too composed such music, much of which must have been lost. The first volume of canzonets for three voices of Gastoldi contains a final number called a '*balletto*'; and this piece, *Par che'l ciel brami*, is subtitled '*Intermedio de Pescatori*' — in other words it was part of an *intermezzo* with fisherman. This *intermezzo* was surely an interlude in a play; and Monteverdi, as we know from his letters,[2] composed many dances for such enter-

[1] Luigi Torchi, *L'arte musicale in Italia*, I (Milan, 1897), p. 183.
[2] Cf. *supra*, pp. 23–4, etc.

tainments. Nor is it a far cry from these to the first two acts of *Orfeo*, not to mention such obviously ballet-like episodes as the final *moresca* to accompany the ascent of Apollo and Orpheus to the heavens. The song of the shepherds 'Lasciate i monti' in Act I, with its interplay between the two upper voices and the role of filling in the harmony taken by the lower parts, is very Gastoldian; so are the regular rhythms and the very diatonic melody. Admittedly the working-out of short imitative tags in the three lower voices is a typically Monteverdian complication, but the delicious orchestration using both wind and strings may tell us what the Gastoldi dance-songs really sounded like. Monteverdi's pastoral chorus is surely one of the finest examples of a ballett 'for singing, playing and dancing' and taken out of its context might well have appeared in a volume of Gastoldi or Vecchi.

Certainly on the occasions when he did contribute to two volumes of this kind, in 1594 when Antonio Morsolino (in his *Primo libro delle canzonette a tre voci*) printed four pieces, and in 1607, when Monteverdi's colleague Amante Franzoni put one of his canzonets in his *Nuovi fioretti musicali a tre voci*, Monteverdi followed Gastoldi's style quite closely. In the earlier pieces[1] especially he found delight in the texture favoured by Gastoldi in his canzonets for three voices. Two sopranos are widely separated from a bass to give an airy sound, and for the most part a homophonic texture stresses the strong dance rhythms. The tunefulness is emphasized by the sweetly moving thirds of the sopranos and the short, memorable phrases. The same things are to be found in Monteverdi's own volume of *Scherzi musicali* of 1607. Academic discussion of this volume has been bedevilled by Giulio Cesare Monteverdi's preface, which mysteriously refers to his brother's use of a French manner of singing or composition (*canto alla francese*). If there is any detectable French influence (and admittedly some of the *Scherzi* begin with the chanson ♩ ♫ motif — but then so did many Italian pieces of the time) it is swamped by the Gastoldian atmosphere. The rhythms of, say, *I bei legami*, the opening number of the volume, are so like those of

[1] *Tutte le Opere,* supplementary volume (Venice, 1966), p. 1. They are also reprinted in W. Osthoff (ed.), *12 composizioni vocali profane e sacre* (Milan, 1958).

Gastoldi's canzonets,[1] the texture and method of phrasing are so similar, that these *Scherzi* seem Mantuan rather than Gallic. And if the extensive use of the hemiola patterns has no exact precedent in Gastoldi, it must have been known to Monteverdi from the work of Vecchi, whose own *Canzonette a quattro voci* of 1593 contains balletts or 'scherzi' which use this essential feature of the galliard — and Vecchi was an Emilian from Modena, and no Frenchman. That this was fully acclimatized in Mantua can be seen from a canzonet of Franzoni, the gentle modulatory harmony of which might have been written by either Gastoldi or Monteverdi:

Ex. 7

(Sweet, serene lights [= eyes], cause of my delight.)

Monteverdi was perhaps not as attractive a composer in this style as was Gastoldi, or as Salomone Rossi, who adapted the ballett manner to instrumental music to become one of the first composers of the trio sonata. In *Prima vedrò* from Franzoni's collection of 1607, Monteverdi seems to be showing his impatience with the restrictions of the canzonet when he interpolates passages of chanting in the manner of *Sfogava con le stelle*, which, however appropriate to the madrigal, ruin the dance rhythms of light music. In this, he may well have influenced Franzoni, who tries out this *falso bordone* usage in two numbers of his second book of *Fioretti Musicali* (Venice, 1607) — *Ecco l'alba* and *Si rid' amor*.

If Franzoni was influenced in this way, he was one of the earliest composers to be really affected by Monteverdi's music, for there is little evidence that Monteverdi had left much of a mark on the world at large. He was still at this time mainly a local celebrity

---

[1] A good example is *Il Invaghito* in Achille Schinelli, *Collana di composizioni polifoniche vocali sacre e profane*, II (Milan, 1960), p. 109.

rather than an international figure. He had been swimming with the tide rather than striking out on his own. Most of his colleagues had been older men, and even a nearer contemporary such as Salomone Rossi probably was not much aware of the greatness of the Mantuan *maestro di cappella*. Certainly Rossi's continuo madrigals, printed before Monteverdi published his fifth book but perhaps (in view of the known delay in the production of this volume) composed contemporaneously, show a quite different approach to the problems of a new manner of composition.

The change came in 1608 with the opera festival at Mantua. Already a year earlier his Venetian publisher had thought it worth while to bring out new editions of Monteverdi's older madrigal-books, as a result of the publicity acquired by the dispute with Artusi. With the production of two operas and a major ballet, Monteverdi became really famous; and it was *Arianna*, more than any other work, which made it impossible for any progressive composer to ignore his style. The lament in this opera became the model for countless compositions. Those which appeared in the secular song-books indeed demand some mention in different surroundings, and this will be found in a later chapter.[1] Here it need only be said that the vogue lasted, especially in opera, until the very end of the century. Even such a composition as the lament in Purcell's *Dido and Aeneas* can trace its ancestry directly to Monteverdi's piece; and perhaps Handel was not untouched by the same fashion in the following century. Nor was religious music unaffected. Especially after the publication of a religious contrafactum in which Ariadne has been transformed into the Blessed Virgin, sacred music took to the genre like a duck to water, and such pieces as Frescobaldi's *A piè della gran Croce* from his *Primo libro d'arie Musicali* (Florence, 1630) and Mazzocchi's *Lamento della B.Vergine* in his *Musiche Sacre e Morali* of 1640 derive directly from Monteverdi's first great popular *scena*; not to mention the great set pieces in Carissimi's oratorios and dialogues, of which the 'Pianto della figlia' in *Jephtha* and the central aria in the *Historia di Ezechia* must be mentioned in this context as two of the best examples of the genre.

[1] Cf. *infra*, pp. 203–4.

What clearly cannot be derived directly from Ariadne's lament are the great variety of styles in which these pieces are written, for even by the 1640's Monteverdi's work was a masterpiece of an older musical manner; but a number of monodists were affected by its technique of melodic expression, and without its superb transmutation of the continuo madrigal into expressive arioso, the serious solo song might well have remained mannerist and purely virtuosic, incapable of further progress into the cantata. Something of the variety in Monteverdi's imitators can be seen by examining the music of two of his closest followers. Of these, Claudio Saracini was a noble Sienese, a dilettante typically attracted towards monody, and, because of the simplicity of the solo song, rather more successful than he would have been in the previous century, when he would have had to master the contrapuntal techniques of the madrigal. In his serious books of songs, there are several pieces which are virtually laments, one of which in *Le Seconde Musiche* of 1620[1] is 'dedicated to the most illustrious Claudio Monteverdi, Maestro di Cappella of the Most Serene Signory of Venice'. It is a setting of *Udite lagrimosi spirti* from Guarini's *Il Pastor Fido* (reminding us from where Monteverdi obtained the idea of the lament); and in many details it shows the sincerest form of flattery. The repetition of the word 'perchè', the irregular movement between melody and bass, the resolution of a seventh by a leap on to a consonant note of the next chord in the following example (Ex. 8) require no comment. A later passage in the same piece equally has a marked similarity to a section of *Nigra sum*, Monteverdi's first published monody, but the taut organization of the original is beyond Saracini's grasp. Monteverdi's professionalism is a deciding factor in the quality of his monodic as well as his polyphonic compositions.

Saracini was not incapable of improvement, and a later lament, *Io parto* (*Le Quinte Musiche,* Venice, 1624), is much more concentrated in its handling of what again is Monteverdian material, this time showing an understanding of the art of repeating phrases which was Monteverdi's main contribution to the arioso style. But for an equally vital handling of the genre we have to turn to

[1] Facsimile edition (Siena, 1933).

Ex. 8

(Why cannot one single death satisfy her fierce desire....)

another professional composer, Sigismondo d'India, whose noble origins and good voice do not seem to have diverted him from a mastery of his craft. The lament was for him a favourite medium, and his last two song-books contain no fewer than five of them, all surely deriving their inspiration from *Arianna*. The similarities of their technical detail have already been discussed elsewhere.[1] Here it may be said that d'India's basic attitude to monodic composition was reasonably like Monteverdi's. Both were concerned with the problems of finding a technique by which the recitative style of the Camerata was made capable of the highest emotional power, without relapsing into pretty tunes or being stolidly academic. Both succeeded to an astonishing degree. D'India's version of Dido's lament at first sight looks like the severest type of operatic recitative. In performance, it proves a worthy successor to the lament of Ariadne.[2] Like Monteverdi, d'India understood not only how to organize his material so that it never becomes amorphous but also how excitement in a deliberately un-melodious style is achieved mainly by variations of speed and tessitura. While dissonance and awkward intervals have their part to play in keeping up the intensity, the overall control of emotional power is revealed in the contrast of pace and

[1] Nigel Fortune, 'Sigismondo d'India, an introduction to his life and works', *Proceedings of the Royal Musical Association*, LXXXI (1954–5), p. 29.

[2] There is a recording of this by Helen Watts and Thurston Dart on L'Oiseau Lyre, OL 50128.

vocal registers in the following passage, which is too like the fourth part of Monteverdi's piece for the resemblance to be pure coincidence:

Ex. 9

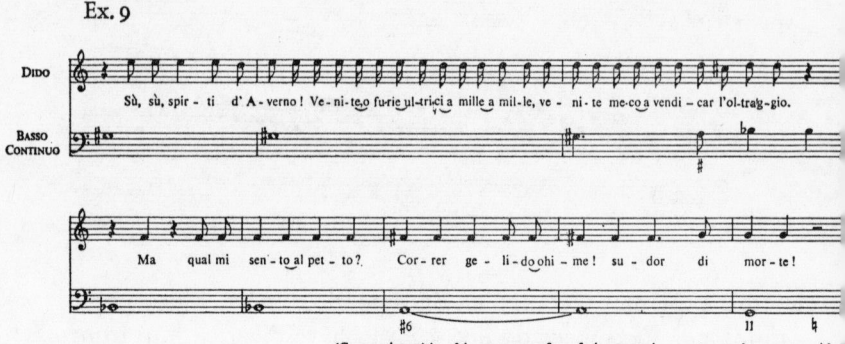

(Come, arise, spirits of Avernus, come fierce furies, come in your thousands to avenge with the foul deed: but, what do I feel in my breast? I feel the sweat of death run within me!)

When Monteverdi wrote *Arianna*, he was by no means half way through his career. Nevertheless, it is the music he composed in the years around this time that had most effect on the musical world. The madrigals of his 'mannerist' style (which include those of Book VI, which represent its culmination) were reprinted time and again. His later music was less well diffused. In part the reason for this must be that tastes were changing more rapidly than was Monteverdi; and in part another reason must be found in his change from being primarily a composer of secular to one of church music. It was much more difficult to be a composer of mannerist church music, and it was perhaps because of this that the music of the Vespers volume never really became popular. Not that it was so revolutionary as has been sometimes thought. The actual ingredients of the music were common enough in Mantuan church music. After all, Viadana was *maestro di cappella* at Mantua Cathedral when he published the first volume of concertato church music ever printed, so that this was no novelty. The use of *falso bordone* chanting, which is so much a feature of the psalm-settings, was seemingly the usual practice in Mantua, if we may judge from Viadana's *Vespertina omnium solemnitatum Psalmodia* (1588) and Gastoldi's *Salmi intieri che nelle solennità dell'anno al Vespro si canta* of 1607. The polychoral manner from which Monteverdi's work was to spring was not unknown there either, for not only was Viadana again one of its exponents, but Pallavicino's *Sacrae Dei Laudes*, published posthumously in 1605, are worthy examples of the style. The *Sonata sopra Sancta Maria* was no unique piece in the region, for it was Francesco Crotti, a monk from Ferrara, who published a similar item in his *Concerti Ecclesiastici* of 1608[1] (it was also imitated by Franzoni in 1619). Even the elaborate ornamentation of the 'solo' motets has its counterpart in the Lamentations of Giovanni Francesco Capello, a Veronese who published these works in this same year of 1610. Nevertheless, the mixture of elements is unique to Monteverdi, and apparently not all that successful in worldly terms, for it was the 'pure' work of the collection, the *Missa in illo tempore*, which achieved wider circulation,[2] not the Vespers music which has fascinated the twentieth century.

And when Monteverdi took up his appointment in Venice, he again seems to have swum with the tide. The concertato pieces which were published in the collections of Bianchi in 1620 closely resemble those of the composers left over from the Gabrielian period in St. Mark's. Giovanni Battista Grillo's *Sacri Concentus ac Symphoniae* of 1617 reveals a pupil of the younger Gabrieli, even to the extent of providing another *Sonata pian e forte*. Nevertheless, the concertato pieces resemble Monteverdi's early Venetian church music quite strongly, the more especially since Grillo has brought the traditional style a little more up to date by making the solo sections (inherited from such works as Gabrieli's *In ecclesiis*) into ornamented duets in the manner of Monteverdi's continuo madrigals from Book V.

The atmosphere in Venice began to change radically only a few years later when Monteverdi began to surround himself with his own discoveries — Alessandro Grandi and Francesco Cavalli,

[1] Cf. Arnold, 'Notes on two movements of the Monteverdi Vespers', *Monthly Musical Record*, LXXXIV (1954).

[2] Whereas the whole mass achieved a reprint in 1612 in a collection published by Phalèse, only two items of the Vespers music were reprinted (in Georg Gruber, *Reliquae Sacrorum Concentum Giovan. Gabrielis, Johan-Leonis Hasleri*, Nuremberg, 1615).

who were appointed in St. Mark's as singers in the period around 1617, Giovanni Rovetta, who started in the orchestra about the same time, and later Giovanni Pietro Berti, who became an organist of the basilica in 1624. These and some others who worked elsewhere in the city made its religious music thoroughly modern, to lead the world in adapting methods developed in secular works to the needs of the church. How much of this change of style can be attributed to the arrival of Monteverdi is problematical, for although his 1610 volume had been a pioneering venture, it was not unique in this way. But it is significant that Venetian music had been tending towards the conservative and was becoming out of touch with the 'modern' schools of Florence, Ferrara and Mantua before 1612. Its acquisition of the greatest of the progressive composers had its effect.

A great deal of this change of heart can only vaguely be ascribed to the influence of Monteverdi. Only in certain composers are the signs clear. Of these, Grandi was one who without doubt learned a great deal from the master and made good use of his knowledge. Although he can scarcely have been more than ten years younger than Monteverdi, he had never composed in the older pre-continuo style, and his first volume of motets published in 1610 was already an accomplished collection in the post-Viadana manner. He produced a considerable amount of church music before he left Ferrara for Venice, but none of it shows anything much more than competence and a certain lyrical gift. Then, in Venice, this gift becomes something more, and since it flowers most particularly in his solo motets, Grandi's development can be ascribed either to the incentive given by the virtuoso singers of St. Mark's or to Monteverdi — or perhaps to both. For the virtuoso nature of these motets is not of the arid kind which stressed florid *gorgie*, but rather, like Monteverdi's, one which needs legato singing and understanding of the words. In *Vulnerasti cor meum*, published four years after coming into Monteverdi's circle, the sensuous climax, with its repeated phrase, chromatics, and subtle dissonance, has the authentic mastery of arioso that stems from *Arianna* and another motet setting a passage from the Song of Songs — Monteverdi's *Nigra sum*:

Ex. 10

(......for I am sick with love.).

And Grandi's version of the plainsong hymn *Veni Sancte Spiritus* could hardly have been written without knowing the solo verses of that other part of the Vespers volume, the hymn *Ave Maris Stella*. Both use triple time and the rhythmic variety of the hemiolas to make a genuine tune which could well belong to the popular song-books of the time:

Ex. 11

This tunefulness indeed may have had its effect on Monteverdi himself, for the young men who were his colleagues were masters of it; and if we compare the 'alleluia' of two motets published in Simonetti's *Ghirlanda Sacra* in 1625 the explanation of Monteverdi's newly found gaiety may be found. (See Ex. 12.)

But an invention which is Monteverdi's alone and which did intrigue the Venetian musical world was the *stile concitato*. He had developed it in the dramatic cantata (which is perhaps the nearest

Exx. 12a and 12b

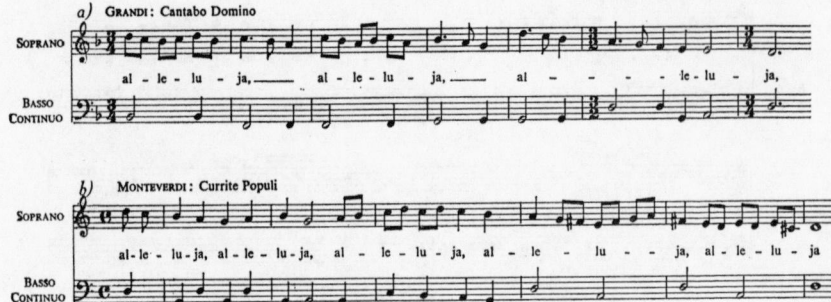

short description of it which seems apt) *Il Combattimento di Tancredi e Clorinda,* where it had a particular significance, and in his last madrigal book the style seems to be part of an academic manifesto, a demonstration of principles learned long ago which had dominated his thinking. To other composers, it was more of a trick, not to be taken seriously or employed with any consistency. Tarquinio Merula, in his *Curtio Precipitato* published in 1638, starts his extended cantata *Curtio, ove vai* with a '*sinfonia ad immitatione d'un Cavallo*' (a symphony to imitate the sound of a horse) and proceeds to express the word 'armato' with the same sort of triple-time vocal arpeggios to which Monteverdi was so attached:

(From head to feet, armed......)

Earlier Grandi had found it a happy way to provide a realistic setting for the word 'conquassabit' in the psalm *Dixit Dominus,*[1]

[1] *Salmi a otto brevi con il primo coro concertato* (Venice, 1629).

a usage justified by Monteverdi in his own settings of the Magnificat, where it is equally appropriate to 'put down the mighty from their seat'.[1] Schütz's use in his duet motet *Der Herr ist mein Licht und mein Heil* in his second book of *Symphoniae Sacrae* is very similar and equally effective, for it is provided first by the phrase 'Wenn sich schon ein Heer wider mich leget' ('Though an host of men were laid against me') and then by 'Wenn sich wider mich erhebet' ('though there rose up war against me'), a reasonably logical use of pictorialism. Less satisfying was his contrafactum of Monteverdi's *Armato il cor* and *Zefiro torna* in the same volume. Schütz was clearly fascinated by the novelty of it all, on his second sabbatical year in Venice. He may well have met Monteverdi, but it was the younger men whose style he really assimilated. His sacred symphonies are offshoots of the motets of Grandi, Rovetta and the rest, and *Es steh Gott auf*, for all its external trappings, shows a liking for the trick rather than the substance of the *stile concitato*. *Armato il cor* takes the phrases based on common chords about as far as they will go. Schütz needs two violins to add a new dimension of colour, for he makes the composition much longer than its original; and it is doubtful whether the material really can stand this. Its second part, an adaptation of Monteverdi's virtuoso chaconne, is more modestly treated, with good reason, for the original stretches its basic idea as far as it can, and Schütz's shorter version matches his shorter text. Yet one must wonder why he chose this composition to parody. *Zefiro torna* is essentially an illustrative piece, tolerable only when the aptness of each musical image for the image of the verse is appreciated. In fact, it is the very piece to avoid when adapting something to another text.

Schütz's relationship to Monteverdi is significant of the position of the old man (for such was a sexagenarian at this time) in 1628. In secular music his juniors were writing pretty melodies and forgetting the mannerism of the early years of the century. In their operas they were no longer to attempt to envelop 'Renaissance man' in an art which wanted to create a whole new world. They were content to entertain a lesser mortal, and if to

[1] *Tutte le Opere*, XV, p. 659.

this end they were willing to borrow the external features of the Monteverdian art, it is doubtful whether they appreciated the philosophy behind it. A glance at a large choral lament from Loreto Vittori's *La Galatea*,[1] a Roman opera produced in 1639, is sufficient to recognize the opening of the madrigal version of Ariadne's lament; another glance is sufficient to realize, not necessarily that it is feebler, but that it is different. It has lost the sustained emotionalism so characteristic of the period of the younger Monteverdi:

Ex. 14

(Let us weep, let us sigh, faithful companions.)

Nor is it hard to find the echoes of the *stile concitato* in dramatic music in the last decade of Monteverdi's life. A chorus of soldiers in Michelangelo Rossi's *Erminia* (1633) has the same sort of fanfare motives, the same consonant harmony — but little sign of understanding of the strict rhythmic patterns which Monteverdi had

[1] Cf. Hugo Goldschmidt, *Studien zur Geschichte der italienischen Oper im 17. Jahrhundert*, I (Leipzig, 1901), p. 288.

derived from Platonic ideas. Even when the basic knowledge of Monteverdi's style is clearly there, some change of atmosphere is always to be found. Cavalli was surely as close a pupil as anyone could have been, employed by Monteverdi in St. Mark's from an early age. In both his church music and his stage works he shows evidence of learning from the master. His concertato motets, and the *Magnificat* which was published in the posthumous collection of Monteverdi's church music are in some ways very similar to the older man's work. The lament from his opera *L'Egisto* (1643) is so like Monteverdi that at its dissonant climax the illusion of its being from *Poppea* or some other work of that period is almost complete:

Ex. 15

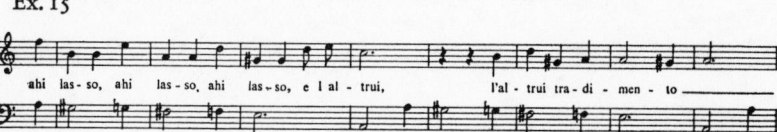

(Alas, it is the treachery of others......)

But only almost complete. A recollection of the 'Lament of the Nymph', with its background of men interjecting 'Ah, miserella', establishes at once the difference. Monteverdi is more complicated, more extravagant and more powerful. Cavalli's magnificence is colder, more Venetian. It is not surprising that he was one of the first composers to take opera to France.

The quintessential Monteverdi is to be seen in *L'Incoronazione di Poppea*. Its composer is not blind to any element in his environment. He has learned from the young men, he has remembered his older colleagues and even his teachers. He is fully aware of what was successful in his earlier works. No doubt if we possessed the scores of those lost operas and *intermezzi* from Mantua and Parma we could trace every part of this masterpiece to some particular circumstance of his musical life. Certainly the smouldering, illogical, immoral and very human atmosphere could not have been produced except by a man who had been through the agonies of the Gonzaga court (we may suspect that there is more than a trace of Vincenzo in the cruelty of Nero). In that power to

I A.F.M.C.

transcribe human experience into music lies the greatness of Monteverdi. For this, much was clearly forgiven him in his lifetime; and we must be grateful to many now forgotten composers who stimulated his overwhelming imagination and provided the means for its musical expression.

III

Thinker and
Musician

CLAUDE V. PALISCA

The Artusi-Monteverdi Controversy

The debt music history owes to Giovanni Maria Artusi is only grudgingly recognized. Yet it is a great one, for he focused attention on one of the deepest crises in musical composition and stimulated the composer who most squarely confronted it to clarify his position. Without Claudio Monteverdi's letter in the Fifth Book of Madrigals and his brother's glosses upon it in the *Scherzi musicali* (1607), Monteverdi's youthful creative thrust would have left a blunter mark in history. His stylistic profile without Artusi's criticism would be set less boldly in relief.

If the controversy between Artusi and Monteverdi gave us a valuable commentary upon music history in the making, it also affected the course of musical evolution. Claudio and his brother Giulio Cesare by publishing their manifestoes for the new or second practice held up a banner for others to rally around. Their slogans echoed for half a century in the prefaces and pamphlets of the avant-garde. Nor is this the only significance of the controversy: it also gives us a glimpse into the way composers thought about certain points of technique, how they justified them, what precedents they recognized, how they viewed the act of composition itself.

What are the real issues of this debate? In one sense it was the usual battle of the generations. Monteverdi rebelled against the strictures of his masters; Artusi, a generation older, stood by the standards of composition taught by Gioseffo Zarlino, among whose followers he was one of the most eminent. He expected dissonances to be introduced according to the rules of counterpoint, and he insisted upon unity of modality within a piece. These conventions had been challenged already in the middle of the sixteenth century, and Artusi's offensive — or rather counter-offensive — was only one of a chain of attacks and counter-attacks that can be traced back to the debate between Nicola Vicentino and Vincenzo Lusitano in 1551. Artusi was not an arch-conservative through and through. His own books on counterpoint relaxed unnecessarily strict rules that were often honoured in the breach. He recognized, as Zarlino did not, that dissonances were of primary importance in composition and devoted a whole volume to them. He was one of the first to take a strong position in favour of equal temperament as a standard tuning for instrumental music. Yet it grieved him to see counter-point, which had reached a point of ultimate refinement and control, become a prey to caprice and expediency. He honestly believed that the patiently erected structure was under siege.

In another sense it was a battle between two contemporary points of view. On one side were those like Monteverdi who accepted the advances of concerted instrumental music, improvised counterpoint, ornamented singing, the rhythms of dance music, and the enlarged vocabulary of chromaticism blended with the diatonic. On the other side were those like Artusi who felt that these innovations, mainly products of relatively unschooled musicians, corrupted a pure, noble, and learned art. In one camp were those who held to a single standard of counterpoint; in the other those who followed a double standard, one for everyday sacred compositions and another for compositions on texts expressing violent passions. From a long view, neither side won an absolute victory. The strict standards backed by Artusi returned by the mid-seventeenth century in a modified form, and the modifications represented concessions to the other side.

Artusi printed and analyzed in his dialogue of 1600 nine examples from two madrigals of Monteverdi that he knew from manuscript copies. He withheld both the composer's name and the texts. The dialogue is divided into two *ragionamenti* or discourses, of which the first, dealing with tuning, was probably Artusi's main pretext for publishing the book. The second dealt with the anonymous composer's madrigals.[1] Artusi saw no reason to print the words, because he did not recognize a double standard of contrapuntal correctness. To omit them also helped conceal the authorship of the madrigals. Although Artusi knew the name of the composer, he refrained from revealing it, because in view of his criticism to do so would have been indelicate. To soften the blow further the author expressed his opinion through one of the interlocutors, a fictitious musician named Vario, who converses with a cultivated amateur named Luca.

Three years after this dialogue Artusi, having received letters from a defender of the anonymous composer who signs himself l'Ottuso Accademico, published a second book. In the first part of this he answers his correspondent's letters. In the *Considerationi* that follow he defends Francesco Patrizi's statements about Greek music against Ercole Bottrigari's criticisms.[2] Although now the discussion of the anonymous madrigals deals largely with the question of text expression, Artusi again omits texts when he prints examples by the anonymous composer and by l'Ottuso. The composer's identity was not made known in print until Monteverdi answered Artusi in the famous letter that opens the Fifth Book of Madrigals of 1605. Of the madrigals criticized in the 1600 dialogue, *Anima mia, perdona* was not published until 1603 in the Fourth Book of Madrigals and *Cruda Amarilli* and *O Mirtillo* not until 1605 in the fifth book. In addition to these, also under discussion in the 1603 book are *Era l'anima mia* and the second part of *Ecco Silvio*, both from the fifth book.

Throughout the controversy the treatment of dissonances was

[1] *L'Artusi, overo Delle imperfettioni della moderna musica* (Venice, 1600). The first *ragionamento* takes issue with Ercole Bottrigari's conclusions about tuning and concerted instrumental groupings published in *Il Desiderio* (Venice, 1594). A part of the second *ragionamento* is translated in Oliver Strunk, *Source Readings in Music History* (London, 1952), pp. 393–404.

[2] *Seconda parte dell'Artusi overo Delle imperfettioni della moderna musica* (Venice, 1603); Francesco Patrizi, *Della poetica, La deca istoriale* (Ferrara, 1586); Bottrigari, *Il Patricio, ovvero De' tetracordi armonici di Aristosseno* (Bologna, 1593). By 1603 Artusi and Bottrigari had exchanged a number of acrimonious pamphlets and letters, both printed and manuscript. The urge to respond to Bottrigari may have provided a stronger motive for the 1603 book than continuing the criticism of Monteverdi.

the most bitterly contested territory. The dissonant effects Artusi objected to in Monteverdi's madrigals are of three kinds: 1) those caused by the application of ornaments to a consonant framework; 2) those which, though accepted by usage in improvised counterpoint and instrumental music, were outside the norms of the severe style; 3) those outside these two categories that could be justified only in terms of the expressive demands of the text. The text, of course, was the principal motivating force behind all three kinds of dissonances. But it was possible to talk about the first two without the text, and this is what Artusi does in his first critique, even though some of his examples could not be explained adequately without the text.

Each of the examples cited by Artusi in the 1600 book violates one or more rules of the strict style as taught by Zarlino and Artusi in their counterpoint books.[1] Luca, who plays the advocate for Monteverdi, pleads that modern composers excuse these lapses by various pretexts. The defences Luca timidly brings up are very revealing of the thinking of the time.

The composer in Ex. 1 is charged by Vario with failing to accord the upper parts with the bass:

Ex. 1: Monteverdi, *Cruda Amarilli*, bars 12–14

Luca argues that the example should be regarded as 'accented'

[1] Gioseffo Zarlino, *Le Istitutioni harmoniche* (Venice, 1558), Bk. III; Artusi, *L'arte del contraponto ridotta in tavole* (Venice, 1586); *Seconda parte dell'arte del contraponto, nella quale si tratta dell'utile & uso delle dissonanze* (Venice, 1589); *L'arte del contraponto . . . novamente ristampata, & di molte nuove aggiunte, dall' auttore arrichita* (Venice, 1598).

singing: that is, it is a written example of an improvisational practice. Vario protests that no author has yet spoken of accented music or defined what accents are. Actually Lodovico Zacconi had spoken of these at length and defined them as follows: 'The graces (*vaghezze*) and accents (*accenti*) are made by splitting and breaking the note values when in a bar or half-bar is added a number of notes that have the property of being rapidly proffered. These give so much pleasure and delight that it appears to us that we are hearing so many well trained birds which capture our hearts and render us very happy with their singing.'[1] For example, when a part has two semibreves or minims, particularly separated by a skip, the singer may fill the time or pitch interval with shorter notes. 'However, he should know that these notes are accompanied by certain accents caused by certain retardations and sustainings of the voice, which are accomplished by taking away a particle from one value and assigning it to another.'[2] Zacconi gives the following illustration:

Ex. 2

Girolamo dalla Casa, another exponent of florid singing, inserts the runs shown in small notes in the following example:

Ex. 3: Cipriano de Rore, *Tanto mi piacque,* with diminutions from dalla Casa, *Il vero modo di diminuir* (Venice, 1584), II, p. 48.

(.... leaves, and to bring forth fruit....)

If Monteverdi's passage of Ex. 1 is reduced to a hypothetical simpler framework (Ex. 4) and Zacconi's suggested *accenti* and

[1] Lodovico Zacconi, *Prattica di musica* (Venice, 1596), Bk. I, ch. lxvi, f. 58. All the translations in this chapter are mine.

[2] Ibid., I, lxiii, f. 55. The ensuing example is at I, lxvi, f. 62.

runs similar to dalla Casa's are applied, we arrive at a version close to Monteverdi's and just as faulty from Artusi's point of view (Ex. 5):

Ex. 4   Ex. 5

Luca finds the effect of the *accenti* attractive. Compositions embellished by such ornaments 'when played by various instruments or sung by singers skilled in this kind of accented music full of substitutions (*suppositi*) yield a not displeasing harmony at which I marvel'.[1]

Vario's answer is doctrinaire, as expected. Composers and singers who use these portamentoes, delays and turns, while they may avoid by instinct offensive sounds or deceive the ear by the quickness of their embellishments, corrupt the good old rules with their mannerisms.

Another ornamental figure lies at the basis of the dissonances in the following bars quoted by Artusi (Ex. 6). A hypothetical simple version is shown in Ex. 7. Christoph Bernhard in a manuscript treatise of around 1660 shows how a similar passage can be embellished by means of the figure he calls *quaesitio notae* (searching note).[2] (See Ex. 8.)

Only some of Monteverdi's licences can be passed as *accenti*. Luca suggests another defence for others: 'these musicians observe their rule that the part making the dissonance with the lowest part should have a harmonic correspondence with the tenor, and

[1] *L'Artusi*, f. 41v.
[2] Christoph Bernhard, *Tractatus compositionis augmentatus*, ch. 33, printed in Joseph Müller-Blattau, *Die Kompositionslehre Heinrich Schützens*, 2nd. ed. (Kassel, 1963), pp. 81–2.

Exx. 6 and 7: Monteverdi, *Cruda Amarilli*, bars 35–8

(But [more deaf and fierce] than the deaf asp.)

Ex. 8

that it [the first] accord with every other part, while the lowest part also should accord with every other part'.[1]

A situation governed by this rule would arise in *contrapunto a mente* if a bass and a higher voice were improvising against a *cantus firmus* in the tenor. The two improvisers would be obliged to accord with the tenor but not necessarily with each other. Tinctoris states as a rule that in singing *super librum*, that is over a plainchant book, the part-singer needs to observe the laws of consonance with respect to the tenor part alone, while in *res facta*, that is written counterpoint, all parts must have regard to each

[1] *L'Artusi*, f. 43.

other. It is laudable, he says, when all the parts accord with each other even in improvised counterpoint.[1] But this will happen only by accident or through rehearsal. In the sixteenth century it was customary to have the bass sing the *cantus firmus*. To judge by the profusion of manuals or portions of them dedicated to the art of improvised counterpoint towards the end of that century and the beginning of the next, it was a widespread practice, particularly in the principal chapel and cathedral choirs.[2]

Adriano Banchieri recalls with pleasure the wonderful effect, peculiar charm and very tasteful sensation of the *contrapunti a mente*, with their unexpected consecutive fifths and octaves, the dissonant encounters and extravagant turns: 'In Rome in the Chapel of our Holy Father, in the holy mansion of San Loreto and in countless other chapels when they sing *contrapunto alla mente* on a bass, no one knows what his companion is going to sing, but together through certain observances agreed among themselves they give a most tasteful sensation to the hearing. It can be stated as a general maxim that even if a hundred various voices (so to speak) were singing consonantly over a bass, all would agree, and those dissonances, fifths, octaves, extravagances and clashes are all graces that make up the true effect of *contrapunto alla mente.*'[3] So impressed was Banchieri with the possibilities of this effect that he made up a set of ten instructions for counterfeiting such counterpoints in writing. The trick, he shows, is to write each of the parts against the bass independently of the others.

Monteverdi accepts into written composition some of the fortuitous clashes that occur when parts are moving independently around some common focus. One of the passages Vario points to as following the relaxed rules of harmonic correspondence between parts are bars 41-2 of *Cruda Amarilli*. Ex. 9 divides the texture into two groups, each of which corresponds harmonically

[1] Johannes Tinctoris, *Liber de arte contrapuncti*, Bk. II, ch. xx, in Edmond de Coussemaker, *Scriptorum de musica medii aevi*, IV (Paris, 1876, reprinted Hildesheim, 1963), p. 129.

[2] Cf. Ernest T. Ferand, 'Improvised Vocal Counterpoint in the Late Renaissance and Early Baroque', *Annales musicologiques*, IV (1956), pp. 129-74.

[3] Adriano Banchieri, *Cartella musicale nel canto figurato, fermo & contrapunto* (Venice, 1614), p. 230.

with the tenor, but parts of opposing groups may clash with each other:

Ex. 9

The composer takes advantage of the tolerance for free mixtures of intervals acquired through improvised music to introduce a variety of rhetorical effects. This device is particularly fitting to illustrate the word 'elusive' (*fugace*), as it affords at once smooth and independent voice movement. The diminished fifth and seventh on the word 'fierce' (*fera*) serve both the musical function of providing a climactic cadence and to heighten the feeling of the word.

Luca makes another significant remark about how musicians became receptive to the chance combinations that arise from rapidly and independently moving parts. In answering Vario's objection that in bars 42–3 some of the quavers do not correspond either to the bass or tenor, Luca says this licence is derived 'from perceiving that in instruments these [quavers] do not much offend the ear because of the quickness of movement'.[1]

Vincenzo Galilei in his manuscript treatise on counterpoint (1589–91) made precisely this observation about rapidly moving parts, which he found 'more appropriate for instruments than for voices'.[2] 'Whenever two or more parts move over one another gracefully according to the decorum of the art of counterpoint, whatever dissonance occurs among them not only will be tolerated by the sense, but it will take delight in it.'[3] Although it

---

[1] *L'Artusi,* loc. cit.

[2] Vincenzo Galilei, *Il primo libro della prattica del contrapunto intorno all'uso delle consonanze,* Florence, Biblioteca nazionale, MS. Anteriore Galileo I, f. 78. See Claude V. Palisca, 'Vincenzo Galilei's Counterpoint Treatise: a Code for the *Seconda Pratica*', *Journal of the American Musicological Society,* IX (1956), p. 88.

[3] Ibid., p. 89, quoted from *Discorso intorno all'uso delle dissonanze,* MS. Anteriore Galileo I, f. 143.

was customary, he said, to alternate consonance and dissonance in writing such runs, he declined to make a hard-and-fast rule, showing rather that as many as three dissonances may occur in succession with impunity. By coincidence his example uses the very same progression as Monteverdi does in bars 42–3 of *Cruda Amarilli* between the two uppermost parts and the bass:[1]

Ex. 10

Up to now I have been reviewing some of the arguments on behalf of Monteverdi adduced by Luca in the second discourse of Artusi's dialogue of 1600. In 1603, as we saw, Artusi published a defence of his criticism of Monteverdi in reply to letters from l'Ottuso Accademico. This book begins with the text of a letter Artusi purportedly wrote to l'Ottuso in response to one from him of 1599. In his letter Artusi quotes selectively from l'Ottuso's reply, which, though not dated, is obviously subsequent to Artusi's dialogue of 1600, as it counters some points made there.

The mystery of l'Ottuso's identity has not been satisfactorily solved. Emil Vogel and others before him[2] simply assumed that he was Monteverdi, and later writers have generally followed suit. Several circumstances, however, militate against this assumption. Monteverdi begins his foreword to *Il quinto libro de' madrigali* (1605) with the remark: 'be not surprised that I am giving these

---

[1] Ibid., f. 126.

[2] Cf. Emil Vogel, 'Claudio Monteverdi', *Vierteljahrsschrift für Musikwissenschaft*, III (1887), p. 315. On p. 332 Vogel cites the authority of Zaccaria Tevo, *Il musico testore* (Venice, 1706), p. 175, to support the attribution of the letters to Monteverdi. Gaetano Gaspari (*d.* 1881) in his manuscript notes appended to his own copy of the *Seconda parte dell'Artusi* now in Bologna, Civico museo bibliografico musicale, also expressed the opinion that l'Ottuso was Monteverdi. This copy, which was the one used in this study, bears the signature of the official censor at the end of the *Considerationi* on p. 54 and the note that the author should be required to place his name and surname and native city on the title page. All of the more personally offensive passages, including the entire sarcastic letter of dedication addressed to Bottrigari and the letter to the reader, are struck out in this copy with a single stroke of the pen.

madrigals to the press without first replying to the objections that Artusi made against some very minute portions of them . . .' He could not have made such a plea if his reply had already appeared in print under the name l'Ottuso. There is no resemblance between l'Ottuso's letter and Monteverdi's style of writing. Further, Artusi prints (ff. 50v–51) fourteen breve-bars taken from five-part madrigals of l'Ottuso — 'passaggi fatti dall'Ottuso ne suoi Madrigali' — and these cannot be reconciled with any known works of Monteverdi. Besides, when Monteverdi is referred to in the correspondence it is always as 'Signor Etc.', not as l'Ottuso.

If l'Ottuso is not Monteverdi, who is he? Several possibilities need to be examined.

(1) L'Ottuso is a straw man contrived by Artusi to be knocked down as he refutes objections made to his earlier critique of Monteverdi.

(2) L'Ottuso is Ercole Bottrigari, to whom the book is dedicated and against whose *Patricio* half of it is directed.

(3) L'Ottuso is a composer and academician probably from Ferrara or Mantua.

Is l'Ottuso Artusi's creation? Just as Artusi invented the interlocutors Vario and Luca to argue the merits of the questions discussed in the 1600 dialogue, it is reasonable that he would invent an opponent against whom he could debate in the first person about Monteverdi's modernisms. L'Ottuso writes garrulously and redundantly like Artusi himself. He cites many classical and modern authors and has a command of the calculations of proportions every theorist, but not necessarily every composer, had to know. He makes a moderately good case for Monteverdi, something Artusi was perfectly capable of doing, because he understood the modernists even if he disagreed with them. It is even conceivable that Artusi might have gone to such lengths as fabricating excerpts from non-existent madrigals, which he claimed were sent to him from l'Ottuso's academy. If l'Ottuso's letter of 1599 was not faked later, why did Artusi not produce it in the dialogue of 1600, when it would have made a good pretext for attacking the modernist point of view in the first place? The dedication in Venice on 20 November 1600 shows that he had ample time to do so. The possibility that l'Ottuso was an invention of Artusi is, therefore, not to be excluded.

May l'Ottuso be Bottrigari, to whom the 1603 book is dedicated? The whole second part of the book is a defence of statements about music, particularly on the Greek tunings, made by Francesco Patrizi in his *Della poetica, La deca istoriale* (1586) against the objections of Bottrigari in his *Il Patricio, overo De' tetrachordi armonici di Aristosseno* (1593).[1] At the same time Artusi answers a pamphlet by Bottrigari entitled *Ant-Artusi*.[2] The possibility that l'Ottuso is Bottrigari is made unlikely by the fact that Bottrigari treats him as a real person. In his *Aletelogia*,[3] an answer to Artusi's book of 1603, Bottrigari says he will not refute what Artusi writes against l'Ottuso in his ninth 'Inconsideratione', because the academician is wise and capable and will defend himself with sagacity and valour. Bottrigari may have known his identity, having lived a long time in Ferrara and now in Artusi's own city of Bologna.

The most likely possibility is that l'Ottuso was a composer active in Ferrara or Mantua. Artusi introduces the first quotation from l'Ottuso's letter with the words: '. . . finding myself in Ferrara in the year 1599, I was given a letter without proper name but with the signature *L'Ottuso Academico*. Later from a good source I had the information that this was a man of much authority and that he was very much a musician. . . .'[4] The pseudonym, meaning 'the obtuse one', fits the current style of academic names, which were often teasingly self-derogatory, like 'L'Ebbro' (the drunken one), 'L'Incruscato' (the crusty one, Giovanni Bardi's name in the Alterati), 'L'Affannato' (the breathless one, Marco da Gagliano's name in the Elevati and Scipione Gonzaga's in the Invaghiti), 'Lo Smemorato' (the forgetful one), and so on. As to which

[1] Cf. note 2 on p. 135.

[2] This pamphlet was mentioned by Artusi in his letter dedicating the *Seconda parte dell'Artusi* to Bottrigari.

[3] Bottrigari, *Aletelogia di Leonardo Gallucio ai benigni, e sinceri Lettori, lettera apologetica D.M.I.S.C.H.B.* (1604), Bologna, Civico museo bibliografico musicale, MS. B–43, p. 72.

[4] *Seconda parte dell'Artusi*, p. 5.

Veduta del. Piaza di S.ͭ Marco di Venezia vista verſo il porto

4 View of St. Mark's, Venice, from a 17th-century engraving

academy he may have belonged to there is no clue. The Accademia degli Intrepidi of Ferrara, founded around 1600, is a likely one. Monteverdi dedicated to it his fourth book of madrigals. In his dedicatory letter, dated 1 March 1603, he acknowledges his debt to the academicians for 'the many favours' and various friendly gestures towards him. Another Ferrarese academy, whose name is not known, had as one of its councillors the composer Count Alfonso Fontanella and as its musical censors Count Alfonso Fogliani and Luigi Putti.[1] Fontanella, a man of culture and an accomplished composer, may well be l'Ottuso. Another good candidate is the Ferrarese composer Antonio Goretti, at whose salon Artusi's dialogists Vario and Luca are represented as hearing Monteverdi's not yet published madrigals.[2]

Although Artusi's credibility on this subject is naturally suspect, it should be recalled that he claims in his last discourse, written under the pseudonym Antonio Braccino da Todi, that the whole quarrel began because a number of friendly and civil letters Artusi wrote to Monteverdi remained unanswered, and instead Monteverdi replied through a third person, obviously meaning l'Ottuso.[3] It is clear, in any case, that Artusi never pretended that l'Ottuso was Monteverdi or that he was calling the composer a blockhead.

Whoever he was, l'Ottuso finally brought the debate around to the main point — why the new harmonic effects were necessary. He is quoted as saying in his letter of 1599: 'The purpose of this new movement of the parts (*modulatione*) is to discover through its novelty a new consensus (*concenti*) and new affections, and this without departing in any way from good reason, even if it leaves behind somehow the ancient traditions of some excellent com-

[1] Cf. Michele Maylender, *Storia delle accademie d'Italia* (Bologna, 1926–30), III, p. 417.

[2] There is a possibility, though not a strong one, that the correspondent was a member of an academy called 'degli Ottusi'. If he had been a member of such an academy, 'Accademico Ottuso' would have been more normal usage than 'l'Ottuso Accademico'. There were two academies so named. One was the Accademia degli Ottusi in Bologna, of which, unfortunately, nothing is known (cf. Maylender, op. cit., IV, p. 173). The Accademia degli Ottusi of Spoleto seems to go no farther back than 1610 (ibid., p. 176).

[3] *Discorso secondo di Antonio Braccino da Todi* (Venice, 1608), p. 6.

posers.'[1] New affections call for new harmonic combinations to express them. This is the crux of the matter.

Artusi's retort deals in semantics. He first defines 'concento': 'it is a mixture of low and high notes intermediated in such a way that when sounded they produce an infinite sweetness to the ear.'[2] There are only four ways of mediating the interval between a low and high sound, through the arithmetic, geometric, harmonic and counterharmonic divisions. None of these will divide a seventh, one of the new combinations defended by l'Ottuso, consonantly. Therefore the new combinations are not *concenti*. Indeed no new *concenti* are possible, because the number of consonances is limited. So no new affections can be expressed by them.

L'Ottuso's second letter, written a month after Artusi's reply, is printed in full by Artusi.[3] L'Ottuso, not intimidated by Artusi's sophistry, insists that if Artusi can find something in Signor Etc.'s madrigals to complain about, it must come from the progression of the parts (*modulatione*), the consensus (*concenti*) resulting from it, or from the lines (*arie*) assigned to the various voices. If he finds these unusual and new, they are so because they must express new affections. The central argument is in this passage of l'Ottuso's letter: 'It is therefore true that the new progression of the parts (*modulatione*) makes a new consensus (*concento*) and a new affection, and not (as you say) new confusion and discord. But Your Lordship himself admits in his [letter] that there is a new air (*aria*), a new stimulation to the ear, which, struck by the quickness and tardiness of movement, is affected now harshly, now sweetly according to the air that [Signor] Etc. has given to the parts. What is this, then, if not new part-movement (*modulatione*) full of new affection, imitating the nature of the verse and justly representing the true meaning of the poet? And if it appears that this somehow contradicts the authority of the very learned Monsignor Zarlino of reverent memory in the Second Part of the *Institutioni harmoniche*, nevertheless he himself confesses at the end of the [twelfth] chapter

---

[1] *Seconda parte dell'Artusi,* loc. cit.
[2] Ibid., p. 6.
[3] Ibid., pp. 13–21.

that from this movement of the parts (*modulatione*) is born melody (*melodia*).'[1]

The major communication-barrier between the two writers now becomes apparent. Artusi follows the terminology of Zarlino, while l'Ottuso uses such terms as *modulatione*, *concento* and *aria* loosely in the manner of the current musical jargon. By *modulatione* Zarlino meant the movement from pitch to pitch through various intervals by one or more parts with or without measured rhythm. *Modulatione*, properly speaking, that is *modulatione propria*, is the movement of two or more parts meeting in consonances through measured rhythm. This kind of *modulatione* produces *harmonia*.[2] *Harmonia*, according to Zarlino, can be of several kinds: *propria*, a mixture of two or more moving lines of low and high sounds that strikes the ear smoothly; *non propria*, a mixture of low and high sounds without any change of pitch; *perfetta*, in which the outer voices are mediated by one or more inner parts; *imperfetta*, when the outer two parts are not so mediated. When the parts meet in consonances, this is called *concento*. *Harmonia propria* has more power to move the passions than *harmonia non propria*, but it does not acquire its full power except through rhythm and text. 'Therefore from these three things joined together, that is *harmonia propria*, rhythm (*rithmo*) and text (*oratione*), arise (as Plato would have it) *melodia*.'[3] *Melodia*, then, is not melody but the synthesis of the musical, textual and expressive content of a composition. This usage of *melodia* not only clarifies what l'Ottuso wants to say in the excerpt quote above but is also, as we shall see, a key to Monteverdi's preface.

So the difficulty was that l'Ottuso, though he had read Zarlino, had garbled his terms. Properly translated into Zarlinian, what he was saying is this. Monteverdi was striving for a *harmonia*, which when combined with the other two elements of Plato's triad, rhythm and text, would produce a *melodia* expressive of a particular text. When this text expressed new and violent

---

[1] Ibid., p. 14.   [2] Cf. Zarlino, op. cit., II, xiv, p. 81.

[3] Ibid., II, xii, p. 80. Artusi summarizes these definitions, paraphrasing Zarlino (*Seconda parte dell'Artusi*, pp. 24ff.). Melody in the sense of a line that an individual part makes as it is 'modulated' is called '*aria*'.

passions, the *modulatione* that made up the *harmonia* had to be new to produce a new *melodia*.

The contradiction that bothered Artusi now becomes evident. Only mixtures of several lines that strike the ear smoothly can be considered *harmonia propria*. Monteverdi's mixtures sometimes did not. Moreover, the *modulatione* was sometimes faulty by Zarlino's criteria; it used intervals not accepted into vocal music. So Artusi could say that Monteverdi's new *melodia* was no *melodia* at all, because it violated the standards of good *modulatione* and *harmonia propria*.

The usages to which Artusi took exception may be considered in two categories, then: irregularities of 'modulation' or melody-writing, and irregularities of 'harmony' or vertical combination.

Artusi objected to the following interval because it passes from a diatonic note to a chromatic one and is therefore unnatural to the voice, which, unlike instruments, is limited to a small number of consonant and dissonant intervals, through which it passes from one consonance to another:[1]

Ex. 11

This interval is made up of one tone (A–B) and two semitones (B–C and A–G♯). A 9/8 tone added to two 16/15 semitones results in an interval in the ratio 32/25. Artusi is assuming the syntonic diatonic tuning of Ptolemy advocated by Zarlino as the only possible tuning for voices singing unaccompanied. The interval C–G♯ is therefore a most dissonant interval. It is neither a major nor a minor third, and Artusi defies his correspondent to tell him what it is.

Whereas l'Ottuso should have challenged Artusi's assumption of the syntonic diatonic tuning, by then proved unserviceable by several authors,[2] he replies feebly: 'It is a new voice progression

---

[1] This example appears in Artusi as follows: , p. 9. I have assumed a soprano clef.

[2] Cf. Vincenzo Galilei in *Dialogo della musica antica et della moderna* (Florence, 1581) and Giovanni Battista Benedetti in *Diversarum speculationum mathemati-*

(*modulatione*) for the sake of finding through its novelty a new consensus (*concento*) and a new affection'.[1]

The interval occurs twice in the madrigal under discussion in these pages, *Era l'anima mia* (Book V) — at bars 28–9 in the quinto part at the words 'Deh perchè ti consumi?' (Say, why do you waste yourself?') and at bars 58–9 in the tenor at the words 'Non mori tu, mor'io' ('Don't die yourself, I shall die'):

Ex. 12

Although l'Ottuso calls it new, he goes on to defend it by precedents (an inconsistency Artusi was quick to point out). Cipriano de Rore uses it in *Poichè m'invita amore* at the words 'dolce mia vita'[2] and Giaches de Wert in *Misera, non credea* at the word 'essangue' (bars 79–84):[3]

Ex. 13

(Kissing these pale and bloodless lips....)

corum & phisicorum liber (Turin, 1585). Cf. Palisca, 'Scientific Empiricism in Musical Thought', in Hedley Howell Rhys (ed.), *Seventeenth Century Science and the Arts* (Princeton, 1961), pp. 133ff.

[1] *Seconda parte dell'Artusi*, p. 15.

[2] *Vive fiamme* (Venice, 1565). L'Ottuso quotes a fragment of the soprano, p. 15.

[3] *Ottavo libro de' madrigali a cinque voci* (Venice, 1586); L'Ottuso quotes fragments of the soprano, tenor and alto, p. 15. A modern edition of this madrigal appears in *Vier Madrigale von Mantuaner Komponisten,* ed. Denis Arnold, *Das Chorwerk,* LXXX (Wolfenbüttel, 1961), p. 10.

Another usage that Artusi criticizes and l'Ottuso defends is that of following a sharpened note by a descending interval and a flattened note by a rising one. Artusi does not cite any examples in Monteverdi; but many can be found.[1] All the *moderni* are doing it, says l'Ottuso, 'most of all those who have embraced this new second practice' (*questa nuova seconda pratica*)[2]. This is the first time the expression '*seconda pratica*' appears in the controversy, and it is introduced without fanfare, as if the term were already current in oral if not written discussions. The particular examples cited by l'Ottuso[3] are: the beginning of Marenzio's *Dura legge* and *S'io parto*;[4] and Wert's *Misera, non credea* at the words 'parte tornò'.[5] In *S'io parto*[6] the step Bb–C is used constantly, as is to be expected in any G minor piece. In the following example from Wert's madrigal the progression to the dominant of D minor is entirely fitting to the modern minor mode (bars 86–7):

Ex. 14

But it does not belong in the First or Second Mode, and Artusi expected a composition to remain within the steps of a mode and its plagal form. In this he was a loyal follower of Zarlino, who denounced inflections and chromaticism in vocal music.

The issue of modal purity and unity had already come up in the

[1] For example, in the fourth book: *Anima mia, perdona,* bars 38ff., second part, bar 17; *Luci serene e chiare,* bars 31, 34–5; *Voi pur da me partite; Ohimè, se tanto amate,* bar 6, flat rising, etc.

[2] *Seconda parte dell'Artusi,* p. 16.

[3] Ibid., p. 18; Artusi prints only fragments of the offending parts.

[4] Both from *Il nono libro de madrigali a 5* (Venice, 1599).

[5] Cf. note 3 on p. 149.

[6] Printed in Carl Parrish and John F. Ohl (eds.), *Masterpieces of Music before 1750* (London, 1952), p. 102.

dialogue of 1600, when Artusi singled out O Mirtillo for attack because it seemed to begin in one mode and end in another.[1] Then in his letter to l'Ottuso, Artusi criticised Cruda Amarilli for having more cadences in the Twelfth Mode (C plagal) than in the mode of its closing or opening, namely the Seventh (G authentic). L'Ottuso's answer is weak. Everybody knows, he says, 'that a mode is determined from the first and last notes and not from the median cadences'.[2] Giulio Cesare Monteverdi's gloss on his brother's letter is similarly naïve in replying to the first attack. He justifies the disunity of mode in O Mirtillo on the precedents of the mixed modes of plainchant and the mixtures of modes in compositions of Josquin, Willaert, Rore and Alessandro Striggio the elder.[3] The latter's Nasce la pena mia[4] is cited as being built upon four modes.

Artusi had reason to be shocked at this mixed bag of examples, which left him wondering if the commentator understood what mixed modes were. He replied for the traditionalists forcefully through 'Braccino da Todi' in 1608: 'Now for the mixture of tones or modes, which the commentator seems to reproach Artusi for not knowing. What it is, how many kinds there are, what is rational and what is irrational, I shall tell you. If Monteverdi wished to write a composition in a single mode (Tono) such as the First, he could not, because perforce there would be a mixture of modes. For when a composer constructs a piece in the First Mode, he must keep to the following order. The tenor should proceed or 'modulate' by way of the notes of the First natural Mode or whichever mode he intends to construct it in ... and the bass by way of its collateral [the plagal mode]. The cantus corresponds and 'modulates' an octave higher and by the same steps [and mode] as the tenor. The contralto regularly corresponds to the bass, but an octave higher. So all vocal compositions are mixtures of the authentic and plagal. But the mixtures of Monteverdi are

[1] L'Artusi, f. 48v.

[2] Seconda parte dell'Artusi, p. 21.

[3] Dichiaratione della lettera stampata nel quinto libro de suoi madrigali in G. Francesco Malipiero, Claudio Monteverdi (Milan, 1929), pp. 83–4, trans. in Strunk, op. cit., pp. 411–12.

[4] Striggio, Il primo libro de madrigali a 6 (Venice, 1560).

not regular like these, but irregular. If he sets out to give one form to his composition, he ends up giving it another, because he exceeds the bounds of mixture. Therefore one may say that he throws the pumpkins in with the lanterns.'¹ Modal unity was of some moment to Artusi, because he, like Zarlino and Glareanus before him, believed that each mode had its special character. In his dialogue of 1600 Artusi had assigned an ethos to each of the modes and urged the composer to choose one suited to the subject of a composition and stick to it.¹

Giulio Cesare's reply did not come to terms with the issue, because he lacked either the courage or conviction to proclaim the end of the tyranny of the modes. Galilei had already prepared their demise when he exposed the false humanism of the modal theorists in 1581³ and again ten years later. In his counterpoint treatise he asserted that modality had become more a matter for the eye than the ear, for no one now paid any attention to the internal cadences: '. . . the best and most famous contrapuntists have used cadences on any step at all [of the mode] in their vocal compositions. Moreover . . . the sure identification of the mode is derived from the last note in the bass. That this is true is obvious every time this last note is hidden from the sight of the person studying the piece. . . . With the eyes, therefore, and not with the ears, do modern practitioners know the modes of their pieces. . . . Moreover, take any modern vocal piece in whatever mode and remove or add one or two notes at the end to make it terminate in other notes than the previous ones (without going to extremes, though), and practitioners today will say that there has been a mutation of mode. . . . And when Zarlino too would wish to persuade me again of the simplicities he writes, saying that among our modes one has a quiet nature, another deprecatory, others querulous, excited, lascivious, cheerful, somnolent, tranquil or infuriated and others yet different natures and characters, and finally that the modes as practitioners

¹ *Discorso secondo musicale,* pp. 11-12.
² *L'Artusi,* f. 68v.
³ One of the main points of the *Dialogo* was that the ecclesiastical modes had none of the virtues claimed for them by Glareanus and Zarlino.

use them today have the same capacities as those he mentioned the ancient modes possessed, I would answer, convinced by experience, which teaches us the contrary, that these are all tales intended to confuse dunderheads. If our practice retains the smallest part of these aptitudes it does not derive them from the mode or the final note or the harmonic and arithmetic divisions but from the way contrapuntists make the parts progress in any of the modes according to 'what suits them best.'[1]

It is usual to compose a sonnet, he continues, so that 'each quatrain and tercet, indeed each particular verse, is of a different mode from the rest. Whoever does differently is taken for a satrap and is accused of indolence and of lacking inventiveness. The ancients sang a history, an action of a hero and an entire book in one same tone (*Tono*), but the goal of the ancients was to make men moderate and virtuous, and that of the moderns is to amuse them, if not to make them effeminate.'[2]

Galilei's objective in criticizing the loose modality practised by composers in his time was the opposite of Artusi's. Galilei wanted to see modality abandoned in favour of tonal unity based on pitch level, on the model of the ancient Greeks. Monteverdi was heading pragmatically in the same direction, though unencumbered by Galilei's theoretical bias. To judge by Giulio Cesare's reply, which must have had his approval, Claudio could not yet foresee the theoretical implications of his creative impulses.

The controversy had begun around the use of dissonance. Luca's rationalizations for their free employment fit only those combinations that seem to come about casually as a by-product of independent part-movement. But more characteristic of Monteverdi's style are dissonances deliberately planted in exposed situations. Some of the exposed dissonances illustrated in Artusi's eighth and ninth examples, both from *Anima mia, perdona*,[3] are the result of suspension. But the suspended note instead of being held is sounded again. Artusi fails to make this clear, because he omits bar 59 of the second part of this madrigal in the second of

[1] *Il primo libro della prattica del contrapunto*, I, ff. 100–100v.
[2] Ibid., f. 101.
[3] Cf. Strunk, op. cit., p. 395.

his examples; the repetition of the suspended C in the alto in bar 60 can be seen in my example (bars 59–62):

Ex. 15

(.... not your torments.)

This repetition violated the regular suspension usage as analyzed in Artusi's own counterpoint text, where one of the notes of a suspension is regarded as the 'patient' (*paziente*) and the other as the 'agent' (*agente*). The 'patient' remains stationary as it suffers the 'agent' causing the dissonance to move and strike against it.[1]

The reasons traditionally given for tolerating the suspension depend on this absorption of the shock of the dissonance by the sustained voice. Franchino Gaffurio speaks of the hidden and dulled nature of this dissonance.[2] Zarlino finds such a dissonance tolerable 'because in singing the syncopated semibreve the voice holds firm, and a certain suspension is heard (*si ode quasi una sospensione*), a taciturnity that is noticed amidst the percussions that produce the tones and make them distinguishable from one another in time. So the ear barely notices this dissonance, not being sufficiently stimulated by it to comprehend it fully'.[3]

Monteverdi's seventh in bar 60 of Ex. 15 does not crouch behind the consonances but steps out to be noticed. As Galilei put it, when a composer uses dissonances in this manner he does not expect them to 'blend in harmony with wonderful effect; but rather that the sense become satisfied with them, not because they harmonize ..., but because of the gentle mixture of the sweet and the strong, which ... affect our ears not unlike the

---

[1] Artusi, *Seconda parte dell'arte del contraponto*, Bk. II, ch. i, pp. 27ff.

[2] *Practicae musicae* (Milan, 1496), Bk. III, ch. iv: 'est item et latens discordia in contrapuncto praeter sincopatam scilicet inter plures cantilenae partes concordes continetur et obtunditur'.

[3] Zarlino, op. cit., III, xlii, p. 197.

way in which taste receives satisfaction from both sugar and vinegar'.[1]

Even more prominent, of course, is the seventh in the top part in bar 61, which is not sounded in the previous bar. L'Ottuso admits that he can offer no theoretical demonstration to justify these usages. Yet he is convinced they are admissible, not only on grounds of precedent, but also by virtue of the context, or as a poetic licence. He is not driven, as Artusi implied, to call a dissonance a consonance — he realizes that a dissonance would always be a dissonance: 'but by circumstance (*per accidente*) it can well be otherwise, for there is no dissonant interval which is in itself one that by circumstance cannot be made good with reference to the accompaniments among which it is placed. As an accent, as a deception, or indeed as a dissonance, though sweetened by the accompaniment of the other parts, it [a seventh] will undoubtedly not only have a good effect but, being something new, will give greater delight to the ear than would the supposed octave. And since you desire a proof, you will draw it very easily from this: you allow an excellent poet the metaphor purposefully used; similarly the seventh is taken in place of the octave.'[2]

The octave is understood or 'supposed' (*supposta*), but the seventh is heard in its stead. As the poet metaphorically takes one word for another, the composer takes one note for another. For example Marenzio 'who was not in the habit of staying within the narrow prescriptions of music theory', used the seventh above the bass in two of the madrigals of his ninth book of five-part madrigals:[3] in *E so come in un punto* at the words 'per le guancie' and 'ascoso langue', and in *E così nel mio parlare*[4] at the words 'maggior

[1] Quoted in Palisca, 'Vincenzo Galilei's Counterpoint Treatise', p. 87.

[2] *Seconda parte dell'Artusi*, p. 16. Angelo Berardi paraphrased this passage in his *Miscellanea musicale* (Bologna, 1689), Part II, ch. xii, p. 39: 'the moderns use the bare seventh (*settima nuda*) as a deception (*inganno*) and accent (*accento*), or as a dissonance, yes, but sweetened by the accompaniment of the other parts, as something new that produces a new affection in the ear . . .' He then cites the madrigals of Marenzio named by l'Ottuso.

[3] *Il nono libro de madrigali a 5* (Venice, 1599).

[4] Printed in Alfred Einstein, 'Dante im Madrigal', *Archiv für Musikwissenschaft*, III (1921), pp. 414–20. From the four places in these two madrigals cited Artusi, p. 17, prints the two voice parts that form the seventh.

durezze' and in the second part at 'da i colpi mortali'. Here is the last of these:

Ex. 16

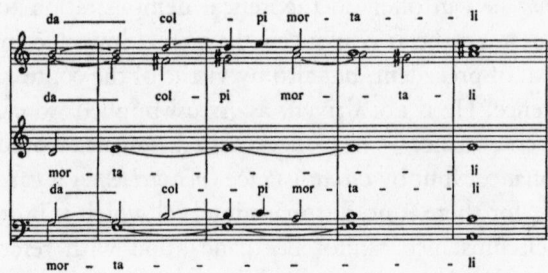

The word 'colpi' (blows) is accompanied by a second and seventh above the bass instead of a third and octave. Like the figure of speech in which a word with stronger and richer associations replaces the normal one, the composer, l'Ottuso would have us believe, substitutes a sharp dissonance for the normal consonance. This notion has great potential, as Bernhard shows when he classifies many irregular uses of dissonance as rhetorical figures. But l'Ottuso fails to develop the thought. Nevertheless he is one of the very few Italian writers who associates musical licences with rhetorical figures.

The two principal sources for Monteverdi's free treatment of dissonance that emerge from Artusi's dialogue and the letters of l'Ottuso are the impromptu practices of singers and the pioneering efforts of Rore and his followers, and they are corroborated by Zacconi in the second part of his *Prattica di musica*, published in 1622. If someone were to ask him, he writes, whence came the practice of placing dissonances on the downbeat in the manner found throughout Monteverdi's works, 'I would say that he took it from the second part of the motet of Cipriano Bora [i.e. Rore] *O altitudo divitiarum*, which uses this arrangement of notes. The first minim [see bar 94 of Ex. 17] is made dissonant as an affectation [*per affetto*], thereby making the second minim awaited by the melody so much the better. Or shall we say that, although he [Monteverdi] may have taken this practice from the forenamed

Ex. 17: Rore, *O altitudo divitiarum*, from *Il terzo libro di motetti a 5* (Venice, 1549) (bars 93–4)

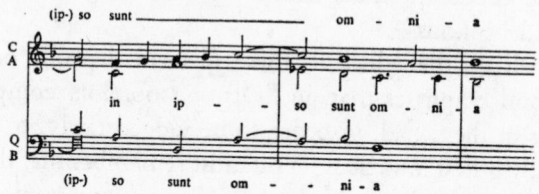

composer, he was not moved entirely by this, but by that every-day habit singers have today of performing things with the most grateful affectations (*affetti*) possibly to make themselves as pleasing as they can to listeners.'[1]

Throughout his replies, Artusi insists upon the rules, because, he says, they are based on nature, demonstration and the models of excellent composers. Although l'Ottuso too has recourse to the example of excellent composers, he challenges the principle of imitation. Every good painter, sculptor, poet or orator seeks to imitate the ancients and particularly the excellent ones, but there are also those who esteem invention more than imitation. Indeed, in music invention is much more esteemed than imitation, because only through invention can musical art advance. Signor Etc. (Monteverdi) is one of those dedicated to invention. *Era l'anima mia*, for example, in whose opening, staying for four bars on the chord of D minor, Artusi found nothing new, but rather a reminiscence of the *giustiniana*,[2] l'Ottuso defends as full of new harmonic progressions, elegant passages from plagal to authentic, ascents after accidental flats and descents after sharps, substitutions of unexpected notes for the expected, and other artful devices. 'If your Lordship considered the madrigals of Signor Etc.', he

[1] *Prattica di musica seconda parte* (Venice, 1622), Bk. II, ch. x, p. 63. Zacconi quotes of the alto and quinto parts the second half of bar 93 and the first half of 94. The motet is published in Rore, *Opera omnia*, ed. Bernhard Meier, I (Rome, 1959), p. 122.

[2] A type of villanella, common in Venice. On the opening of *Era l'anima mia* cf. also *infra*, p. 217. Similarly, Artusi asks if the first eight bars, which he quotes, of *Ma se con la pietà*, the second part of *Ecco Silvio* in the fifth book, is the beginning of a *giustiniana* or a *spifarata mantovana: Seconda parte dell'Artusi*, p. 5.

pleaded, 'you will find them full of such flowers, embellished with such terse modulation, far from the common, indeed full of judicious deceptions.'[1]

So much of the effect of these licences depends on subtle nuances and emphases that, in l'Ottuso's opinion, compositions indulging in them had, in order to be judged fairly, to be sung by specially gifted musicians. 'You must remember that the singer is the soul of music, and it is he who, in sum, represents the true meaning of the composer to us. In this representation, according to the variety of the subject, the voice is sometimes reinforced, at other times sweetened. For this reason you have to hear this manner of clever composition sung by singers who are out of the ordinary. Your Lordship's grounds [for criticism] would then cease to exist, in that the harshness of these madrigals would be covered in such a way that the dissonances would not be heard . . .'[2]

For Artusi l'Ottuso relied too much on deluding the ear and the judgment with deceptions, suppositions and artifices that have no basis in reality. 'All those things that the modern confounders call suppositions, flowers (*fioretti*), deceptions, accents and artifices, which are against the good rules, the student knows for false, false suppositions against the nature of the thing, false deceptions, false flowers, false artifices, false accents, and never true things and true suppositions.'[3] Modern composers take too much refuge in the deficiencies of the senses. In their ambition to sway the emotions they resort to means that are unnatural and therefore cannot stimulate a natural process like moving the affections, for like responds to like. The only new effects that come across are those the singers do when they 'turn the head slowly, bend their eyebrows, roll their eyes, twist their shoulders, let themselves go as if they want to die, and their many other metamorphoses, the likes of which Ovid never imagined. Indeed they make these grimaces just when they arrive at those dissonances that offend the sense to show what others ought to be doing. But instead of being moved [the listeners] are ruffled by the bitterness and dis-

[1] Ibid., p. 19.
[2] Ibid., pp. 19–20.   [3] Ibid., p. 47.

content they feel, and, turning their heads, depart dissatisfied.'[1]

The following concise and eloquent statement, printed in the Fifth Book of Madrigals (1605), is the only public reply Claudio Monteverdi made to Artusi's criticisms.

'Studious Readers:

'Be not surprised that I am giving these madrigals to the press without first replying to the objections that Artusi made against some very minute portions of them. Being in the service of this Serene Highness of Mantua, I am not master of the time I would require. Nevertheless I wrote a reply to let it be known that I do not do things by chance, and as soon as it is rewritten it will see the light with the title in front, *Seconda pratica overo Perfettione della moderna musica*. Some will wonder at this, not believing that there is any other practice than that taught by Zerlino [*sic*]. But let them be assured concerning consonances and dissonances that there is a different way of considering them from that already determined which defends the modern manner of composition with the assent of the reason and the senses. I wanted to say this both so that the expression *Seconda pratica* would not be appropriated by others and so that men of intellect might meanwhile consider other second thoughts concerning harmony. And have faith that the modern composer builds on foundations of truth.

'Live happily.'[2]

This is a statement full of promise. Monteverdi, though confident of his musical instinct, recognized the need for a theoretical rationalization of his new way of dealing with dissonances if it was to be generally accepted.[3] Like his predecessors Zarlino and Francisco de Salinas, he aimed to appeal to both the reason and the senses. The letter does not imply, as has sometimes been suggested, that Monteverdi considered the rules of the first practice a theory, while the second was a mere practice. He

---

[1] Ibid., pp. 40–1.

[2] Italian text in Malipiero, op. cit., pp. 71–2.

[3] Monteverdi was apparently unaware of Galilei's counterpoint treatise, which for polyphonic music at least presents a new set of rules and considerations about consonance and dissonance on the basis of the works of some of the composers Giulio Cesare Monteverdi names as founders of the *seconda prattica*. See Palisca, 'Vincenzo Galilei's Counterpoint Treatise'.

obviously knew the difference between *musica theorica* and *musica practica*. Zarlino's *Istitutioni* is a union of both, but its Book III, which deals with the use of consonances and dissonances in counterpoint, is essentially a *musica practica*. Monteverdi promised to replace it with a second and different *musica practica*.[1]

Giulio Cesare Monteverdi's commentary on his brother's letter, published in the *Scherzi musicali* (1607), is one of the most important manifestoes in the history of music. As with most manifestoes it is richer in slogans than in original aesthetic ideas. But it does illuminate some of Claudio's remarks, even if we cannot assume that he would have stood behind every word of it.

From the first paragraph we learn that Monteverdi's letter of 1605 was answered by a discourse printed under the name of Antonio Braccino da Todi. No copy of this is extant, but its existence is further corroborated by the title of the discourse published under the same name in 1608, *Discorso secondo musicale di Antonio Braccino da Todi per la dichiaratione della lettera posta ne Scherzi musicali del Sig. Claudio Monteverde*.[2] The author of these discourses has always been assumed to be Artusi, and there is no reason to contest this attribution. The explanation for Artusi's hiding behind a pseudonym is probably that here for the first time he names the composer whose madrigals he attacked and out of delicacy wished to remain anonymous, as before he kept the composer anonymous.

The principal contribution of Giulio Cesare's commentary is that he informs us of the *seconda prattica*'s pedigree, both in practice and philosophy. He names Rore the founder and lists the composers who developed it before his brother,[3] and he aligns it with the famous dictum of Plato, which put the text ahead of the other

---

[1] This numbering of the 'practices' is obviously short in hindsight, as Artusi points out in the *Discorso secondo*, p. 15; but the latter's suggestion of calling it the third or fourth practice, depending on whether that of the Greeks and Romans is considered the first or the first and second, is not much better.

[2] Venice, 1608; facsimile reprint, Milan, 1934.

[3] These are Marc'Antonio Ingegneri, Marenzio, Wert, Luzzasco Luzzaschi, Jacopo Peri, Giulio Caccini, and the 'Heroic School' of gentlemen-composers, which includes Carlo Gesualdo, Prince of Venosa, Emilio de' Cavalieri, Fontanella, 'the Count of the Camerata' (i.e. Bardi), Cavaliere Turchi and Tommaso Pecci.

Turchi   Inglese

Intartenimento che dano ogni giorno li Ciarlatani in Piazza di S. Marco al Populo
d'ogni natione che mattina e sera ordinariamente, ui concore
Giacomo Franco Forma con Priuilegio

5 Players in St. Mark's Square, from Giacomo Franco's *Habiti e feste* of 1598

two components of music, 'harmony' and rhythm. Giulio Cesare and, we may assume, Claudio, conceived the second practice as a revival of Plato's ideal music. It renewed or revived this lost art through 'our notation', that is the mensural notation used in polyphonic music. Both Zarlino and Artusi had quoted the relevant passage from the *Republic*, but neither had emphasized the order Plato gave to the three elements. One writer who did call attention to the priority of the text was Giulio Caccini,[1] who, as we have just seen, significantly figured among those Giulio Cesare named as developers of the second practice.

Caccini was not the first to note this side of Plato's definition. Johannes Ott pointed to it briefly in a foreword to his masses of 1539,[2] and Bishop Jacopo Sadoleto commented upon it at length in a sweeping condemnation of the polyphonic music of his time in his *De liberis recte instituendis* (Concerning the Proper Education of Free Men) in 1533. A humanist churchman who as cardinal was a member of the pontifical commission for the reform of the church and the Council of Trent, he appealed to musicians to restore the verbal message to its sovereignty among the components of music. Elaborating on the famous Platonian passage in his dialogue, Sadoleto has the father, Jacopus, tell his son Paullus: 'If we inquire into what style is to be maintained in music, I believe that we should bear all the following in mind. A chorus consists of three elements, the sense of the words, the rhythm (which we call number) and tone. The words are the first and most important of the three as being the very basis and foundation of the others. By themselves the words have no mean influence upon the mind, whether to persuade or restrain. Accommodated to rhythm (*numerus*) and meter (*modus*) they penetrate much more deeply. If in addition they are given a melodic setting, they take possession of the inner feelings and of the whole man.'[3] Sadoleto missed this persuasiveness and feeling

---

[1] In his foreword to *Le Nuove Musiche* (Florence, 1602); trans. in Strunk, op. cit., p. 378.

[2] Cf. ibid., p. 256, note k.

[3] *Iac. Sadoleti De liberis recte instituendis liber* (Venice, 1533), f. 42v: 'Quod si quaeratur qui modus sit in musicis tenendus, haec ego omnia attendenda esse puto: cum constet chorus ex tribus, sententia, rhythmo (hic enim numerus

in the vocal music of his day, which he characterized as consisting of nothing but variation and patterns of notes. The music with text that he heard served only the sense of hearing, and this made the mind a slave of the body.

Giulio Cesare proclaims that the second practice has restored the supremacy of the text, subordinating 'harmony' and leading to the perfection of 'melody'. Without perhaps intending to, he gave a new twist to Plato's words. He assigned to the word 'harmony' a modern meaning, while attempting to cling to the ancient concept of 'melody'. Zarlino had already planted the seed for this confusion, when he said 'from proper harmony (*harmonia propria*), rhythm (*rithmo*) and text (*oratione*) arise (as Plato would have it) melody (*melodia*)'.[1]

The confusion resulted from the scant comprehension of Greek music on the part of the early translators of Plato. The translation most current in Italy was the Latin of Marsilio Ficino. Plato's phrase is rendered: '. . . melodia ex tribus constare, oratione, harmonia, rhythmus'.[2] And later: 'atqui harmonia et rhythmus orationem sequi debent'.[3]

In the original Greek, however, we read that *melos* (song) consists of three things, *logos* (the word, or that by which the inward thought is expressed), *harmonia* (agreement or relation of sounds) and *rhythmos* (time or rhythm). Plato was saying simply that a song consists of a text, an agreeable arrangement of intervals, and measured time; and of these the text is the leader.

But Giulio Cesare, and l'Ottuso with him, are saying that a modern polyphonic composition, like the ancient song or *melos*, should subordinate to the text (its meaning and rhythm) the arrangement of tones both successive and simultaneous (broadening of the concept of *harmonia*) and rhythm (now broadened to

nobis est) & uoce, primum quidem omnium & potissimum sententiam esse, utpote quae si sedes & fundamentum reliquorum, & per se ipsa ualeat non minimum ad suadendum animo uel dissuadendum: numeris autem modisque contorta penetret multo acrius: si uero etiam cantu & uoce fuerit modulata, iam omnis intus sensus & hominem totum possideat'.

[1] op. cit., II, xii, 80.

[2] *Republic* 398*c*: Plato, *Opera,* trans. Marsilio Ficino (Venice, 1491), f. 201.

[3] *Republic* 398*d*.

include tempo, metre and rhythm). This results in the perfection of 'melody', that is, expressive composition. He is not saying, as has sometimes been inferred, that melody in the sense of tune or monody should now take precedence over counterpoint or harmony. Melody in this sense is not even in question.[1]

The recognition that Monteverdi gave to the existence of two practices and their definition by Giulio Cesare were of resonant importance. Hardly a theoretical book was published after 1608 that did not help to confirm this dichotomy. It should be recalled, however, that the Monteverdi brothers underscored a dualism that already existed in both the music and the literature about it from the middle of the sixteenth century. The *musica nova* and *musica reservata* of the 1540's and 1550's broke the ground for the tradition that Giulio Cesare dates back to the madrigals of Rore.[2] Galilei in his counterpoint treatise contrasted the composers who followed the rules — the *osservatori* — and those who, like the painters Michelangelo and Raphael, were guided only by their own judgment based on both reason and sense.[3]

---

[1] Artusi quite rightly, if unduly harshly, scolded Giulio Cesare for distorting Plato's meaning: 'Plato does not treat nor ever did, nor had he any thought of treating of modern melodies or music, but I believe, rather, that he discussed those melodies that flourished in his time. It was possible to say then that the text had greater force than the harmony or rhythm, because that history, tale or whatever it may have been was recited to the sound of a single instrument. . . But the melodies of Monteverde of which the commentator writes are not similar to those used in the time of Plato; they are deformed. In those [of the ancients] the text was stirring, in these, if anything, the harmony; in those the text was intelligible, in these the harmony; then they worked many effects, now none . . . There is no conformity or resemblance between the melody used in the time of Plato and that of our day. It is too diverse, too different. The quoted passage is out of the seminary, out of context, a chimera, malapropos' (*Discorso secondo musicale*, p. 9).

[2] Cf. Palisca, 'A Clarification of "Musica Reservata" in Jean Taisnier's "Astrologiae," 1559', *Acta musicologica*, XXXI (1959), p. 133.

[3] *Discorso intorno all'uso delle dissonanze*, I, f. 142v: 'The greatness and majesty that is contained in that Canzone which begins *Hor ch'il cielo, et la Terra, e'l vento tace* [*Li madrigali cromatici a 5, Libro I*, Venice, 1562], the loveliness and grace of *Anchor che col partire* [*Il primo libro de madrigali a 4*, Ferrara, 1550], the varied sweetness and unusual sonority of *Cantai mentre ch'io arsi del mio foco* [*Li madrigali cromatici*], the sombreness of *Come havran fin le dolorose tempre* [*Primo libro a 5*, 1550] expressed with so much artfulness without any affectation: Cipriano did not learn the art of turning out such works as these in the

Girolamo Diruta in 1597[1] and Adriano Banchieri in 1614 distinguished between the *contrapunto osservato* and the modern freer *contrapunto commune*. The *osservato*, Banchieri notes, was explained both as to theory and practice by Zarlino, Artusi and other writers, but of the *contrapunto misto* or *commune* writers had not produced a single rule or precept for accommodating the affections. Nor does he consider the subject one that could be written about.[2]

The writer who most faithfully communicates both the language and spirit of the Monteverdi brothers is Marco Scacchi. He synthesizes the ideas of the 1605, 1607 and 1638 prefaces in a single system of style-classification. While the 'musica antica', Scacchi asserts, maintained the same style for all serious subjects, whether meant for sacred or secular functions, modern music employs two practices and three styles. In the first practice the composer is guided by the principle *ut harmonia sit domina orationis* (that harmony be the mistress of the text). In the second practice he obeys the rule *ut oratio sit domina harmoniae* (that the text be the

---

books written about the rules of counterpoint, but it rested entirely on his own judgment'.

[1] *Il Transilvano Dialogo sopra il vero modo di sonar organi & istromenti da penna* (Venice, 1597).

[2] Adriano Banchieri, *Cartella musicale nel canto figurato, fermo & contrapunto . . . novamente in questa terza impressione ridotta dall'antica alla moderna pratica* (Venice, 1614), pp. 161ff. Already in an earlier publication, *Conclusioni nel suono dell'organo* (Bologna, 1609), pp. 58–9, Banchieri had complained that the authors on counterpoint never gave 'any rule or precept that would show how in practice to imitate the affections when setting any kind of words [to music], whether Latin or vernacular, and in particular words signifying pains, passions, sighing, tears, laughter, question, error and similar circumstances . . . There is no doubt that music, so far as harmony (*harmonia*) is concerned, must be subject to the words, since the words are those that express the conceit . . .' Galilei in 1591 made a similar complaint: 'In the variety of books which are in print today written on the subject of the art of modern counterpoint, which I have read diligently many times, I have never been able to know two very principal things. One of these pertains to the soul of harmony, which is the meaning of the words; and the other pertains to the body, which is the diversity of successive sounds and notes by which the parts proceed. Regarding the soul, no one so far as I know, as I have said, has yet taught the way to accompany the words, or rather the ideas behind them, with notes . . .' (*Discorso intorno all'uso delle dissonanze*, I, f. 105v).

mistress of the harmony).[1] Scacchi's three styles of music are indebted to the letter that precedes the *Madrigali guerrieri, et amorosi* (Venice, 1638). Here Monteverdi states: '. . . the music of grand princes is used in their royal chambers in three manners to please their delicate tastes, namely [music for] the theatre, for the chamber and for the dance . . .'[2]

Scacchi built upon this base a broader scheme of classification. The three styles of the modern or second practice are the church style (*ecclesiasticus*), the chamber style (*cubicularis*) and the theatrical style (*scenicus seu theatralis*). These categories break down into further divisions, as shown in the following chart:[3]

Ecclesiasticus	*Cubicularis*	*Scenicus seu Theatralis*
1. 4 to 8 voices, no organ	1. madrigals *da tavolino* (*a cappella*)	1. *stile semplice recitativo* (without gestures)
2. polychoral with organ	2. madrigals with basso continuo	2. *stile recitativo* (with gestures)
3. *in concerto* (with instruments)	3. compositions for voices and instruments	
4. motets in modern style in *stile misto* (recitative with florid passages and arias)		

Scacchi's style-system underwent further development at the

---

[1] Marco Scacchi, *Breve discorso sopra la musica moderna* (Warsaw, 1649), ff. 10v–11. This pamphlet is essentially a commentary on Giulio Cesare's *Dichiaratione* in response to an opponent of the modern style, namely Romano Micheli. Scacchi comments on the Artusi–Monteverdi feud also in his *Cribrum musicum* (Venice, 1643).

[2] Malipiero, op. cit., p. 91.

[3] In this chart I have incorporated into the classification presented in the *Breve discorso* the more detailed division of church music Scacchi makes in a letter to Christoph Werner, published in Erich Katz, *Die musikalischen Stilbegriffe des 17. Jahrhunderts* (Freiburg, 1926), pp. 83–7. This classification of church music is adopted by Berardi, a pupil of Scacchi, in his *Ragionamenti musicali* (Bologna, 1681), p. 134.

hands of Christoph Bernhard,[1] who partly reconciled it with the terminology of Diruta and Banchieri:

Contrapunctus gravis	*Contrapunctus luxurians*
or *stylus antiquus*	or *stylus modernus*
or *a capella* or *ecclesiasticus*	1. *communis*
(*Harmonia Orationis*	(*Oratio* as well as *Harmonia Domina*)
Domina)	2. *comicus* or *theatralis*
	or *recitativus* or *oratorius*
	(*Oratio Harmoniae Domina*
	absolutissima)

Thus the slogans of Giulio Cesare Monteverdi still ring in the treatises and pamphlets of the mid-seventeenth century. The ripple started by Artusi's first stone reaches ever wider circles as the controversy over the two styles is stirred up in Rome, Danzig, Warsaw and Hamburg, among other places. In Rome Romano Micheli takes up Artusi's role as defender of the first practice, while Marco Scacchi challenges him from Warsaw.[2] Their quarrel grows out of a local difference between the composers Paul Seyfert and Kaspar Förster the Elder in Danzig. Then, as Scacchi gathers testimonials for his point of view throughout Germany and Poland, many of the other musical centres of northern Europe are drawn into the fray. In the heat of these debates were tempered and forged the rules of the neo-severe style of the late seventeenth century.

[1] *Tractatus compositionis augmentatus,* chs. 3 and 35, pp. 42–3 and 82–3.
[2] See my articles 'Micheli' and 'Scacchi' in *Die Musik in Geschichte und Gegenwart,* IX (1961), cols. 273–4, and XI (1963), cols. 1466–9, respectively.

JEROME ROCHE

Monteverdi and the *Prima Prattica*

'By First Practice he understands the one that turns on the perfection of the harmony, that is, the one that considers the harmony not commanded, but commanding, not the servant, but the mistress of the words, and this was founded by those first men who composed in our notation music for more than one voice, was then followed and amplified by Ockeghem, Josquin Desprez, Pierre de la Rue, Jean Mouton, Crequillon, Clemens non Papa, Gombert, and others of those times, and was finally perfected by Messer Adriano with actual composition and by the most excellent Zarlino with most judicious rules.'[1]

Thus Monteverdi's brother, Giulio Cesare, outlines what Claudio himself meant by the term *prima prattica*, in a manifesto printed with the *Scherzi Musicali* published in 1607. But what is our conception of the term? Is it synonymous with *stile antico* or *a cappella*? These questions inevitably pose themselves at the outset of a consideration of Monteverdi's relationship with the *prima prattica*, for the three terms have been used rather loosely and have even become interchangeable in writings on early seventeenth-century church music. The problem can be stated in another way: if we agree that the *prima prattica* represents seventeenth-century music written deliberately in a style that belongs to the previous century, then surely we shall have to decide at what date the style becomes anachronistic, at what date a composer writing polyphonically ceases to be with the times and becomes a reactionary? This crude over-simplification can lead us dangerously near to the viewpoint of historians several generations ago who treated

[1] Oliver Strunk, *Source Readings in Music History* (London, 1952), p. 408.

1600 as a 'great divide', whereas in reality the transition from late sixteenth-century church music to the *seconda prattica* is not nearly so abrupt. Just as the former has its anticipations of concertato techniques, the latter in its early stages still preserves characteristics of the older music. For instance, the motets of Viadana's *Cento Concerti* of 1602, while breaking new ground as small-scale church music for a handful of solo voices with an indispensable *basso continuo* accompaniment, were composed with an attitude to the text that savoured of the *prima prattica*: that is, they had none of the emotionalism in their approach to the text that was essential to music of the Second Practice. The very reason why *prima prattica* is confined to church music is that the greater part of the liturgical texts of the mass and psalms were of a neutral nature, not calling for the dramatic word-painting of the newer music. This is not to say that the best church music was composed according to the *prima prattica*; on the contrary most of the finest early seventeenth-century church music is essentially of the Second Practice.

Can the musical environment of Monteverdi's youth in Cremona and Mantua cast some light on his future development as a composer of *prima prattica* church music? His teacher in the 1580's was Ingegneri, who was not among the most progressive north Italian church musicians of the time, preferring a more flowing polyphony to the chordal tendencies in the music of Ruffo or Andrea Gabrieli. Monteverdi's *Sacrae Cantiunculae* of 1582, which can be looked upon as contrapuntal exercises or possibly as spiritual madrigals — a form popular at the time — show a predilection for strict polyphony and are independent of musical trends in Venice. Had Monteverdi been born ten years later in Venice his whole musical upbringing, especially his attitude to polyphony, could have been utterly different. His style in the *Sacrae Cantiunculae* was orientated towards the purer Roman kind of counterpoint. But in fact his concern during the period of his youth was less with church music than with the madrigal, in which field he was more progressive. It was probably not necessary for him to compose much church music for use until towards 1610, by which time the *Sacrae Cantiunculae* were of the past.

It was by about this time that the transition to the concertato style in north Italian church music was more or less complete. Viadana's new conception of the small-scale motet for from one to four voices and organ, written for the ordinary unambitious church choir, was beginning to have a wide influence precisely because it was a practical proposition in the average church where money was not plentiful. In Rome, on the other hand, the stylistic issue was still open: the *stile antico* was not a lost cause, since the full choirs necessary to its performance were more easily maintained financially. Thus the two manners in church music were beginning to crystallize. 1610 was the year of Monteverdi's first publication of church music, historically unique in that it was the first to include *prima* and *seconda prattica* music within one cover. The publication of music in the two idioms within the same collection was to be a somewhat rare event, as a glance through a list of mass publications after 1610[1] will show. In the first decade we find only two collections of masses, by Pietro Lappi and Stefano Bernardi, and in the 1620's four, by Ghizzolo, Ignazio Donati, Aloisi and Bellazzi. An interesting point is that three of these publications include parody masses upon madrigals; the parody mass was still very much the norm where the concertato style was not adopted. More important is the designation of the older-style masses as 'da cappella', used in antithesis to 'concertato'. The term is also applied to the six-part mass in Monteverdi's 1610 collection: its exact meaning has been widely misconstrued. This is understandable since around this date it was changing its meaning. Praetorius[2] tells us that in Italy 'cappella' signifies a choir with voices and instruments mixed, and Viadana, in prefacing his polychoral psalms of 1612, asserts that unless the 'cappella', or foundation choir, has at least twenty voices and instruments, it will produce a poor sound. This is the notion of 'cappella' that had been prevalent in the sixteenth century, when instruments never did more than double the voices; but now that instruments were acquiring their own obbligato parts,

---

[1] Taken from Gaetano Gaspari, *Catalogo della Biblioteca Musicale G.B. Martini di Bologna* (repr. Bologna, 1961), II.
[2] *Syntagma Musicum*, III (Wolfenbüttel, 1619), p. 113.

written in idiomatic style, the term 'cappella' ceased to have any particular relevance to their use and slowly came to mean simply full choir music without soloists. It was but a short step to its modern, conventional meaning of unaccompanied choral music. Thus, in these mass settings with the two idioms side by side, 'da cappella' implies that soloists were not used.

The most striking difference between the *da cappella* style of Monteverdi — at least in both the 1610 and *Selva Morale* masses — and that of his contemporaries is that he tried to be far more conservative. A glance at one or two of the mass collections noted above will show that the older-style masses stand at a point much closer along a line of continuous evolution to the concertato ones: one or two of Bernardi's works will be mentioned later. Monteverdi, on the other hand, went right back to a motet of Gombert for the model of his parody mass *In illo tempore* of 1610. At the time of composing it he was intent on proving to the Roman world in general and Pope Paul V in particular that he had mastered the intricacies of classic Netherlands polyphony. And yet why should he consider that *this* was the kind of music the Romans would like to see him writing? What really was the kind of music being written for the mass in Rome in 1610? The answer to this question can fortunately be found in a work that affords a most illuminating comparison with Monteverdi's Gombert mass — the Hexachord Mass (*Super voces musicales*) by Francesco Soriano, whose music Monteverdi must have got to know through his Mantuan connections.[1] This is written in the same Ionian mode and for the same six voices, and the 'Christe eleison' motif even bears a resemblance to the first of Gombert's points that Monteverdi uses (see Ex. 1).

Hereafter the likeness rapidly diminishes: Soriano displays the progressive trends typical of Palestrina's late manner — the interest in pure sonority rather than polyphony, especially in the *Gloria*, where rhythmic motives replace conventional imitation points, as at 'Domine Deus' (see Ex. 2).

[1] Karl Proske, *Selectus Novus Missarum*, II (Regensburg, 1857), p. 205. Monteverdi's first mass and the Gombert motet *In illo tempore* on which it is based are printed in an Eulenburg score, ed. Hans F. Redlich (London, 1962).

Ex. 1[1]

Ex. 2

The *Gloria* begins chordally rather than imitatively and almost at once the diatonic C major is tarnished by an unexpected A major harmony:

Ex. 3

S. I and II

Et   in   ter - ra pax

A. and T. I

This use of a strange chord is comparable with the sudden flat-wards lean in bars 25–8 of Monteverdi's *Gloria*, though it is more

[1] All musical examples except those in triple rhythm have (where necessary) been adjusted to 4/4 or 4/2 time with *crotchet* tactus to facilitate comparison. The words have not always been fully underlaid, nor have organ continuo parts been quoted except when independent of the voices.

dramatic because it comes so near the beginning. At 'Domine Deus Agnus Dei' Soriano actually juxtaposes the C and A major chords as a coloristic effect; the chromatic alteration in the top part is typical of the compromise of the Palestrina style with modern expressiveness:

Ex. 4

The whole wayward chord progression is thrown into relief by a return within three bars to a diatonic C major. It will be seen from these two quotations from Soriano's *Gloria* how much more angular and harmonically-conceived is his bass line than Monteverdi's. His use of a modal B flat chord at 'Pater omnipotens' is similar to Monteverdi's at 'Jesu Christe':

Exx. 5*a* and 5*b*

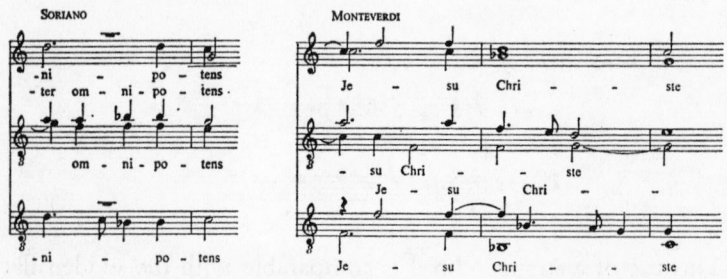

But the 'Amen' of his *Gloria* is full of clashes caused by the held G in the top part, again prompted by the desire for a touch of colour.

Soriano's melismas, in Palestrina's vein, have the effect of emphasizing the text, whereas Monteverdi's are more syncopated and rhythmically tortuous and recall earlier music: the type of writing can be seen at 'extollens vocem' or 'quinimo', in bars 14 and 31 of the Gombert motet:

Exx. 6a, 6b, 6c

There is certainly no hint in Soriano's music of Monteverdi's obsession with sequences — the only suggestion of it occurs for three bars at 'resurrectionem mortuorum' in the *Credo*, where the patterns are almost exactly repeated, allowing minor differences demanded by the word-setting:

Ex. 7

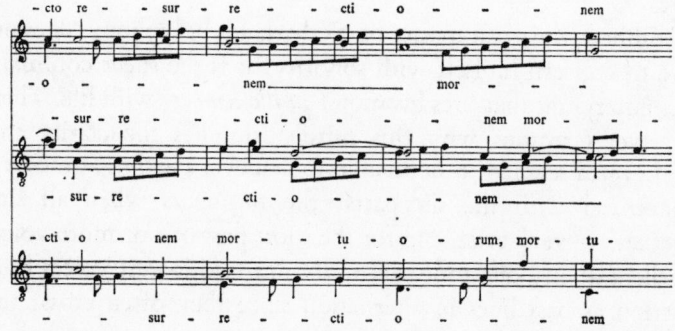

There is also a sequence in actual sound if not part by part at the 'Amen'; both these instances, however, arise from the use of the hexachord motive, which invites sequential treatment, whereas Monteverdi evolves his sequences from non-sequential material, detaching and extending the first four notes of Gombert's second 'subject':

Ex. 8

Soriano's style, apart from the occasional chromatic alterations, reflects that of late Palestrina. A mass like the latter's upon the motet *Assumpta est Maria*[1] is even simpler harmonically, with a good deal of homophony in the *Gloria* and *Credo*, which is rare in Soriano. Palestrina's harmonic outline, as also his counterpoint, is infinitely clearer to the ear than Monteverdi's. The fact is that to a contrapuntist six parts are really less ideal for strict polyphonic writing than four;[2] the six-part texture allows for a more sonorous writing with extra, non-contrapuntal voices filling out the chording. This explains why Monteverdi's valiant attempt at completely independent part-writing results in a constantly lush texture lacking to some degree in clarity. He considered six parts to imply more, rather than less, complication. A study of his 'Crucifixus' section will demonstrate how much more clarity there is with just four parts and similar strictness of style.

Gombert, the great master of Netherlands polyphony, does not have to concern himself with sonority; it is the sheer command of counterpoint that fires his motet *In illo tempore* with life. There are several reasons why this music, too, has the clarity that Monteverdi seemed to be unable to achieve. Firstly, Gombert is economical with the six parts: the moments when all sing together are very brief, and for the most part one or more voices are silent at any one time. Secondly, his two lowest voices both function as bass lines in alternation since they often cross: this means that a harmonic bottom line can be contrived when,

---

[1] *Opere Complete*, XXV, ed. Lino Bianchi (Rome, 1958), p. 209.
[2] Cf. Redlich, *Claudio Monteverdi* (London, 1952), p. 123.

for instance, one part becomes conjunct and the other has a leap:

Exx. 9*a* and 9*b*

Here the lower bass has risen a fifth and relinquished harmonic control to the quintus with its falling fourth; in bars 22–3 the momentary modulation to F is supported by the quintus (Ex. 9*b*). Of course, many of Gombert's 'subjects' contain rising fourths and fifths that function harmonically in the lower parts. His over-all harmonic motion is more regular, cadences occurring on the strong beats of 4/4 in Redlich's transcription. His economy with the voices leads to a clearer chording; one has only to look at part of Monteverdi's *Kyrie II* to notice some of the extraordinary clashes — some strangely beautiful — into which an over-lush texture can lead him:

Exx. 10*a* and 10*b*

Monteverdi, used to the high level of unprepared dissonance in his *seconda prattica* madrigals, evidently finds it hard to reacquire the technique of conventional dissonance treatment and falls back on sequences as a solution (see Ex. 10*c*).

This use of sequences gives rise to some of the clearest articula-

Ex. 10*c*

tion in the Monteverdi mass, though such an apparently modern device has no precedent in Gombert's motet. Tillman Merritt[1] explains that Gombert's music proceeds by constant imitations resulting in a continuous flow and that Palestrina's motet construction was to be an outgrowth of this style. Gombert stands midway in the stylistic transition from Josquin to Palestrina, and it was in fact Josquin who made use of the sequence to preserve symmetry: an example of the device as he used it can be seen in Ex. 11:

Ex. 11: Josquin, *Missa Hercules Dux Ferrariae, Agnus*

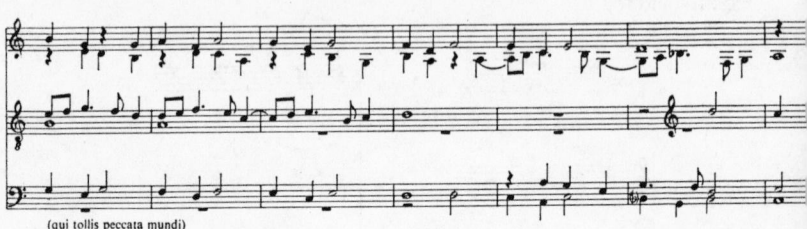

(qui tollis peccata mundi)

Even so, sequences are on the whole a feature that further removes Monteverdi's music from the purity of Gombert's manner. His sequences are sometimes inspired by a strong feeling for modern tonality, especially at 'Domine Deus Agnus Dei' in the

[1] Cf. A. Tillman Merritt, 'The Motet at the time of Gombert', *Bulletin of the American Musicological Society*, VII (October 1943), p. 19. Ex. 11 is from *Werken van Josquin Des Prés*, Masses II, ed. Albert Smijers (Leipzig, 1937), p. 38.

Gloria, or they may be laid out with a vocal ornamentation typical of his madrigal style, as in *Agnus I*:

Exx. 12*a* and 12*b*

(Domine Deus Agnus Dei Filius Patris)

mi — — se - re — — — re no — — — bis —

But unlike other important madrigal composers of the time, such as Wert, Vecchi and Marenzio, Monteverdi did not allow the madrigalian idiom to influence his 1610 mass. Instead he put in a great amount of tiring work undergoing extensive studies to familiarize himself with an early style to which he was opposed: in choosing that of Gombert, of all the Flemings, he displayed great discrimination.[1] Why should he choose Gombert as a model for a music that he hoped would be acceptable in Rome rather than the actual Roman music of the time? Firstly, because the collection of music at S. Barbara in Mantua contained motets of Gombert, but more significantly because this model would force him to adopt an old-fashioned style. The 'subjects' of the motet *In illo tempore* were the very stuff of classical polyphony, and the six-part scoring quite normal for *da cappella* music as Monteverdi would have known it in his youth. But the difficulties of composing the mass were immense, and the result is somewhat of a hotchpotch, not linked with anything else Monteverdi did, and falling short in several ways of being the perfect reincarnation of the music of the Netherlands master.

A point that has been overlooked in the efforts of some writers

---

[1] Cf. Leo Schrade, *Monteverdi* (repr. London, 1964), pp. 249–50.

to prove that the vespers psalms of Monteverdi's 1610 collection were the most revolutionary church compositions of the time is that these psalms have at times a faint connection with the learned style of the mass: this can be seen from a comparison between 'et in Spiritum Sanctum' in the *Credo* and the 'Amen' of the psalm *Laudate pueri*:

Exx. 13*a* and 13*b*

(Et in Spiritum Sanctum)

(Amen) Tenor Parts omitted

Likewise the vast polyphonic tuttis of the psalm *Nisi Dominus* are not at all a 'modern' sound; they resemble parts of the Gombert mass in texture, especially with their supernumerary syncopated inner parts. The vespers psalms are not essentially ultra-progressive large-scale church music like the later motets of Giovanni Gabrieli; they are rather a synthesis between the boldness of Monteverdi's madrigal and operatic writing (in *Orfeo*) and a late sixteenth-century type of *stile antico*. The basic pull of styles can be witnessed in the way that the 'Amen' of *Laudate pueri* is twisted back into a modern style by the intrusion of sequences and then the florid duet manner.[1]

[1] *Tutte le Opere*, ed. Gian Francesco Malipiero, XIV. i, p. 168.

When he arrived in Venice to take up the post of *maestro di cappella* at St. Mark's, Monteverdi was entrusted with the restoration of a '*canto polifonico*' which served to intensify his interest in what had by now definitely become an old-fashioned church style.[1] As has already been explained, the term '*da cappella*' was altering its meaning and becoming more synonymous with '*stile antico*'. It no longer signified merely the type of ensemble required but implied a certain archaism of style as well. The *stile antico* was now a deliberate phenomenon, in opposition to the modern concertato style. The two four-part masses in the old style that Monteverdi wrote during his Venetian period (1613–43) are more natural and unforced than the Gombert mass: the four-part scoring is now normal for the old style. Indeed, the publication by Felice Anerio of six-part Palestrina masses reduced to four-part scoring confirms that the six-part texture was becoming less common. If colour and sonority were desired, the modern mixed vocal and instrumental ensembles would provide it in the form of large-scale music for big feasts. But for lesser Sundays or ferial days *stile antico* masses filled the bill where the choir was still big enough to tackle them, as in the larger churches of cathedral status. In these places the *stile antico* was synonymous with an old-fashioned dignity, though lacking the musical colour of Palestrina's style.

The Palestrinian polyphonic ideal inspires Monteverdi's *da cappella* mass in the *Selva Morale*[2] at the roots. If we compare it with a typical Palestrina mass in four parts — the *Veni sponsa Christi* mass[3] is a good example of a fairly late work — we find that Monteverdi has the same introduction of a point of imitation in pairs of voices: two parts state the point in close canon, the other two following several bars later. Close entry of all four parts is reserved for climaxes. Canzona-like points on repeated notes (Ex. 14*a*), independent harmonically-angled bass lines (Ex. 14*b*), the use of homophony at 'Et incarnatus' in the *Credo* and lively triple time at 'Et resurrexit', and the greater smooth-

---

[1] Domenico de' Paoli, *Claudio Monteverdi* (Milan, 1945), p. 192.
[2] Reprinted as an Eulenburg score, ed. Denis Arnold (London, 1962).
[3] Palestrina, op. cit., p. 30.

ness of writing in the *Sanctus*: all conform to the late Palestrina practice.

Exx. 14*a* and 14*b*

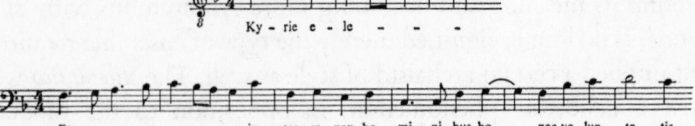

But there are significant differences, of which the most important is that Monteverdi is not in the least bit modal: in fact his mass is written in an F major that is much more diatonic than the C major of the Gombert mass. There is not one E flat in the whole work to suggest the subdominant colouring, and only a few A major chords to hint at the relative minor. Indeed the only point where a D minor feeling persists for any length of time comes at 'Quoniam' in the *Gloria*, where it is clearly ushered in by block chords:

Ex. 15

Monteverdi's rhythms are obsessively four-square, possessing none of the suppleness of Palestrina's, where there are perpetual cross-accents in individual lines. The start of the 'Crucifixus' is an instance of a rhythmic interplay that is all too rare in Monteverdi's mass:

Ex. 16

This central part of the *Credo* lacks any of the pathos that its text suggests, whereas Palestrina has melismas for 'Pilato' and a fine descending 'passus' idea, with the soprano moving through an octave. Again, Palestrina varies his *Sanctus* in the conventional manner, with a *tricinium* at 'Pleni sunt' and a triple-time 'Osanna', but Monteverdi stays in 4/4 and in four parts throughout, setting the 'Osanna' to yet another statement of the cyclic theme which dominates the mass. Much of the *seconda prattica* music that Monteverdi wrote during his Venetian period shows his concern for thematic unity, but such a concern is somewhat unnecessary in old-style polyphonic music: Palestrina, in the *Veni sponsa Christi* mass, uses his cyclic theme only at the openings of movements, and in the opening *Kyrie* has three different ideas treated in imitation. Monteverdi's three sections of the *Kyrie* are, however, monothematic, treating the ideas in various combinations in what is really a manner more suited to the concertato idiom.

How does Monteverdi's four-part *Selva Morale* mass compare with other Italian masses in the *stile antico* for the same number of voices? The only similarities between it and Felice Anerio's four-part mass[1] (another typical contemporary Roman composition) consist in the short, thwarted triple time interjections in each *Gloria*:

Exx. 17*a* and 17*b*

[1] Proske, op. cit., I (Regensburg, 1855), p. 35.

Again, in the 'Amens' of the same movement, both have an interrupted-plus-perfect cadence:

Exx. 18*a* and 18*b*

Monteverdi's endings are, however, curiously long-drawn-out, occasionally involving infelicitous harmony or awkward leaps. Anerio's mass is generally thicker in texture, reflecting the Roman interest in sonority. It has both the supple rhythms and the triple 'Osanna' movement of Palestrina, the former well exemplified in the opening of the work (Ex. 19*a*), where Anerio exercises a free approach to the duration of each note of the point, and in *Kyrie II*, where the canon is at a beat's distance (Ex. 19*b*):

Exx. 19*a* and 19*b*

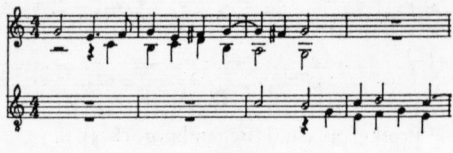

The important *prima prattica* composer in the north of Italy to whom Monteverdi can be compared is Bernardi, whose mixed publication of 1615 has already been mentioned. His mass on *Preparate corda vestra*[1] is clearly in a modal D minor typical of the previous century, although the harmonies at the end of the *Kyrie* and in the anguished 'Crucifixus' are 'affective':

Exx. 20*a* and 20*b*

Bernardi is again more interested in sonority than Monteverdi, using the four parts more continuously. His mass on *Il bianco e dolce cigno* is a *missa brevis* in type, often chordal in the long movements; its tonality is not so obsessively F major as Monteverdi's, though it is perhaps more committed than that of Roman-school masses, so that a sudden A major chord at 'Et incarnatus' is very striking (this same point in Monteverdi's Gombert mass is marked by a mediant major chord). Here the 'Crucifixus' is a consciously Palestrina-like *tricinium*, more modal and polyphonic than the rest and showing how the old style as in the rest of the mass had altered since about 1575. Despite its more old-fashioned sound, at least the conventional reduction in scoring is applied to this

[1] *Denkmäler der Tonkunst in Österreich*, XXXVI. i (Vienna, 1929), p. 1.

section of the *Credo*, whereas in the Monteverdi mass the music proceeds continuously in four parts. Although Bernardi did not completely succeed in capturing Palestrina's felicity of style, he showed a greater regard than Monteverdi for the true *stile antico* by avoiding four-square rhythms and by introducing modal colours into the tonality.

The third of Monteverdi's complete masses that survive, which was published posthumously by Vincenti in 1651 along with more modern-style psalm settings, is probably the finest *prima prattica* work of the whole early seventeenth century, and certainly Monteverdi's best.[1] For here he is, as it were, being himself and not trying desperately to be somebody else. If this results in the old style being compromised on all sides by the use of sequence, chromaticism, madrigalian part-writing and even occasional independence of the organ bass line, there is no cause for worry, since the music succeeds so much more than that of the other two masses. To couple this mass with the F major one and to assign both to 'the austere manner of Palestrina' is surely to do no justice to the vast difference between the two compositions. The F major mass is so austere that it bears less relation to Palestrina's music than some historians have perhaps imagined. On the other hand the G minor mass, far from being a lifeless copy, constitutes a real reincarnation in seventeenth-century language of Palestrina's own intensity. Palestrina's restrained, mystical harmonic and rhythmic excitement is transformed, by a technical compromise of style, into the full-bloodedness to which seventeenth-century churchgoers had become accustomed; still definitely *antico* in flavour yet having an immediacy relevant to the age; distinct in manner from the *seconda prattica*, yet with its own kind of up-to-date intensity. A strong characteristic of this mass is its consciously *thematic* musical development of a number of related ideas, of which the chromatic sequence figure that first occurs in the 'Christe' is the most striking. The perfect use of the Dorian mode preserves the old spirit of Palestrina's modal colour; its E natural and associated harmonies are thrown into relief by the contradictory E flats in the chromatic sequence figure.

[1] Reprinted as an Eulenburg score, ed. Redlich (London, 1952).

The madrigalian nature of some of the music can well be seen in the 'Christe', a perfectly balanced section opening and closing with the same succession of harmonies; it also uses the ornamental melismas of the madrigal style for the contrapuntal middle passage, at the start of which the imitation is treated by pairs of voices *à la* Palestrina. *Kyrie II* is concerned with sequences in many guises, including the lively cross-rhythms (bar 56) that were sadly lacking in the F major mass. In the *Gloria*, 'Qui tollis' (bar 32) has a madrigalian contrast of registers that can also be found in late Palestrina, followed by an imitative build-up to a homophonic climax at 'deprecationem nostram'. The 'Crucifixus' of the *Credo* has real pathos and respects the conventional reduction to three voices; the dovetailing of 'sepultus est' with the triple-time 'et resurrexit', though musically deft, makes rather strange sense of the text without the ritual pause to represent Christ's sojourn in the depths. Two passages show the middle baroque feeling that sometimes comes out in the *Credo*: the varied triple time is much more advanced than in the old style:

Exx. 21*a* and 21*b*

On the other hand Monteverdi's dissonance treatment is orderly and conventional. Most of the harmonic stringency is caused by typically sixteenth-century false relations, as at the heartfelt 'miserere' of the *Agnus Dei* (bar 16), which is characteristic of Monteverdi at his best. The use of sequence is in complete harmony with the overall style, not conflicting with its purity as in the Gombert mass. The G minor mass represents the real *prima prattica* Monteverdi, borrowing from a *da cappella* manner of which he had had genuine experience in his early madrigals.

We are now left with the five *da cappella* psalm settings, three in the *Selva Morale* of 1640 and two in the posthumous 1651 publication.[1] The three double-choir psalms pose special problems, while the other two are more comparable with the masses in their scoring. The four-part Magnificat from the *Selva Morale* is a conventional *alternatim* psalm (polyphonic verses alternating with plainsong ones) in what would have been bold polyphony for the late sixteenth century. The *nota cambiata* figures at 'deposuit' are very similar to the setting of 'reges' in the *Dixit Dominus* of the 1610 Vespers, showing how Monteverdi unwittingly absorbed the traits of the *prima prattica* into his earlier concertato church music:

Exx. 22*a* and 22*b*

Besides a more lively rhythmic life than the F major mass, the Magnificat has added musical variety through its alternation with plainsong. The intermittent working of a plainsong *canto fermo* into the top part is more convincing. It is also more consistent with the practice of the previous century than his attempt

[1] These five works can be found in Malipiero's complete edition thus: *Credidi*, XV. ii, p. 544; *Memento*, XV. ii, p. 567; *Magnificat*, XV. ii, p. 703; *Dixit*, XVI, p. 94; *Laudate pueri*, XVI, p. 211.

to graft it on to *seconda prattica* music, as in the 1610 Vespers, where its use militates against modernity of style. This Magnificat could well have been written early in Monteverdi's Venetian period, for there is little of the compromise with seventeenth-century idiom that we find in the G minor mass, nor indeed in the five-part *Laudate pueri* from the posthumous publication. This latter is a through-composed, not an alternating, psalm setting: sequences, bolder word-painting, homophony, sectionalization by well-defined pauses, and fine textural crescendos are well in evidence (Ex. 23*a*), though a slight archaism is maintained by the fact that the motives are not in a thoroughly concertato vein. The 'Amen' sequences (Ex. 23*b*) are notably like those at the end of the *Gloria* of the G minor mass, with the written-out ritenuto implied in the decrease of movement.

Both the mass and the *Laudate pueri* seem to belong to the same creative period of Monteverdi's life, probably a late one: they show a maturity of invention, and a coming-to-terms with a *da cappella* idiom that he made his own — a genuine re-interpretation of the *prima prattica*.

Of the three *cori spezzati* psalm settings, the *Credidi* in the *Selva Morale* is in a staid sixteenth-century Venetian manner, with much block chordal writing, syncopated entries and a lively triple-time 'Gloria Patri'. No plainsong *canto fermo* is used except at the beginning in the top part, where it answers the plainsong intonation. Printed immediately following this is a setting of *Memento*, which has a crotchet rather than a minim tactus but is otherwise similar to the *Credidi*. Both use a *coro grave* (A.T.T.B.) for the second choir; neither is really *prima prattica* music in the polyphonic sense. They are conceived in the lively double-choir style of the late sixteenth century, which is very close in spirit to the modern manner in all features except the use of soloists and was being used for non-concertato psalms by several lesser composers (such as Bellazzi, Leoni and Girelli) as late as the 1620's. The transition from this style to concertato was very smooth, although different cities had reached different stages along it. Girelli's psalms of 1620 include both *da cappella* and concertato psalms, but apart from the use of soloists in the latter pieces the musical ethos of the two

Exx. 23*a* and 23*b*

types is much the same in double-choir music. In music for single choir, both masses and psalms, two distinct idioms could co-exist, especially in Venice; not only Monteverdi, but also Rovetta and Rigatti, included *da cappella* psalms in their publications of 1626 and 1640 respectively. Even so, not all these psalms are as entirely alien in conception to the seventeenth century as Monteverdi's first two masses seem to be.

Monteverdi shows himself to be a master of double-choir

writing in the *da cappella Dixit* of the 1651 publication (marked 'alla breve'). The style is rendered more expressive by chromatic alterations ('confregit' and 'conquassabit'), contrasts between long and short notes, and harmonic chromaticism:

Exx. 24*a*, 24*b* and 24*c*

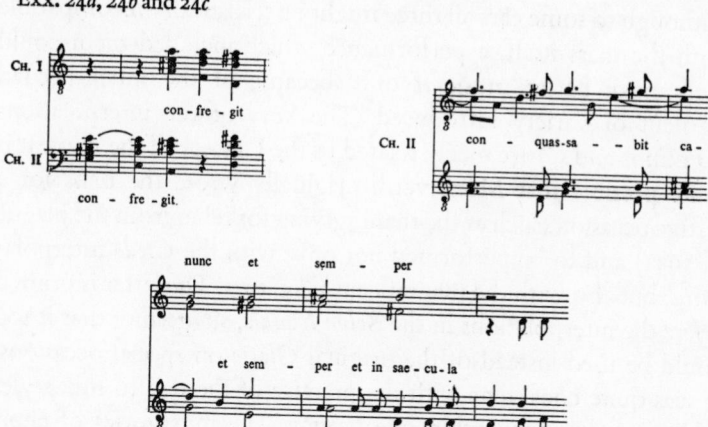

Monteverdi is clearly much more imaginative with the forces at his disposal than the lesser church composers. Certainly these three double-choir psalms cannot be assigned to the *prima prattica*, although they are called *da cappella*, because the latter term is here used in the sense understood by Praetorius: it signifies the type of ensemble required, not the style in which the work is conceived, which, as we have seen, is not necessarily archaic in *cori spezzati* music. In single-choir music, however, the term became identified with *stile antico*, or indeed *prima prattica*. These signify any style that has its roots in the single-choir polyphony of the sixteenth century, used in deliberate antithesis to modern idioms by church composers from the time of Monteverdi's Gombert mass onwards. Monteverdi's own works show the various old styles that it was possible to select. He was surely the only composer to write in such divergent idioms with such unparalleled versatility: in this connection the interpolations for the *Credo* of the F major mass, also published in the *Selva Morale*, are of great interest. Monteverdi indicates that these three short pieces may be inserted in place of the original settings of the relevant part of the text. All three are *seconda prattica* in conception: the 'Crucifixus' section is inspired by Monteverdi's madrigalian manner and is smoother than the more brilliant concertato of the 'Et resurrexit' and 'et iterum' sections, which are in the most up-to-date church style. Although to some ears all three might be stylistically incompatible with the mass itself, a performance which included them could well make better music if only because of the much-needed element of variety introduced. The keys of the interpolations (D minor and C) are nicely related to the F major of the mass. It is quite possible that Monteverdi originally wrote the mass for a festive occasion (such as the thanksgiving for relief from the plague in 1631) and to be performed not only with the *Credo* interpolations, but also with the magnificent *Gloria a 7*. The latter is printed *before* the interpolations in the *Selva Morale*, suggesting that it too could be used instead of the original *Gloria* on special occasions. It was quite consistent with the practice of the day to mix styles of liturgical music within one service. The inventories of choir music in northern Italy, which contain modern motets but no modern masses, testify that concertato motets were often sung during masses in which the ordinary was rendered in *stile antico*.[1] Today this idea is for example perpetuated in the Anglican cathedral service, with responses, anthems, services and voluntaries drawn from different periods of music.

The mixing of styles in one movement — such as would happen if these *Credo* interpolations were sung — can be seen in the ceremonial mass of 1639 by Monteverdi's disciple Rovetta, where in a generally modern-sounding *Credo* there is a reversion to the *stile antico* at 'Et in Spiritum Sanctum' — the precise point where Monteverdi's modern insertions finish. This duality of style has already been discussed in relation to Monteverdi's vespers psalms of 1610, and it still persists in some of the other *Selva*

---

[1] Cf. also the fact that several composers wrote in different idioms for different forces or kinds of music; e.g., Frescobaldi wrote *antico* masses but up-to-date organ music, and Francesco Turini, who also wrote old-style masses (in his publication of 1643), wrote progressive church sonatas and canzonas.

Morale music. The large setting of the Magnificat[1] has odd moments of old-style part writing:

Ex. 25

It seems to have been a characteristic of baroque church music generally to have included passages in a more learned, contrapuntal idiom than the rest of the music: this can be seen in Carissimi and Vivaldi, and it persists, indeed, in some of Haydn's earlier masses. Once the *stile antico* had become a deliberate phenomenon, its shadow could haunt composers whose work was otherwise 'modern' in manner.

[1] *Tutte le Opere*, XV. ii, p. 639.

NIGEL FORTUNE

Monteverdi and the *Seconda Prattica*

i: MONODY

In his secular vocal music Monteverdi presents an apparent paradox. Here was an enthusiastic advocate of the *seconda prattica*, none more so, who constantly strove to illuminate and project words through music of the utmost expressiveness and who never bothered to write instrumental works at all. Yet he wrote very few solo songs at a time when song was so obvious a medium for the dissemination of the new style that after about 1600 it attracted all the Italian composers who shared his progressive humanist views, in some cases to the exclusion of all other music. Instead of writing songs Monteverdi first of all remained faithful to polyphonic madrigals. But even before he adopted the *basso continuo* in his fifth book he tended more and more to break up the traditional texture into smaller groups and to make the movement more discontinuous; this process was hastened in his continuo madrigals, in which he could also include contrasting solo sections; and in his later years it developed so radically that publications such as the seventh and ninth books of madrigals are packed with duets and trios that are really no longer madrigals at all.

The present chapter offers a survey of Monteverdi's songs in the context of the songs of the period and also shows how his operatic lament of Ariadne prompted other composers to write laments, the only type of song in which his influence can significantly be seen. The next chapter follows on from this. Its purpose is to show that by reacting as he did — by preferring ensemble music to monody — Monteverdi was probably indulging his love of sonorous textures not only for their own sake but also because they helped him to another of his chief concerns: the creation of satisfying large-scale forms that could also be enhanced by tonal contrasts. Some of his best monodies show the same tendencies, especially the convincing form that so many by lesser men fatally lack.

Hundreds of solo songs — or monodies, as they are often called — were published in Italy in the first four decades of the seventeenth century, the product of one of the most insistent crazes in the history of music.[1] Their two principal forms were still those of the ensemble music of the later sixteenth century: through-composed madrigals, which were particularly popular at first, and strophic forms such as aria and canzonet. The epoch-making collection *Le Nuove Musiche* (1602) by Giulio Caccini, which decisively inaugurated the vogue, is prefaced by a long essay in which Caccini emphasizes the novelty of his songs, the madrigals in particular.[2] The words, he claims, are all-important. Solo performance with an accompanying instrument playing simple chords means that all the words can be clearly heard: this, he found, never happened in polyphonic madrigals. He was introducing 'a kind of music by which men might, as it were, talk in harmony'[3] in an arioso vocal line midway between the recitative of opera and the rhythmically defined tunes of arias. The sovereignty of the words demands that the music be sung in free time, and the more emotive ones are heightened by all manner of subtle embellishments. Caccini is acting here as polemic spokesman for the Camerata, the group of Florentine noblemen, thinkers, poets and musicians who after 1580 forcefully argued the superior qualities of monodic music. He was also a singer, and singers such as Jacopo Peri (in Florence, like Caccini) and Francesco Rasi (at Mantua, like Monteverdi) were prominent among the composers who before long published monodies. They un-

[1] Cf. Nigel Fortune, 'A Handlist of printed Italian secular Monody books, 1600–1635', *R.M.A. Research Chronicle*, III (1963), p. 27.
[2] Translated in Oliver Strunk, *Source Readings in Music History* (London, 1952), p. 377.
[3] Ibid., p. 378.

doubtedly sang them themselves, an incentive to their composition denied to Monteverdi, who was not a singer.

Amateurs — both noblemen, like Claudio Saracini, and those who, like Domenico Maria Megli and Pietro Benedetti, followed other professions — were another sort of men who quickly took to writing monodies. It is quite likely that professional composers of Monteverdi's generation who had had a hard grounding in the intricacies of polyphony considered monodies beneath them, because they were so 'easy' to write as to be within the powers of the dilettante and the part-time composer. Here, then, is another possible reason for Monteverdi's comparative indifference. It may be significant that the eminent theorist Giovanni Battista Doni, who championed monody, felt it necessary to ask, through rather a specious analogy, if it were really easier to paint a nude than a clothed body[1] and that even the best composers of vocal music born shortly after Monteverdi — Marco da Gagliano (born *c.* 1575) and Sigismondo d'India (born *c.* 1580?) — though sympathetic to the 'new music' still composed more ensemble madrigals than songs in the heyday of monody. Gesualdo (born *c.* 1560) wrote no monodies at all, though he lived until 1613.

Solo arias were at first less self-consciously canvassed as 'new'. The meticulous expression of emotive words here yielded, in Caccini's phrase, to 'a lively, cheerful kind of singing which is carried and ruled by the air itself',[2] and indeed many of their texts have been aptly summed up as amorous baby-talk. Some of Caccini's arias, however, are more serious and in mood are rather like strophic madrigals. In one or two he hinted at the technique of strophic variation, in which the vocal line varies from verse to verse over a more or less unchanged bass. This form proved to be a fruitful one for several later composers, especially in Rome, and with the bass moving briskly in crotchets it also characterized the earliest pieces to be called cantatas: these were published in the 1620's by Venetians such as Alessandro Grandi and

[1] Cf. Giovanni Battista Doni, *Compendio del Trattato de' Generi e de' Modi della Musica* (Rome, 1635), p. 124.

[2] Cf. Strunk, op. cit., p. 384.

Giovanni Pietro Berti, who worked under Monteverdi at St. Mark's.[1]

Only some fifteen monodies by Monteverdi survive, and it is perhaps not surprising that five or six of them have overtones from the world of opera, where he was obviously so much at home. Nor is it surprising, in view of his preoccupation with formal unity, that in five songs he adopted the principle of strophic variation. Of the others, only one is a madrigal, and that for quite exceptional forces; one is a lament (of Olympia), which, like Monteverdi's other laments, whether lost or in his last operas, doubtless stemmed from the immense success of his lament in *Arianna*; two are somewhat austere recitatives in the surprisingly popular genre of the *lettera amorosa* or musical love-letter (one of them originally called *partenza amorosa*); another, *Voglio di vita uscir*, is a suave and rounded aria, significantly (if it *is* by Monteverdi) founded on the strict form of the chaconne bass;[2] and six are simple canzonets. Hundreds of canzonets, most of them in triple time, poured from the Venetian printing-presses in cheap books from 1618 onwards, and so popular were they that Monteverdi, the greatest musician in Venice, could hardly avoid writing a few, even if he rather despised them. But he left it to other men to publish them for him; indeed the only solo songs he bothered to see through the press himself are the four in the seventh book of madrigals.

It is worth looking at a few of these songs to see how far they reflect Monteverdi's principal preoccupations. His refusal to write conventional solo madrigals is extremely pointed, for they were the monodists' favourite fare before being quickly superseded after about 1618 by the passion for canzonets and arias. Since their non-strophic poems seemed to afford few opportunities for refrain-

---

[1] Cf. Fortune, 'Solo Song and Cantata', *New Oxford History of Music*, IV (London, 1968), pp. 172–4.

[2] This aria and the lament of Olympia do not appear in Gian Francesco Malipiero's complete edition but may be found in *Monteverdi: 12 Composizioni vocali profane e sacre (inedite)*, ed. Wolfgang Osthoff (Milan, 1958), pp. 18 and 10 respectively. The lament is quite probably genuine Monteverdi, but I have reservations about the aria, which I am not otherwise considering in this chapter.

like repetitions, composers found it difficult to impose formal order on their madrigals; since, moreover, polyphony could no longer be used to conceal perfect cadences, continuity as often eluded them; and the amorphous and halting music that frequently resulted could no longer be enlivened by textural contrasts, which were beyond the power of a single voice and a neutral instrumental background to provide. Monteverdi was therefore perhaps unimpressed by whatever solo madrigals he knew. It is noteworthy that the masterly *Lamento d'Arianna* in its original solo version in the opera was interrupted from time to time by a chorus of fishermen (whose music is lost)[1] and is unified by reprises of two intensely despairing phrases which have a strong 'personal' quality on the lips of one who by that stage in the work must have been established as a compelling tragic character.

There are over 50 pieces in the three madrigal books Monteverdi brought out — in 1605, 1614 and 1619 — during the first wave of enthusiasm for monody, and the only solo madrigal among them is *Con che soavità* (1619).[2] The poem is a typical amorous conceit by Giovanni Battista Guarini in praise of the beloved's lips as the source of both sweet words and kisses. Any other composer would have set it straightforwardly for the usual forces without worrying about problems of form and texture. But Monteverdi, possibly prompted in the first place by the seductive words, accompanied his soprano with three instrumental 'choirs', whose clefs are those favoured by Giovanni Gabrieli and other composers in polychoral works. The first is a continuo ensemble of two chitarroni, harpsichord and spinet; the second consists of three stringed instruments and harpsichord; and the third is a darker-hued string trio with an unspecified continuo instrument. From its scoring, the piece could be an offshoot from *Orfeo*; possibly it was written for the Accademia degli Invaghiti shortly after they had staged the opera. The movement of the vocal line is nicely varied between gently moving arioso and more rhythmic writing and is unusual in being almost entirely un-

---

[1] Cf. J. A. Westrup, 'Monteverdi's "Lamento d'Arianna" ', *Music Review*, I (1940), p. 147.

[2] Claudio Monteverdi, *Tutte le Opere*, ed. Malipiero, VII, p. 137.

ornamented; the harmonic rhythm, too, is unusually slow, no doubt so that the instrumental sonorities could be heard to advantage. Monteverdi opens his setting with his first group of instruments. When the movement becomes livelier he adds his second group after half-a-bar's rest, and these upper strings tend to be used throughout to underscore the more incisive rhythms in the vocal part with a 'biting' homophonic texture. In his setting of the last seven lines of the poem he makes even more telling structural use of his instrumental forces. This is the text:

> *Che soave armonia*
> *Fareste, O cari baci,*
> *Che soave armonia*
> *Fareste, O dolci detti,*
> *Se foste unitamente*
> *D'ambedue le dolcezze ambo capaci,*
> *Baciando i detti e ragionando i baci!*

(What sweet harmony you would make, O beloved kisses, and you, O sweet words, if you were both together capable of both sweetnesses, words kissing and kisses speaking!)

At the important first pair of lines Monteverdi first of all brings in his third instrumental group for the first time, again after a half-bar's rest, and immediately adds the other two to reinforce a long-held note on 'O' with the first sound of his complete ensemble; he repeats all this a tone higher for the next matching pair of lines. He also uses his instrumental groups to organize his extended setting of the last three lines: he reserves his full ensemble for the idea of 'both together' and accompanies four statements of the final line with the first two groups in turn before again bringing everyone in for the last two repetitions of it. The exceptional length of the piece is entirely consistent with the size of the 'orchestra', which wonderfully illuminates the sentiments of the poem.

In the first of his strophic variations, *Tempro la cetra* (also from Book VII),[1] Monteverdi once again added rich instrumental sonorities to a conventional vocal form, which he had previously

---

[1] Ibid., p. 1.

used in the better-known prologue to *Orfeo*. The instruments are an unspecified quintet with continuo. The poem opposes images of love and war, a theme that Monteverdi was of course to develop in his later madrigals; it is by Giambattista Marino, who, with Guarini, was the poet most often set by the early seventeenth-century monodists. The setting has something in common with the great song 'Possente spirto' in Act III of *Orfeo*,[1] especially in its still, portentous atmosphere and in the way the vocal embellishments become more elaborate from verse to verse as the variations unfold over the unchanging bass. The four verses are separated by a ritornello, which is the last of the three six-bar phrases of an introductory sinfonia; this sinfonia is also heard twice at the end, where, with a contrasting central dance, it forms a satisfying ternary structure that provides a fine culmination to the song.

It was to be expected that Monteverdi would continue to employ a form in which the bass was so powerful a force for formal unity. Three more examples appear in the *Scherzi Musicali* of 1632, a small collection mainly of solo songs assembled by the publisher Bartolommeo Magni almost as if he thought it about time so important a composer as Monteverdi had a few more songs in print. The best of them is *Et è pur dunque vero*,[2] in which variations appear over two basses, each heard seven times: one underpins the vocal sections, the other a ritornello whose varying melody is entrusted to a single unnamed instrument. The music of the seven verses has the characteristic madrigalian movement of strophic variations, and there is room for 'madrigalisms' such as the chromatic cadence expressing the jilted lover's tears, a clash of C natural and C sharp for his torments, and slurred quavers for the murmuring of breezes. The brisk crotchet-and-quaver movement of the bass of the ritornello approaches the 'walking' bass usually found in the earliest strophic-bass cantatas. Monteverdi wrote one of these too, possibly the most distinguished of all, *Ohimè, ch'io cado*;[3] it appeared in either 1623 or 1624 in the *Quarto Scherzo delle Ariose Vaghezze* of the minor composer

---

[1] *Tutte le Opere*, XI, p. 84.
[2] *Tutte le Opere*, X, p. 82. [3] *Tutte le Opere*, IX, p. 111.

Carlo Milanuzii, who was then working in Venice. There are six verses, each preceded by the same short ritornello, of which we have only the bass. As in most strophic-bass cantatas,[1] the strict and steady progress of the bass, which moves almost entirely in crotchets, precludes the use of expansive 'madrigalisms'. But such a bass obviously acted as a challenge to Monteverdi, who triumphantly succeeded in devising over it six different melodies with the same general character, though there are here and there similarities in the lines from verse to verse. Ex. 1 shows the opening bars of each verse:

Ex. 1

Unless manuscript copies have not survived Monteverdi must have been unwilling to develop his gifts as a writer of independent songs even in the 1620's when strophic songs were all the rage in Venice; but he was kept very busy in St. Mark's and wrote a

[1] Cf. the example by Berti given by Fortune, 'Solo Song and Cantata', loc. cit.

great deal of stage music, most of which is lost. He wrote no more strophic-bass cantatas and played no part in transforming the simple canzonet into the rounded and sensuous triple-time aria, as junior associates such as Berti did with such success. However, we have of course the arias in his last operas, and the duet *Zefiro torna*, discussed in the next chapter, is to some extent a piece of this new kind. Monteverdi's six strophic songs are all quite simple, though one or two unusual, less simple features disrupt the innocuous tunes and tripping rhythms. For instance, he sets the last verse of *Più lieto il guardo*[1] as a recitative presumably because the words seemed to demand it, a step analogous to the contemporary development of the recitative and aria; and it was a madrigalian touch, for rather madrigalian words, to prolong and retard with chromatic minims the refrain '... languendo moro' of *La mia turca*.[2] Once at least, with the charming throwaway tune of *Maledetto*,[3] Monteverdi rivals the more self-conscious purveyors of tunes on their own ground, and the asymmetrical phrases and ternary form show that he could not help bringing craftsmanship and imagination to even the humblest task. But we may well wonder, I think, whether Monteverdi's lack of interest in arias and canzonets, so conspicuously at odds with the musical climate in which he lived, was not connected with a dominant impression one gets from his work as a whole: that he was not really interested in what we understand by 'good tunes'. He wrote very few of them; matters of dramatic impact, form and texture, which I have already stressed, seem to have been much more important to him; and it must have been feelings such as these that kept him writing duets rather than monodies in his middle and later years. One instance should not be made to bear too much weight, but his setting of Gabriello Chiabrera's poem *Damigella* in the *Scherzi Musicali* of 1607 and that by the minor Florentine Vincenzio Calestani illustrate succinctly the difference between an apt, quite attractive tune

[1] Domenico de'Paoli, *Claudio Monteverdi* (Milan, 1945), appendix; it was first published in *Arie de'Diversi* (1634), edited by Alessandro Vincenti.

[2] *Tutte le Opere*, IX, p. 117; it was first published in Milanuzii's *Quarto Scherzo* referred to above.

[3] *Tutte le Opere*, X, p. 76.

and a really catchy one and at the same time seem to sum up the difference between Monteverdi's attitude to tunes and those of a host of lesser contemporaries:

Exx. 2*a* and 2*b*[1]

(Pretty girl, pour out that good wine; make the dew fall distilled with rubies.)

It might of course be added that no great composer before this period had ever seen it as a main part of his function to write self-conscious tunes. As the first great composer influenced by the new 'harmonic' approach to composition Monteverdi did so more readily than his forerunners. But Purcell is the first great master in the history of music whom we value as highly for his melodic gifts as for any other quality.

[1] Cf. respectively ibid., p. 40, and Vincenzio Calestani, *Madrigali et Arie* (Venice, 1617), p. 35.

The two *lettere amorose* have never been among Monteverdi's most admired compositions and are hardly ever performed. They are unusually long stretches of the kind of recitative devised by the Florentines for the earliest operas and rarely found outside operas before the Venetians developed the pairing of recitative and aria in their songs of the 1620's; and in these songs the recitatives are generally short. It is quite likely, as Leo Schrade hints,[1] that Monteverdi wrote these pieces several years before he published them in 1619: they could indeed have been studies for the recitative in *Orfeo*, especially as he describes them as being 'in genere rappresentativo', a definition that he and his contemporaries normally reserved for stage music. But it is worth noting that they are settings of prose and that their vocal range is unemotionally narrow. Schrade probably exaggerates when he says that the style of the pieces was 'rather generally disapproved of by composers' by 1619, since they reappeared in print in 1623 and the other six *lettere amorose* I have been able to discover were printed between 1618 and 1633. These may well have been written in emulation of Monteverdi's: even Biagio Marini, who published the first of them in his *Madrigali e Symfonie* of 1618, may have known Monteverdi's pieces in manuscript or have heard them. Since they appeared in the print of 1623 only with the *Lamento d'Arianna*, then, as now, Monteverdi's most famous piece, it might be inferred that they also were included as being among his most popular works and not simply as makeweights; however, they were his only songs for voice and continuo available in print to the publisher Magni, and they are mentioned on the title-page in type far smaller than that announcing the lament. But they certainly made an impression on at least one composer, Filippo Vitali, who published one of his own in 1629, when he was living in Florence or Rome: it is headed in terms almost identical with Monteverdi's and appears in a publication with the same title, *Concerto*, as the one (the seventh book of madrigals) in which Monteverdi's *lettere* were first printed. Monteverdi clearly took some trouble over these pieces: he continually varies his pace, judiciously repeats short phrases and is

[1] Cf. Leo Schrade, *Monteverdi* (repr. London, 1964), pp. 290–1.

not afraid to introduce expressive roulades at one or two cadences.

Monteverdi's *lettere*, then, may have given impetus to a very minor sort of monody. There can be no doubt at all that the resounding fame of the great lament of Ariadne initiated a much more rewarding kind of song, which enjoyed undiminished popularity throughout the seventeenth century and beyond, and in other countries besides Italy: before very long no opera was thought to be complete without its lament, and a number of composers wrote chamber laments vividly portraying the predicaments of those same characters — Dido, Olympia, Jason — whose tragic stories dominated so many baroque operas. Although it was never published, *Arianna* was repeatedly admired by eye-witnesses, composers, poets and theorists, whereas *Orfeo*, published twice, was hardly discussed in print at all. It was clearly Ariadne's lament that prompted these people to enthusiasm: for most of them the rest of the score need hardly have existed. Alas, for us it does not; but at least the activities of opportunist publishers and eager scribes ensured that we have six copies of the solo sections of the lament.

It is worth indicating briefly the enormous impact of this piece. It was published twice in 1623, as well as in Monteverdi's *Selva Morale* in 1640 (with sacred words) and in his five-part arrangement in 1614. At least three composers published their own infinitely feebler settings, Severo Bonini and Francesco Costa monodic ones in 1613 and 1626 respectively, Antonio Il Verso a polyphonic one in his fourteenth book of five-part madrigals in far-off Palermo in 1619. Marino wrote his own *Lamento d'Arianna*, *Misera, e chi m'ha tolto*, of which Pellegrino Possenti published a monodic setting in 1623 together with a fulsome eulogy of Monteverdi. Marino also refers to the original in his long poem *Adone* (VII, 68). Bonini, writing some thirty years after he tried to emulate Monteverdi as a composer, says that no musical household lacked its copy of the lament and refers to Monteverdi's 'peregrini pensieri' ('exquisite invention') in *Arianna*,[1] a

---

[1] Cf. Severo Bonini, *Prima Parte de'Discorsi e Regole sovra la Musica*: Florence, Biblioteca Riccardiana MS. 2218, quoted in Angelo Solerti, *Le Origini del Melodramma* (Turin, 1903), p. 139.

phrase already used of it in 1620 by Vitali in the preface to his opera *Aretusa*.[1] Gagliano's preface to his *Dafne* (1608) reveals a fellow-composer's first flush of enthusiasm.[2] For Doni, writing about stage music, the lament was 'forse la più bella Composizione che sia stata fatta a'tempi nostri in questo genere' ('perhaps the most beautiful composition of our time in this field').[3] Esteban Arteaga was still talking about it in 1783, likening its fame in its day to that of Pergolesi's *La Serva Padrona* in his own.[4] Nor do these references exhaust the catalogue. Mention should be made too of laments by other composers clearly inspired by Monteverdi's example. The finest are undoubtedly five by d'India, two published in 1621 and three in 1623. They represent probably the most fruitful influence of Monteverdi on any composer of the time and are worthy companions to Monteverdi's own laments.[5] Another of the best monodists, Saracini, published in his *Le Seconde Musiche* in 1620 not only a *Lamento della Madonna* of Monteverdian cast but also an intensely sombre madrigal, *Udite, lagrimosi spiriti d'Averno*, which he dedicated to Monteverdi.[6] There is another fine arioso lament, *Le Lagrime d'Erminia*, in the *Madrigali Concertati* of 1629 by Giovanni Rovetta, Monteverdi's deputy at St. Mark's. In the 1630's the number of laments increases, if anything. They now tend to become aria-like pieces and are often built on ground basses, the start of a tradition that was later to embrace, in Purcell's lament of Dido, the only lament seriously to challenge the supremacy of Monteverdi's great original.

Monteverdi was no doubt pressed for sequels. We know that

[1] Reprinted in Emil Vogel, *Bibliothek der gedruckten weltlichen Vocalmusik Italiens* (repr. Hildesheim, 1962), II, p. 332.

[2] Reprinted in ibid., I, p. 265.

[3] Cf. Doni, *Trattato della Musica scenica*, chap. IX, printed in his *De'Trattati di Musica*, ed. Antonio Francesco Gori (Florence, 1763), II, p. 25.

[4] Cf. Esteban Arteaga, *Le Rivoluzioni del Teatro musicale italiano*, I (Bologna, 1783), pp. 254–5.

[5] Cf. Fortune, 'Sigismondo d'India', *Proceedings of the Royal Musical Association*, LXXXI (1954–5), pp. 41–4. Also cf. *supra*, pp. 120–2

[6] Facsimile of the complete volume published at Siena in 1933; the two pieces are at pp. 25 and 1, respectively. The whole of the second piece and extracts from the first in Robert Haas, *Die Musik des Barocks* (Potsdam, 1928), pp. 53–5. For further discussion of Saracini's laments cf. *supra*, pp. 120–1.

in 1610 he intended the five-part version of the *Lamento d'Arianna*
to form a trilogy of laments with *Incenerite spoglie* and a setting of
Marino's lament of Hero and Leander. The first of these other
two pieces is the one he wrote in memory of Caterina Martinelli,
who had she lived would have sung the part of Ariadne, and he
published it with Ariadne's lament in his sixth book of madrigals;[1]
the Marino lament he either did not finish or it has been lost.[2]
Of solo laments we have some magnificent examples in the last
operas, those of Penelope in *Il Ritorno d'Ulisse* and Octavia in
L'Incoronazione di Poppea,[3] and we have lost those of Apollo and
Armida of which we read in Monteverdi's letters.[4] We also have
the little-known *Lamento d'Olimpia* in a manuscript in the hand
of Luigi Rossi, composer to the Borghese family. Osthoff plausibly
suggests that Monteverdi could have written this lament for the
great contralto Adriana Basile, who lived at Mantua between 1610
and 1616 and after 1623 and who had connections in Rome with
Cardinal Scipione Borghese. Like so many sequels, the new lament
falls short of its model. But it is still a remarkably compelling work
which owes a good deal to its predecessor in text and organization.
And even in musical invention, as Ex. 3 shows. Here we see the
opening of each lament, (*a*) Ariadne's, (*b*) Olimpia's, and also
(*c*) that of a madrigal from d'India's third book of *Musiche* (1618)
to give an idea of the powerful impression that Monteverdi's
'peregrino pensiero' must have made on a responsive spirit:[5]

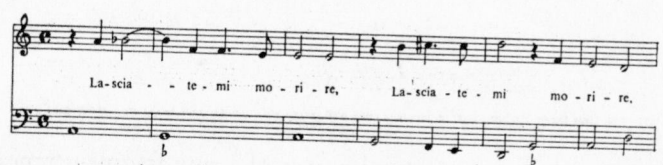

---

[1] *Tutte le Opere*, VI, p. 46.
[2] Cf. Don Bassano Casola's letter to Cardinal Ferdinando Gonzaga, printed
in Vogel, 'Claudio Monteverdi', *Vierteljahrsschrift für Musikwissenschaft*, III
(1887), p. 430.
[3] Cf. *Tutte le Opere*, XII, p. 14, and XIII, pp. 49 and 229, respectively.
[4] Cf. *supra*, pp. 47, 49–51 and 62.
[5] Cf. respectively *Tutte le Opere*, XI, p. 161; Osthoff edition, p. 10; and
Sijismondo d'India, *Le Musiche . . . Libro terzo* (Milan, 1618), p. 6.

(a) Let me die... ; (b) I wish to die; (c) Weep, my eyes....

The common feature here is a drooping cadential figure, and so Monteverdi, in Olympia's lament as in Ariadne's, is able quite naturally to return to it at cadences as a unifying motif. In Olympia's lament we again see him building up tension through a mounting series of repeated notes:

Ex. 4[1]

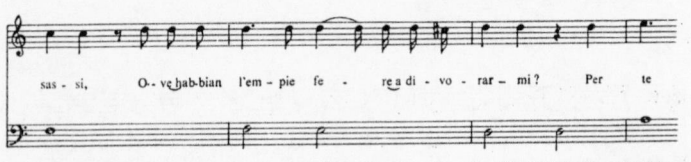

(Can you thus leave me here among desolate cliffs and rough rocks, with wild beasts to devour me? For you.. .)

The emotional and structural power of a tiny fragment repeated in a different melodic context can also be well illustrated at the more relaxed start of the third and last section (see Ex. 5).

In most of his songs we have seen that Monteverdi exploits as far as he can at least one of the features that dominate so much of his music: dramatic possibilities, contrasts of texture, highly

[1] Osthoff edition, p. 11.

Ex. 5[1]

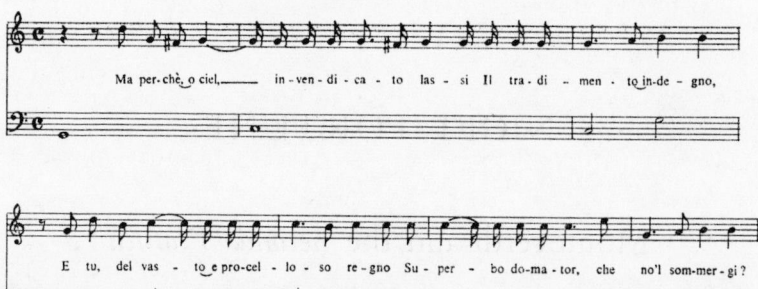

(But why, O heavens, do you allow undeserving betrayal to go unavenged, and you, proud conqueror of the vast and stormy kingdom, who do not drown him?)

organized form. We can now go on to see in the next chapter how much truer this is of the music he wrote as he gradually transformed the traditional madrigal into the concertato textures so typical of the new century.

[1] Ibid., p. 16.

NIGEL FORTUNE

Monteverdi and the *Seconda Prattica*

ii: FROM MADRIGAL TO DUET

The tremendous popularity of monodies in Monteverdi's day is evident from the great quantities printed and from the remarks of theorists and of composers in their prefaces. However, at least 450 volumes of ensemble madrigals appeared in the seventeenth century, and it would be easy to assemble a rival anthology of observations pointing to their continued popularity in the face of competition from monodies.[1] As one would expect, they seem at first to have been favoured by older composers and no doubt by people who preferred to sing themselves rather than listen to professional soloists; in any case, if such people wanted to sing monodies they probably found that many of them were beyond their vocal powers. However, not all madrigals were old-fashioned (nor were they easy to sing). In the later sixteenth century in the hands of the most imaginative, forward-looking composers they responded to influences similar to those that stimulated the art of monody and shaped its development. Madrigalists grew more and more anxious to project words, and so textures became increasingly homophonic, with prominent top parts, more neutral inner parts and a more harmonically conceived bass. As textures gradually became more fragmented too there were more opportunities for varied sonorities and more meaningful structural order; and the more changing sonorities demanded repetition of words, the

[1] Cf. Gloria Rose, 'Polyphonic Italian Madrigals of the seventeenth century', *Music & Letters*, XLVII (1966), p. 153.

longer madrigals grew. Composers such as Giaches de Wert who were Monteverdi's seniors at Mantua were especially interested in developments of this kind and were very likely prompted by such celebrated virtuoso singers as the three ladies of Ferrara, Lucrezia Bendidio, Tarquinia Molza and Laura Peperara.[1] The rise of virtuoso singing and a humanist concern with words were parallel developments that fertilized each other.

Even without his writings on the subject we could see from his middle-period madrigals that Monteverdi shared the ideals of the early monodists; and he convinces us that to transform the art of the madrigal from within instead of abandoning it and going over suddenly to monody was an equally valid way of fulfilling them. There are signs in his second set of madrigals published in 1590 at about the time he settled in Mantua that he had absorbed the new expressiveness of the Mantuans, especially as seen in Wert's eighth book. But for the purposes of this study there is no need to go back beyond his fourth book, published in 1603, to see his lively and sensitive handling of techniques that were soon to permeate so many of his continuo madrigals.

The opening of *Luci serene e chiare*[2] shows Monteverdi's new approach at its most expressive:

Ex. 1

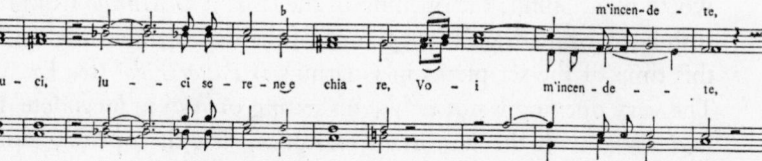

The translucent chords in the first seven bars perfectly reflect the 'serene and clear' eyes. The two top parts sing in thirds, and

[1] Cf. Alfred Einstein, *The Italian Madrigal* (Princeton, 1949), II, pp. 825–35 and 844–7, and Denis Arnold, *Monteverdi* (London and New York, 1963), pp. 56 ff.

[2] *Tutte le Opere*, IV, p. 35.

Monteverdi may have been thinking of them as a duet against a neutral harmonic background; as we shall see, homophony like this is one of the most characteristic textures of his duets. Again, the slight increase in movement from bar 7 in the three upper parts is a perfect match for the lover's exclamation 'You inflame me'. Here the duet texture breaks down, and the highest part becomes a 'solo'. The little lift on 'voi', one of the simplest and most telling of emotional embellishments, is rather like one that graces some early solo madrigals. Monteverdi also used it often. Among other examples in the same book is one in the second bar of *Sfogava con le stelle*, where the jump down of a third reminds one even more forcibly of the form it usually assumes in monodies; in Ex. 2 this passage can be compared with the opening of Caccini's song *Perfidissimo volto*:

Exx. 2*a* and 2*b*[1]

 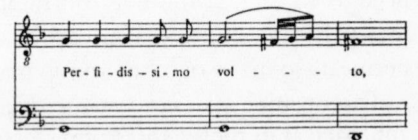

One more of Monteverdi's expressive 'solos' from these years is worth mentioning: the opening of the lament *O Mirtillo* from his fifth book of madrigals (1605), one of the innumerable settings at this time of the set pieces in Guarini's *Il Pastor Fido*[2] (see Ex. 3). The very opening is not unlike his setting of 'Voi m'incendete' in *Luci serene* with the important exception that the opening note of the melody, now harmonized as a concord, launches the new melodic interval of the major sixth, which had hitherto been virtually excluded from polyphony and which Monteverdi was beginning to use as one more way of heightening emotional tension.

Declamatory series of repeated melody notes on the surface of a

---

[1] Cf. respectively ibid., p. 15, and Giulio Caccini, *Le Nuove Musiche* (Florence, 1602), p. 8, where the third note in the vocal part is wrongly printed as a minim; facsimiles of Caccini's publication, Rome, 1930 and 1934.

[2] *Tutte le Opere*, V, p. 5,

Ex. 3

(O Mirtillo, Mirtillo, my life . . .)

homophonic texture are prominent in the last two examples. The words are clearly audible, and the technique has the further advantage that it builds up tension that needs to be released in some arresting dissonance or plangent melodic gesture. In this typical example from *A un giro sol* (Book IV)[1] the alto moves up a semitone to start a chain of dissonant suspensions sparked off by the emotive word 'crudele':

Ex. 4

(Surely when you were born so crue land harsh . . .)

This example also illustrates the duet texture we have already noticed — here on two middle voices, but immediately transferred to the top two with a nice sense of contrasting sonorities. The duet for two sopranos that starts *Ah, dolente partita* in the same book[2] behaves in precisely the same way: a monotone inflamed into acrid dissonance under the stress of the composer's response to doleful words. When Monteverdi was writing true duets with continuo he returned to this highly effective technique, as we can see at the equally poignant opening of *Interrotte speranze* in Book VII:[3]

[1] *Tutte le Opere*, IV, p. 52.
[2] Ibid., p. 1.
[3] *Tutte le Opere*, VII, p. 94.

Ex. 5

(Interrupted hopes, eternal faith, fire and powerful darts in a weak heart)

A good deal of the music in the examples we have been considering could after a fashion be reduced to monody. But this would remove the cunningly placed, affecting dissonances between two equal voices, which are precisely the sort of sound that fascinated Monteverdi and kept him for so long faithful to the duet and away from monody.

The repeated notes in Ex. 2(a) are of course of a peculiar kind: here and in five other places in *Sfogava* Monteverdi indicates only chords and leaves the singers to chant the rhythms freely as though they were singing psalms set in *falso bordone*. The cumulative tension here is even more powerful than that generated through 'normal' note-values, and the release from it when such values return can be all the more overwhelming. Indeed the last two pages of this madrigal are among the most arresting in the whole of Monteverdi. The poet, Ottavio Rinuccini, tells of a lover who is addressing the stars:

> *La fareste col vostr' aureo sembiante*
> *Pietosa sì, come me fate amante.*

(You would surely make her pitying with your golden mien, as you make me a lover.)

The first line and a half are declaimed three times in free chords, and the third is the most thrilling: in the first place the chord clashes with the one ending the previous phrase through the disruptive mediant relationship that Monteverdi so often exploited, and the three-note phrase that burgeons out of it, enhanced by the leaping dissonance, is charged with an emotional intensity that even he never surpassed:[1]

[1] *Tutte le Opere*, IV, p, 19.

Ex. 6

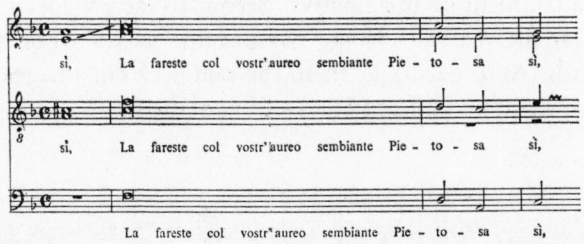

The music subsides to the final cadence through a quiet setting of the last few words in free imitation of a little scalic figure mingling with gently concordant treatment of the three-note outburst. Once again, we can see Monteverdi in one of his later duets, *O come vaghi*,[1] generating emotional power at the same word 'pietosa' by not dissimilar, though simpler, means, after which he handles in a correspondingly bland way the technique of unison followed by dissonance — in this case a standard cadence — that we have just seen in other duets:

Ex. 7

(But if pityingly you turn your glances...)

It is not really true, as has been claimed, that in *Sfogava* Monteverdi reserves free chanting only for the less important parts of the poem. He does, however, distinguish clearly between homophony, which he uses for the setting of the scene at the start, and polyphony, which bursts in with the first direct speech as the poet starts to address the stars. The distinction is one that could within a few years be drawn by means of recitative and aria. Monteverdi possibly felt it a defect of monody that no such distinction could be made while preserving a reasonable degree of musical continuity, and indeed compared with his madrigal Caccini's flat

[1] *Tutte le Opere*, IX, p. 105. The piece was published in 1624 in a collection of *Madrigali . . . posti in Musica da diversi eccellentissimi Spirti.*

setting[1] shows that simply to write for solo voice was no short cut to the attainment of imaginative 'Seconda Prattica' ideals. Ex. 8 shows (*a*) the marked change Monteverdi makes while setting the words 'And, gazing at them, he said, "O fair images..."' and (*b*) Caccini's undifferentiated setting of them:

Exx. 8*a* and 8*b*

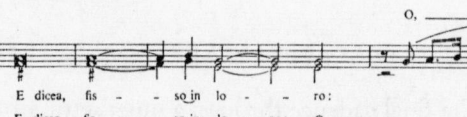

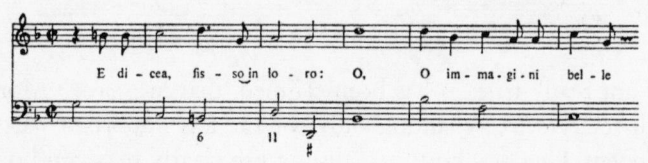

As soon as he introduced an obligatory continuo part into his madrigals Monteverdi began to write monody, but significantly only in alliance with other textures in an attempt to create a new and convincing emotional and structural order. Let us next consider *T'amo, mia vita*, one of the last six madrigals in his fifth book for which the continuo was 'fatto particolarmente'.[2] The words

---

[1] Caccini, op. cit., p. 13; a convenient reprint is in Archibald T. Davison and Willi Apel, *A Historical Anthology of Music*, II (London, 1950), p. 3.

[2] *Tutte le Opere*, V, p. 90.

of the title are sung five times by the first soprano, usually to a scale descending through a fifth, in alternation with homophonic declamation by the three lowest voices, often consisting of clearly articulated repeated notes of the type we have already seen. The two textures are utterly different, the trio rather matter-of-fact, the solo affectingly lyrical, especially when its last three statements come in quick succession in the middle of the piece: remembering *Sfogava*, the reader will not be surprised to learn that the solo represents a lover's direct speech, the trio a commentary. The madrigal is rounded off by nearly twenty bars of free polyphony for the full five-part ensemble. This climax, based on the refrain for 'T'amo, mia vita', now completed by the phrase 'La mia vita sia', indicates an imaginative new role for traditional polyphony when used in this concentrated way to crown and 'complete' a series of contrasting lighter textures. The work as a whole is like a study in the realistic textures of the celebrated *Lamento della Ninfa* in Book VIII:[1] Monteverdi makes naturalistic use of monody but is still primarily intent on a rounded structure enhanced by interplay of textures. To turn the opening words into a refrain does no violence to the meaning of the poem: indeed it makes it more vivid, as do the comparable repetitions of two phrases in the *Lamento d'Arianna* that I mentioned in the last chapter. It is surprising that monodic madrigalists used repetition so rarely. Pietro Benedetti brings back the opening phrase of his madrigal *Ho vist' al pianto mio* as a cadence to his first section, and Sigismondo d'India unifies his madrigal *E pur tu parti, ohimè* with nine more statements of the opening rhythm (Ex. 9), but these are isolated cases.[2]

Ex. 9

(And yet you depart, alas!...)

[1] *Tutte le Opere*, VIII, p. 288.

[2] Cf. Pietro Benedetti, *Musiche ... Libro Quarto* (Florence, 1617), p. 17, and Sigismondo d'India, *Le Musiche ... Libro Terzo* (Milan, 1618), p. 16.

We can definitely say that in *T'amo, mia vita* Monteverdi was writing for solo voices, whatever may be true of his earlier madrigals. *Addio, Florida bella* in Book VI (1614)[1] is another piece obviously meant for one voice to a part. He described it by the fashionable new word 'concertato', and it is indeed more like a typical early seventeenth-century dialogue than a traditional madrigal. Two lovers, Florus and Florida, are saying good-bye on the banks of the Tiber. Dramatic realism now demands that each sing a solo, she as a soprano, he as a tenor; the solos are, moreover, heightened by the florid writing frequent in solo madrigals. Then they continue their farewells in an imitative duet. In between, the full five-part group of voices, again reduced to the role of commentator on the sidelines — or in the bushes, like the voyeurs of so much madrigal verse? — remark in plain words and amusingly 'confused' music on the confused noise of the lovers' sighing, kissing and talking, and they round off the piece by echoing the farewells in a coda as satisfying in terms of sense, form and texture as that of *T'amo, mia vita*.

It is, however, not monody but the two-part textures of his middle madrigal books that Monteverdi later developed so intensively in independent pieces. One should really think of them primarily as three-part textures, certainly after he has adopted an instrumental bass. Even in his earlier books a passage for two adjacent voices is sometimes underpinned by a quasi-instrumental vocal bass. He has only to take the logical step of making the bass purely instrumental to produce the most characteristic forces of his duets — two equal voices and continuo. The vocal writing in his duets varies between homophony and a fairly free polyphony based on short melodic figures that also derives from passages (usually for more than two voices) in his ensemble madrigals; the bass nearly always moves independently. Monteverdi also wrote a number of trios: here the homophonic three-part textures of his ensemble madrigals are found much less often than loosely imitative polyphony for all three voices, and the instrumental bass either doubles the lowest one (nearly always a bass) or reproduces its essential harmony notes in the long values

[1] *Tutte le Opere*, VI, p. 38.

common in continuo lines. Monteverdi also of course wrote in his later years a number of madrigals for four or more voices, which are beyond the scope of this chapter; but, needless to say, in several of them he developed the important features I have pointed to in his earlier madrigals and his duets.

There are plenty of duet- and trio-sections in the madrigals of Monteverdi's fourth book and in those in the fifth book where the continuo is not yet obligatory. We have seen some of them already, and there is no point in multiplying examples. But there is one wonderful beginning, of *Era l'anima mia* in Book V,[1] that is well worth mentioning for its original, varied and outstandingly expressive use of the texture. Guarini's image of the soul at its last hour, in the context of a love poem, summoned from Monteverdi cavernous D minor chords for the three lowest voices in which the middle one acts as a pivot in third-textures with first the voice below and then the one above. The upper voices of this trio then sing drooping thirds, full of disturbing false relations. They also produce dissonances with a bass that from this point takes on an 'instrumental' character with long-held notes that act as successive dominants in a modern tonal way; when it drops out before the final resolution and leaves the other two voices on their own the effect is intensely chilling. Gloom is banished, however, by the sudden bright texture of the three highest voices and bass that follows at the words 'Quand'anima più bella, più gradita' — another striking textural contrast assuming structural importance as the major cadence of the new phrase blossoms into a series of polyphonic entries. Most of the 'trios' in Monteverdi's middle-period madrigals are homophonic and for three adjacent parts conceived as two-against-one. None of his works tells us so eloquently of his delight in this texture as the *Lamento d'Arianna*:[2] when he reworked his celebrated operatic monody as a five-part piece he added 64 bars and scored all but three of them for three voices. Contrasting trios more and more assumed structural functions: the appearance of four different three-part textures during less than twenty successive bars of *Ah,*

[1] *Tutte le Opere*, V, p. 9.
[2] *Tutte le Opere*, VI, p. 1.

dolente partita[1] is only one more example among many in which Monteverdi seems to have been concerned to expand his form in a satisfying way at least as much as to illuminate his text, which, however, certainly remained his starting-point. In the chamber duets in his seventh book of madrigals and elsewhere we constantly find him using homophonic textures of thirds over a free bass for varying emotional and structural ends: for example, as a still contrast to more elaborate imitative writing ('Gentil al par d'ogn'altre havete il core' in *Non è di gentil core*), or to emphasize points of repose or intensify cadences (two examples on the second page of *O come sei gentile*), sometimes creating a feeling of climax after alternating solos (second page of *Io son pur vezzosetta*).[2]

As soon as he adopted the continuo as an essential feature Monteverdi plunged into duet writing more eagerly than into solo writing, not only to exploit its sonorous potentialities but again to seek out new forms. *Ahi, come a un vago sol*, the first of his continuo madrigals,[3] is a marvellous illustration of what he could do with the new medium. The first 23 bars are a duet for the two tenors, now singing imitatively, now in thirds, over a slow-moving bass: the riot of embellishments at the protracted cadence affords a fine climax to those heard earlier in the duet. This proves to be the first of four duet-sections, which get progressively shorter and plainer and are separated by a plaintive refrain to the words 'Ah! che piaga d'amor non sana mai' ('Ah! love's wound never heals') which is a remarkable example of the emotional power Monteverdi could wrest from quite ordinary chord progressions (see Ex. 10).

The first two statements of the refrain are for a trio consisting of the two highest voices and the lowest. The music of the refrain then invades the third duet, which flowers into five-part writing for the third statement proper of the refrain. This is a notably imaginative passage, which fuses the two main formal ideas of the piece: the new warmth generated as a result can burn itself

---

[1] *Tutte le Opere*, IV, pp. 3 (bottom)–5.
[2] *Tutte le Opere*, VII, pp. 10–11, 36 and 42 respectively.
[3] *Tutte le Opere*, V, p. 62.

out only through a development of the refrain in five parts interrupted only by the fourth duet-section, now a mere four bars long. *Qui rise Tirsi*, in the next book,[1] is another fine concertato opposing in a highly satisfying manner a full but plain refrain and sections more lightly but also more exuberantly scored. The symmetrical schemes of these pieces, with their suggestions of rondo form, are of course similar to that of *T'amo, mia vita*, already discussed.

Ex. 10

As I mentioned above, we also find in his earlier madrigals the other important texture which shares the limelight with homophony in Monteverdi's fully-fledged duets, as it also does in the first part of *Ahi, come a un vago sol*. This is the imitation of short, rhythmically incisive melodic phrases which are often developed sequentially and sometimes merge into characteristic textures in thirds. Spirited counterpoint of this nature, never developed at great length, was one of the newer techniques Monteverdi introduced into his earlier madrigals: it was one of the elements through which textures gradually became more discontinuous as composers sought to express the meanings of their texts more and more subjectively and in ever minuter detail.

The first page of *La piaga ch'ho nel core* in Book IV[2] (Ex. 11) vividly illustrates the formal and emotional impact that such a texture can create. Many other instances from Monteverdi's madrigals of this period could be mentioned, all of them perhaps

---

[1] *Tutte le Opere*, VI, p. 77. [2] *Tutte le Opere*, IV, p. 41.

more 'normal': for this is a particularly disruptive passage in which he approaches the neurotic violence of the later Gesualdo:

Ex. 11

'The wound in my heart, lady, makes you happy', says the text, offering the sort of sharp antithesis that must have delighted a composer of Monteverdi's keen dramatic perceptions. So to start with he creates 'wounding' dissonance and harmonic dislocation (bars 2–3) in a context of low spirits emphasized by the long values. The figure denoting the lady's unseemly pleasure bursts in with the utmost force of surprise far removed from the halting discontinuity of the weaker solo madrigals of the day. For in every respect it is the exact opposite of the opening bars: brief, sprightly, incisive, written in short values, repeated several times, treated imitatively. Monteverdi has no time now for strict and expansive imitative polyphony in a piece of this kind; the entries are sequential, and all of them are duets in thirds or tenths. Thus he announces his violently contrasting material at the outset, and he works out the rest of the madrigal as a synthesis of it.

There are innumerable instances in Monteverdi's duets of the imitative technique I have just illustrated in its five-part guise.

Here is just one passage, from *Dice la mia bellissima Licori* in Book VII:[1]

Ex. 12

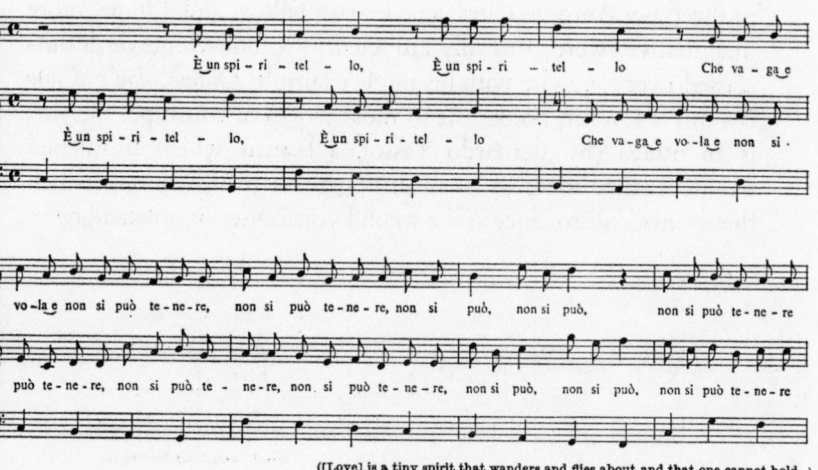

([Love] is a tiny spirit that wanders and flies about and that one cannot hold.)

The vocal parts are a web of short interrelated phrases continuously heard in canon or close imitation, and the 'walking' bass, paralleled in a number of other duets, anticipates the basses of strophic-bass cantatas.

In the secular field Monteverdi wrote 24 duets and 23 trios.[2] The duets in particular belong to a genre that in prestige was second only to monody among many of the composers who were spreading the new music through Italy. There were several kinds of two-part music, two of which need not concern us here: imitative canzonets without independent instrumental bass and thus little to the taste of modern-minded composers; and dialogues often consisting of alternating solos with a final duet. These types were popular, but less so that what are usually referred to as chamber duets — the balanced structure of homophony and imitation I have already referred to, nearly always in common

[1] *Tutte le Opere*, VII, p. 59.
[2] The total of trios leaves out of account, of course, the *Canzonette* of 1584 and the *Scherzi Musicali* of 1607, which are quite different types of piece.

time and sometimes on quite a large scale. Closely related to these works are an important group of duets in which strophic variations unfold from verse to verse over standard popular basses such as the *romanesca* and *ruggiero*. There are more duets than monodies of this type: Antonio Cifra, a pedestrian fellow, and d'India, more imaginative, were especially attracted to it, but Monteverdi outclassed everyone else with his single example, *Ohimè, dov'è il mio ben* in his seventh book.[1] As in most works of this type, the text is an ottava (by Bernardo Tasso), a lament which stimulated Monteverdi to some of his most heartfelt writing, among which the agonized dissonance as the second voice enters is outstanding:

Ex. 13

(Alas! where is my beloved ...)

Apart from this piece Monteverdi wrote fourteen chamber duets fairly strictly of the type I have mentioned; most of them are in his seventh book and account for half its contents. There are seven other duets, which probably date from the 1630's and reflect much more obviously than his solos the contemporary development of monodies into recitatives and triple-time arias and cantatas; the total is completed by two splendid isolated works which are discussed below. Several other composers at this period published collections largely devoted to chamber duets: d'India's *Musiche a due voci* (1615), especially rich in works founded on stock basses, and Giovanni Valentini's *Musiche a doi voci* (1622) are two of the most notable; and half the twenty pieces in Gagliano's fine *Musiche* (1615) are duets.

Duets, then, are the most representative contents of Monteverdi's seventh madrigal book of 1619, as imaginatively discontinuous five-part madrigals are of the fourth book published sixteen years before. They are of course no longer madrigals and

---

[1] *Tutte le Opere*, VII, p. 152.

indeed are designated as such on the title-page only in small type as a sub-title to the significant word *Concerto*, which sums up Monteverdi's approach to the innovations of the new century. Nearly all these duets, and the later ones, are exceptionally fine pieces which are still too little known. There is no space here to analyze them as they deserve. But I must at least put together the various technical features I have been discussing in a study of a single complete piece; in choosing *Non vedrò mai le stelle*[1] I am aware of the equally pressing claims of such masterpieces as *O come sei gentile* and *O sia tranquillo il mare*[2] and two from which I have quoted above, *Interrotte speranze* and *O come vaghi*.

Non vedrò mai is the song of a betrayed lover. It begins with desolate recitative including many repeated notes over a static bass (e.g. eight bars of tonic pedal to start with). Monteverdi intensifies the feeling of grief by the texture in thirds, which stems from the fact that successive phrases enter a third higher; note also the satisfying way in which he completes the second phrase in bar 5 by twice repeating an earlier word:

Ex. 14

(I shall never look at the stars in the heavens, faithless woman, [without thinking of the eyes that attended the harsh cause of my torments or saying to them . . .])

The music progresses sequentially through shorter alternating phrases to a tonic cadence. The lover then addresses the stars,

[1] Ibid., p. 66.

[2] Ibid., p. 35, and *Tutte le Opere*, IX, p. 36, respectively.

begging them to lend some of their light to the benighted mistress. At once Monteverdi introduces three telling changes — to monody, relative major and legato line:

Ex. 15

Then he gives us a little incisive duet of the type I have discussed above before expanding into a typically Venetian triple-time aria still imploring the 'luci belle'. This is a very significant change: it is one of the earliest suggestions of the later pairing of recitative and aria and, in so thoroughly upsetting the traditional movement of a duet, it makes this piece perhaps the most forward-looking in Book VII. Monteverdi returns to common time for the last page or so, during which imitation of short phrases again predominates. But before this there is a particularly cheerless moment when, as the poet still harps on the betrayal, he doubles solo tenor and continuo:

Ex. 16

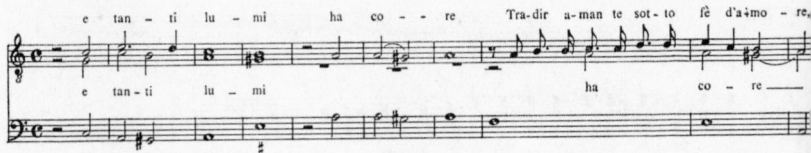

It can be seen from this account that as in the great ensemble madrigals Monteverdi is still able to handle an expanded form with the utmost variety and consistency, to devise brilliant strokes memorable alike for imagination and truth and to reconcile these detailed responses to an emotional text with the claims of the total form.

It only remains to turn to Monteverdi's two most celebrated duets to show how in them he developed two other kinds of composition to new technical and imaginative heights. *Chiome d'oro*[1] is a canzonet and as such appears at the back of Book VII away from the more serious duets; in both vocal and instrumental writing it is not unlike some of the *Scherzi Musicali* of 1607. It is notable for the way in which he enriched a strophic form as he did in *Tempro la cetra*:[2] there are three ritornellos at the beginning for two violins and continuo, and one of them in turn is heard between the five verses; and the entire piece — ritornellos as well as verses — is composed as strophic variations, an unusually serious form for a canzonet. The vocal texture is mainly homophonic, which means that thirds predominate, and the bass throughout is of the 'walking' type found in the first cantatas. The text is very likely a parody of madrigal verse; if so it would make especially appropriate the weighty number of ritornellos and the 'learned' form and would certainly account for the comically exaggerated roulades on 'ferita' (wound) just before the end. The invention all through shows Monteverdi at his happiest and most fertile.

This is of course equally true of *Zefiro torna*,[3] which technically is perhaps Monteverdi's greatest achievement. It is built almost entirely on a short chaconne bass, a type that had by 1630 supplanted in popularity the old type of longer bass such as the *romanesca* among composers interested in this sort of variation. It is the first great chaconne. To continue as long as he does with his bass, apparently so limiting of harmony and phrase-structure, without once flagging is one more illustration of the way in which a stern technical challenge can release a composer's imagination. Monteverdi imposes larger paragraphs on his short-phrased structures and takes all sorts of word-painting in his stride without interrupting the onward flow. Or rather he interrupts it exactly when he wants to, at the only possible places — where the downcast lover can contain no longer the sorrows that contrast so sharply with the joys of spring he has been so lyrically describing. Monteverdi plunges into anguished recitative including at one appearance of the word 'piango' (I weep) perhaps the most

---

[1] *Tutte le Opere*, VII, p. 182.
[2] Cf. *supra*, pp. 197–8. [3] *Tutte le Opere*, IX, p. 9.

arresting and lugubrious of all harmonic progressions in that age of harmonic daring:

Ex. 17

(At the dictates of my fortune, now I weep, now sigh)

This work, first published in 1632, makes a fitting conclusion to the attempt to show the technical and emotional stresses that lay behind a great composer's personal transformation of a great musical genre, and I hope I have shown how strong were the claims of form, interpretation of text, texture and sonority in keeping him loyal to it even when surrounded by the fashionable sounds of monody. While serving and renewing, with such questing distinction, the form through which he grew to musical maturity Monteverdi showed himself to be the most imaginative humanist of his age.

DENIS STEVENS

Madrigali Guerrieri, et Amorosi

If the enviably elastic qualities of certain terms used to describe instrumental forms can occasionally prompt such a question as 'When is a concerto not a concerto?'[1] it might reasonably be supposed that a parallel problem — 'When is a madrigal not a madrigal?' — results naturally from the over-liberal application of an already loose term whose lineage has been lost in the limbo of linguistics. Useful as it may be to define the madrigal by the classical standards of its Italian phase from about 1550 to 1590, there is absolutely no excuse for attempting to rule out its validity, as an evocative and convenient word, in the fourteenth century or indeed in the twentieth, when latter-day Landinis have in their various and devious ways sought to prolong the idea of the madrigal if not the style that is generally associated with it.

Similarly, there is no reason why secular vocal polyphony intended for use as chamber music should be excluded from the madrigalian canon merely because its composer (or his publisher, after the event[2]) added a *basso continuo* part to be sustained and realized by stringed and plucked instruments. As long as the audible impression remains madrigalesque — that is, replete with the thoughtful and artistic interplay of vocal lines — no great damage is done to the texture by the thoroughness of its basis. It may even be argued that a continuous and self-contained harmonic support, by its very nature, helps to free the densely

[1] Cf. David Boyden's article, so entitled, in *The Musical Quarterly*, XLIII (1957), p. 220.

[2] Monteverdi's Book IV was reprinted in 1615 (Phalèse, Antwerp) with a basso continuo added.

interwoven strands of a texture that has in times past shown a decided tendency to clog, causing critics of conservative polyphony to deplore the smothering of individual words and general sense alike.[1]

Words and sense, expressed by one voice only (yet supported harmonically), can easily make their mark; and when tutti follows upon solo, temporarily reviving the classical texture of the madrigal, a slight verbal confusion is of little moment since the poetical phrase or line, if repeated more or less exactly, has already made its impression on the hearers. What they perceive is a musical variant of a literary ostinato. Yet this happy and fruitful marriage of monody and madrigal has for decades given occasion only for diatribes and denigration: the decline of the madrigal, the debasement of the madrigal, the death of the madrigal. It all sounds so much like the objections raised when the scion of a noble house takes it in mind to marry a commoner.

As a madrigalist, Monteverdi evidently considered his terms of reference in the broadest possible light, developing with sureness of touch and brilliance of invention a repertoire of textures and techniques almost without parallel among his predecessors and his contemporaries. Far from dying, the madrigal gained a new lease of life — perhaps with tongue in cheek since most of its dying had been of an amatory nature — and stalked its way across the Piazza San Marco in 1619 barely disguised by the mask of concerto.[2] When is a madrigal not a concerto?

At first glance the nineteen years between Book VII and Book VIII seem to have been neglected by Monteverdi as far as vocal chamber music is concerned, apart from the *Scherzi Musicali* of 1632. In fact it was less a case of neglect than of transferred

---

[1] 'For having left the old style, which was somewhat unpolished, and also the excessive passage-work with which they embellished it, they now devote their attention for the most part to a recitative style. . . . Above all, they now make the words clear, using one note for each syllable; now piano, now forte, now slow, now fast — by the expression of their faces and by their gestures giving meaning to what they are singing, but with moderation and not in excess.' (Vincenzo Giustiniani, *Discorso sopra la Musica*, trans. Carol MacClintock, American Institute of Musicology: *Musicological Studies and Documents*, 9: ii, 1962, p. 76.)

[2] Concerto: the main title of Monteverdi's seventh book of madrigals.

activity, for the madrigals were now well able to look after themselves. Book VII was thrice reprinted, the first six books were each reprinted once, and other secular works appeared in at least four different anthologies.[1] All this was automatic enough to leave Monteverdi time for new compositions, these falling naturally into three main categories — occasional, theatrical, liturgical.

Quite apart from composition, although linked to it as closely as Haydn's concerts at Esterház were linked to his symphonic output, were the evenings of chamber music which Monteverdi was asked to organize and direct in the splendid residences of Venetian noblemen, princes of the church, and foreign ambassadors. These occasions are not well documented, apart from the performance of *Il Combattimento di Tancredi e Clorinda* at the house of Girolamo Mocenigo in 1624; yet the composer's letters give us a glimpse, here and there, of his social popularity and the consequently heavy demands upon his time.

Writing to Alessandro Striggio at Mantua, Monteverdi turns down an offer of employment there by playing up the particular and pecuniary advantages of musical life in Venice, and stressing the fact that church music and chamber music, directed by the *maestro di cappella* of St. Mark's, never lacks a thronging audience.[2] An English traveller, Fynes Morison, tells us not only that the Venetians at this time excelled in music; he actually describes what he heard: '... consortes of grave solemn Musicke, sometimes running so sweetly with soft touching of the strings, as may seem to ravish the hearer's spirit from his body, which music they use at many private and public meetings...'[3] It may seem both a paradox and a disappointment that Monteverdi, whose first professional appointment came to him because of his skill as a violinist, left no instrumental compositions aside from the toccatas, sinfonias and ritornellos that enliven his vocal and choral music. Nevertheless he must have known, rehearsed and per-

[1] For a complete list see Emil Vogel, 'Claudio Monteverdi', *Vierteljahrsschrift für Musikwissenschaft*, III (1887), p. 412–15.

[2] Letter dated 13 March 1620: cf. translation *supra*, p. 53.

[3] Fynes Morison, *Itinerary* (unpublished chapters), ed. Charles Hughes (London, 1903), p. 423.

formed considerable quantities of those consorts of grave solemn music to which Morison lent so attentive an ear, and his skill in using instruments as a foil for voices emerges triumphantly in his Venetian madrigals, canzonets and monodies.

As a director of vocal and instrumental groups he knew what it was to struggle for perfection, and his preface to the eighth book makes it clear that musicians who played only one long note when sixteen successive semiquavers were asked for received very short shrift indeed.[1] If Monteverdi was aware of his limitations (and his letters frequently indicate this) he was also aware of his capabilities, especially as a choral conductor, as his English pupil Walter Porter relates: '. . . the Ignorant judge frequently by the Performance, not by the Composition; which caused that unparallel'd Master of Musick, my good friend and Maestro *Monteverde* to vindicate a good Composition ill performed, affirming *to the Duke of Vennice* that had he been Rector Chori, he would have made that Song before judg'd bad, to have pass'd for good. So advantagious and necessary is the Judicious ordering and management of Musick.'[2] But the struggle for perfection was time-consuming, as Monteverdi complains in a letter to Striggio concerning a busy Saturday in July 1627, when he had to provide chamber music at the house of the English Ambassador from 5 until 8 p.m., then rush off immediately to the Church of the Carmelites for First Vespers of Our Blessed Lady of Mount Carmel, which occupied him until the small hours.[3] It reads rather

[1] Facsimile in Monteverdi, *Tutte le Opere*, VIII; translation in Oliver Strunk, *Source Readings in Music History* (London, 1952), p. 413.

[2] Cf. G. E. P. Arkwright, 'An English Pupil of Monteverdi', *The Musical Antiquary*, IV (1912–13), p. 244. The italicized words indicate handwritten insertions in the copies at Christ Church Library, Oxford, of the volume of motets that Porter published in 1657.

[3] Letter dated 24 July 1627: cf. translation *supra*, p. 72. It has not been hitherto noticed that the 'previous Saturday' referred to by Monteverdi was 15 July, eve of the feast of Our Blessed Lady of Mount Carmel; and that the antiphon to Magnificat at First Vespers (*Sancta Maria, succurre miseris*, with the special ending 'tuam solemnem commemorationem') was set by the composer for two treble voices, or two-part boys' choir, and *basso continuo*. It was printed in the same year, 1627, in the *Promptuarium musicum*, III, of Johannes Donfrid (Strasbourg); see also Monteverdi, *Tutte le Opere*, XVI, p. 511.

like the session-schedule of a conductor or virtuoso in some busy
modern musical metropolis.

Whereas Monteverdi's frequent visits to other Italian cities
and courts are documented at least in outline, his journeys further
afield remain almost unknown. When he asked for leave, the
Procurators granted it; but they invariably showed some anxiety
if he prolonged his stay beyond the point at which the music for
some major feast might run into jeopardy.[1] As a composer,
director and *animateur* in many realms of music, his personal
services continued to be in demand throughout those years of
preparation for the eighth book, whose dedication and contents
display abundant evidence of close artistic ties with the Habsburg
court. But even as he makes his humble offerings to Ferdinand III,
Monteverdi's first thought is for the late Emperor who, 'deigning
through his innate goodness to receive them with favour, and
honour them when they were in manuscript, has granted me as it
were an authoritative passport to entrust them to the printer's
press'.

There are no records after 1595 of Monteverdi visiting Graz,
Innsbruck or Vienna, but the best portrait of him hangs in
the Ferdinandeum at Innsbruck,[2] and his music must have
been known there as well as at Graz, where Ferdinand III
developed his early enthusiasm for Italian music and musicians.
The Mantuan opera-ballet *Il Ballo delle Ingrate* was performed in
Vienna in 1628, twenty years after its first performance and ten
before its first publication.[3] A well-known Venetian ballet-
master was imported to Vienna for the occasion, but there is no
evidence that the composer directed the music, and there was no
real need for his physical presence. On the other hand, he was no

[1] Cf. Denis Arnold, *Monteverdi* (London, 1963), p. 203 (Documents 4, 5 and
6).

[2] This is the portrait that is the frontispiece to this book. Although it has
usually been considered the work of an unknown artist, it can certainly be
identified as the portrait by Bernardo Strozzi (who was living in Venice in
Monteverdi's lifetime) mentioned in Boschini's *Carta del navegar pitoresco*: cf.
Luisa Mortari, *Bernardo Strozzi* (Rome, 1966), *passim*, but especially p. 139 and
plate 436.

[3] Cf. Robert Haas, 'Ferdinand III', *Die Musik in Geschichte und Gegenwart*,
IV, col. 36.

stranger to Eleonora Gonzaga, daughter of Duke Vincenzo and consort of Ferdinand II, and it is not unlikely that she would have invited an eminent musician to provide suitable courtly entertainment.

Other dignitaries of state definitely did so, if we can believe the statement of a Jesuit priest of Cremona, Padre Ansaldo Cotta, whose eloquence might with some justification be said to weigh heavier than his evidence. In an oration given on 16 December 1653, in the church of S. Marcellino, the good padre took as his theme 'Omnia Cremonae summa', spending a generous amount of time on music and of course on Monteverdi. First the Duke of Mantua, then the City of Venice is called upon to bear witness to Monteverdi's many-sided genius, and finally the King of Poland is invoked, presumably the music-loving Sigismund III, 'who at that time would have considered his happiness in all respects perfect, if he had been able to listen with eager ear to the melodies of Claudio summoned to his palace.'[1]

Wave upon wave of Italianate sound had in fact satisfied the eager ear of Sigismund from the time of Gabussi and Marenzio to the newer generation of Pacelli, Giovanni Francesco Anerio and Scacchi, but there is no direct proof of a visit by Monteverdi to Warsaw, where the royal chapel and court exerted their joint artistic influence from 1596 onwards. Monarch and maestro must surely have met, however, when Sigismund came to Venice in 1625, for one of Monteverdi's letters from that year tells of his preoccupation with church and chamber music for 'this Highness of Poland?'[2]

Although the Emperor's political and military campaigning left him little enough time for enjoyment of the peaceful arts, he kept up with evident relish a well-staffed musical establishment no less

---

[1] 'Testatur Poloniae Rex Augustissimus qui tunc felicitatem suam omnibus expletam numeris existimasset, si Claudii numeros saepius in aulam acciti, aure accipere avida potuisset.' Cf. Raffaele Monterosso (ed.), *Mostra Bibliografica dei Musicisti Cremonesi* (Cremona, 1951), p. 3.

[2] '... ma il molto d'affare havuto et che ho tuttavia in servire et in chiesa et alla camera quest'Altezza di Pollonia mi ha levato l'haver potuto pagar in questa picciola parte almeno, il molto debito che ho et haverò per sempre a V.S.III^{ma}...' (Letter dated 15 March 1625, in Malipiero, op. cit., p. 239.)

Italianate in character than that of the Polish king. Warsaw quite naturally boasted some Polish composers and singers, as Graz and Vienna boasted a few Austrians; but no matter what their nationality, they tended to follow the fashions invented and developed in Lombardy and the Veneto. Much less of a musician than his successor, Ferdinand II nevertheless commanded a greater measure of awe and respect not only from his own musicians, but from all who wished to derive some benefit — no matter how small — from the well-stocked imperial coffers. The number of individual works and printed collections dedicated to him is vast, though still not completely catalogued.[1]

It has come to be generally accepted that Monteverdi put together the eighth book with the intention of dedicating it to Ferdinand II, thus following the lead of many of his contemporaries, and the proposed mélange of madrigals embracing both love and war seems perfectly appropriate for the domestic delectation of such an emperor. But the winter of 1636 witnessed one of those smoothly planned transfers of supreme authority by means of which the new replaced the old in a gentle and gradual fashion, avoiding all unseemly haste. The ailing Ferdinand II began to yield his power, and late in December the coronation of Ferdinand III took place amidst festivities generously interspersed with music.[2] The old emperor lingered on for six more weeks, his successor duly inheriting the spacious territorial acquisitions of the Habsburgs and (doubtless with feigned enthusiasm) what remained of the Thirty Years' War.

At this point Monteverdi must have realized that while his original plans for the dedication would have to be modified, there was no immediate necessity for hastily publishing music that could just as well wait until the new régime had had time to settle down. More than eighteen months elapsed, in fact, before the eighth book came off the press, its dedication to the new emperor being dated 1 September 1638. Unfortunately the years

[1] Cf. Hellmut Federhofer, 'Graz Court Musicians and their Contributions to the *Parnassus Musicus Ferdinandaeus* (1615)', *Musica Disciplina*, IX (1955), p. 167.

[2] Cf. Egon Wellesz, *Essays on Opera* (London, 1950), p. 33.

leading up to this event, as far as Monteverdi is concerned, remain an almost complete artistic and biographical void.

From 1630 until 1637, he produced nothing in the way of stage music, whether opera, ballet or *intermezzo*, as far as current research shows. Between the *Scherzi Musicali* of 1632 and the eighth book of 1638 there were no new publications; and there are very few documents (and these few so far unpublished) between the letter of the Procurators written in mid-August 1632[1] and the entry in the registers which tells us that Monteverdi hired two Roman singer-composers, Manelli and Ferrari, for St. Mark's choir on 3 October 1638.[2] The composer's own letters, insofar as we know them today, come to an abrupt end on 2 February 1634.[3] There is another letter, or rather petition to the Procurators (9 June 1637)[4] concerning the insults hurled at him by one of his singers, Domenico Aldegati, who seems to have resembled the common singing-men impaled upon the lively quill of John Earle only a few years before: 'though they never expound the Scripture, they handle it much and pollute the Gospell with two things, their Conversation and their thumbes'.[5]

A septuagenarian enjoying widespread fame and countless honours could afford to brush aside the taunts of a warped and doltish character, and Monteverdi was at pains to point out that — speaking as a priest — he forgave the man, but as *maestro di cappella* of St. Mark's he was concerned that his office should suffer no blemish, especially since the incident took place before a crowd in the piazza. Fortunately the more pleasant aspects of life in Venice helped to compensate for the occasional bothersomeness of daily routine, as for example the return to Italy (after a number of years in the service of Ferdinand II) of an old colleague from Mantua, Giovanni Battista Buonamente.[6] Late in 1637

---

[1] Cf. Arnold, loc. cit. (Document 6).

[2] Ibid., p. 46, footnote 2.

[3] Cf. translation *supra*, pp. 85–7.

[4] Printed in Domenico de'Paoli, *Claudio Monteverdi* (Milan, 1945), pp. 302–4.

[5] Cf. *Micro-cosmographie, Or, a peece of the world discovered; in essayes and characters* (London, 1628), ed. Edward Arber (London, 1868), p. 52.

[6] Cf. Paul Nettl, 'Giovanni Battista Buonamente', *Zeitschrift für Musikwissenschaft*, IX (1926–7), p. 528.

Buonamente's seventh and last book of *Sonate, Sinfonie, Gagliarde, Corrente, et Brandi* emerged from Vincenti's indefatigable presses, and its very first item — a trio sonata in the form of a brilliant canon — must have given considerable pleasure to its dedicatee as well as to his many friends and admirers. Its title was *La Monteverde*.[1]

The early part of 1638 saw Monteverdi engulfed in the demanding task of correcting proofs of the eighth book. His eyesight, which had given him trouble in 1634,[2] could hardly have been at its best, yet there were eight part-books and a *basso continuo* volume in larger format to deal with. Doubtless many errors were corrected, but an even larger number seems to have escaped detection by composer and printer. Some of the mistakes and inconsistencies are of the kind that might be attributed to hasty copying (perhaps by another hand) for the purpose of retaining a reference score or parts, and this is especially true of the string parts of *Hor che'l ciel e la terra* and of the ballet *Movete al mio bel suon*.[3] Had the parts actually been used, the director or players would presumably have made the necessary corrections. Other items, in contrast to this, hint at fairly reliable working copies as originals, and *Il Ballo delle' Ingrate*, which presents the text of the Vienna version rather than that of Mantua, had in all probability been returned after the performances in 1628.[4]

Errors notwithstanding, there is no evidence to show that the eighth book was a hasty compilation. The lost treatise on the *seconda prattica* (referred to by the title of 'Melodia' in Monteverdi's correspondence[5]) surely survives, in part, in the famous preface with its initial bow towards the Greek philosophers and its subsequent anecdotal account of the discovery of the warlike

---

[1] Modern edition published by Hinrichsen–Peters (London and New York, 1962). A further item in the same collection is also dedicated to Monteverdi.

[2] Letter dated 2 February 1634: cf. translation *supra*, pp. 85–6.

[3] See the critical notes to my editions of these two works (respectively *Penn State Music Series*, VII, University Park and London, 1965; and London, 1967).

[4] The text of the Mantuan version (given in the edition published by Schott & Co. Ltd., London, 1960) was printed twice in 1608, first as a libretto, *Mascherata dell'Ingrate*, then as part of Federico Follino's *Compendio delle sontuose feste fatte l'anno M.DC.VIII nella città di Mantova*.

[5] Letter dated 22 October 1633: cf. translation *supra*, p. 84.

genus. No theorist by training or inclination, the composer could nevertheless demonstrate his points persuasively and even forcefully by directing his own music. This he did constantly in Venice and elsewhere, before the general public, the clergy and nobility, before princes and potentates, kings and emperors. His 'Melodia' is to be found in the melodies, harmonies and rhythms of the eighth book, in which he looks back not without pride over nearly forty years of composition and music-making. Far from being hasty, he had in fact decided to save some of his greatest works until the end, publishing them finally in a form which made it clear that the years of grappling with problems of declamation and expression had not been wasted.

These problems proved of vital interest to many of Monteverdi's contemporaries, both famous and obscure, and the challenging words of the preface found an echo in far-distant lands. In the introduction to his *Zangh-Bloemzel*,[1] published in Amsterdam in 1642, Johann Albert Ban speaks of having recently read a statement by Monteverdi concerning the close relationship between rhythm and emotion in music. After recounting the substance of Monteverdi's theories, Ban generously admits that they are of great importance even though they do not go as far as they might. He then distinguishes three main stylistic periods in Monteverdi's work: the first, in which the young composer follows Marenzio's lead; the second, corresponding to the continuo madrigals and the *seconda prattica*; and a third, placed on the loftiest pedestal of all and dating from the 1624 performance of the *Combattimento*. Ban's observation, which simply repeats Monteverdi's preface, nevertheless underlines a piece of evidence which helps to date certain compositions in the eighth book. If the *stile concitato* as exemplified by the 'madrigali guerrieri' emerged in 1624, it follows that all those works grouped together in the first half of the book belong to the period 1624–1638, or (allowing for an average lapse of time between composition and performance, also between assembly and publication) 1623–1637.

'Nothing gives more pleasure to a sincere friend of learning and lover of the arts', says Ban, 'than to find a goodly number of

[1] Vogel, op. cit., pp. 399–400, prints several extracts.

colleagues working in the same field of endeavour.' He feels sure that Monteverdi is still experimenting with ways and means to release the latent power of sound from its source, not only with rhythms but with melodic figuration of one kind or another ('steps and leaps' is his admirably simple and accurate description), for there are still wonderful things to be brought about and perfected. Neither Ban nor Monteverdi could have known it, but the feeling of excitement communicated by that elementary device of hammering out chains of semiquavers was to become the stock-in-trade of classical and romantic composers. True enough, single-note repetitions supplied orchestral strings with the possibility of an increased volume of sound, but the *concitato* element is surely present still when the semiquavers move rapidly or rush headlong, with détaché bowing, to suggest an angry sea, a battle, or a storm. The pity of it is that Monteverdi's effect has been so often confused with a bowed tremolo,[1] which is an un-measured shimmering usually employed for atmospheric reasons.

No comparable striving for intensity and variety of expression can be found in contemporary madrigal-books, although two published in the same year as the eighth book are extensive in scope and rich in instrumental participation. In the dedication of Martino Pesenti's *Quarto Libro de Madrigali*, dated 14 February 1638,[2] the printer Alessandro Vincenti presents the blind com-poser's works as one of the marvels of the city of Venice. Yet there is no hint of the *stile concitato* in the contents, although super-ficial similarities between Monteverdi's and Pesenti's choice of textures and instrumentation point to a recognizably Venetian spirit: two violins are suggested ('se piace', whereas Monteverdi's are always obbligato), room has been found for a ballet, and there is a group of three-voiced canzonets corresponding to the ones in the *madrigali amorosi* of Monteverdi. A few months later Domenico

[1] 'This new effect of rapidly repeated notes, which he dignifies as the symbol of passion is, however, nothing more than the string *tremolo* so well known to us today as to be hackneyed.' (Hans F. Redlich, *Claudio Monteverdi*, London, 1952, p. 107.)

[2] Cf. Vogel, *Bibliothek der gedruckten weltlichen Vocalmusik Italiens* (repr. Hildesheim, 1962), II, p. 74; and Claudio Sartori, *Bibliografia della Musica Strumentale Italiana* (Florence, 1952), p. 359.

Mazzocchi, a Roman, offered to the Barberini in particular and madrigal-lovers in general a collection of pieces, some of them to be sung unaccompanied, others with continuo, and others still 'variamente concertati'.[1] The composer's avowed model is Gesualdo, though there appears no conscious attempt to emulate the species of musical oxymoron so successfully exploited in that composer's last two books of madrigals. Instead, we have a fine setting of Armida's lament, with *ruggiero* as ground and a consort of violins to support the harmony. Mazzocchi does, however, come closer to Monteverdi in his preface, where he shows himself much concerned over subtle distinctions in intonation, as well as with *messa di voce* and marks of dynamic expression. The art of performance clearly influenced the thinking of both composers.

Monteverdi's collection displays, in its neat symmetry, two carefully contrived categories whose individual items often share more than one feature or attribute with a corresponding number in the other category. These by no means tenuous connections between love and war can best be observed in diagrammatic form (see opposite page). Italics are used to make these 'concordances' clear. The title-page does, of course, mention a third category: the compositions 'in genere rappresentativo' (of which there are four), but in fact there is an overlap here, since two stage pieces are included among the warlike madrigals, and two among the amorous. This may be considered yet another aspect of Monteverdi's symmetrical plan. Since the dates of *Il Ballo delle' Ingrate* and *Combattimento* are known, there remains the task of discovering when, approximately or precisely, the rest of the works were written.

Leaving aside for the moment the question of internal stylistic evidence as a determining factor in chronology of a composer's output, it is generally admitted that works of a ceremonial or occasional nature often provide clues in their literary texts. This is certainly true of certain texts in the eighth book hitherto disregarded or unevaluated. First and foremost come the polyphonic paeans in honour of one or the other Ferdinand. The book begins with *Altri canti d'Amor*, based on an anonymous sonnet

[1] Cf. Vogel, *Bibliothek*, I, p. 436.

Madrigali guerrieri			Madrigali amorosi
Altri canti d'Amor	a 6; *strings*	a 6; *strings*	*Altri canti* di Marte (Marino)
Hor che'l ciel (*Petrarch*)	a 6; *strings*	a6 & 7; *strings*	Vago augelletto (*Petrarch*)
Gira il nemico	A.T.B.	T.T.	Mentre vaga Angioletta (Guarini)
Se vittorie si belle } *also in Book IX*	T.T.	T.T.	Ardo } *also in Book IX*
Armato il cor	T.T.	T.T.	O sia tranquillo il mar
Ogni amante è guerrier	T.T.B.	T.T.B.	Ninfa che scalza il piede
Ardo avvampo	a 8; *strings*	a 5	Dolcissimo; Chi vuol haver (Guarini)
Combattimento (Tasso)	*gen. rapp.*	*gen. rapp.*	Non havea Febo ancora (Rinuccini)
		a 3	Perchè; Non partir; Su, su, su
Ballo: Movete al mio bel suon	*gen. rapp.*	*gen. rapp.*	*Ballo* delle Ingrate (Rinuccini)

Note: Compositions in several sections have been counted as one, and the voice designation provides the actual combination needed for performance (*i.e.* the four sections of *Ogni amante è guerrier* call for T.T., B., T., T.T.B.). In the case of *Hor che'l ciel* the octave is followed by the sestet *Così sol*; but the other Petrarch setting gives the octave only. The abbreviation '*gen. rapp.*' stands for '*in genere rappresentativo*'.

written in obvious imitation of Marino's *Altri canti di Marte*. Monteverdi went through his 'Marino period' in a fairly short space of time, setting four poems in Book VI and six poems in Book VII. Since *Altri canti di Marte* is the only Marino setting in the eighth book, it may well belong to the early Venetian period, 1614–19. On the other hand, its omission from Book VII (1619) seems to suggest a slightly later date, though not perhaps one after 1625, for that was the year in which Marino died. A reasonably probable midway point would be 1622, and if this is accepted in view of the appropriate musical style, the imitation could have been written at any subsequent date up till 1637.

At this point we encounter the *Doppelmonarch* Ferdinand. Monteverdi might conceivably have wished to honour both emperors by placing an act of musical homage to the late sovereign at the beginning of his warlike madrigals, and a similar work right at the end in recognition of the new sovereign. A distinguished German scholar implies as much by referring to *Altri canti d'Amor* as 'eine kontrastreiche Huldigung an Kaiser Ferdinand II'.[1] But there is nothing in the text that points clearly and unequivocally to the old or the young emperor: it is necessary to read between the lines:

> *Altri canti d'Amor, tenero arciero,*
> *I dolci vezzi e i sospirati baci*
> *Narri gli sdegni e le bramate paci*
> *Quand'unisce due almi un sol pensiero.*
> *Di Marte io canto furibondo e fiero*
> *I duri incontri e le battaglie audaci;*
> *Strider le spade e bombeggiar le faci*
> *Fo nel mio bellicoso e fiero.*
>
> *Tu, cui tessuta han di Cesareo alloro*
> *La corona immortal Marte e Bellona,*
> *Gradite il verde ancor novo lavoro*
> *Che mentre guerre canta e guerre sona,*

---

[1] Wolfgang Osthoff's notes to the gramophone record *Madrigali e Concerti, 1605–1638* (Telefunken (S)AWT 9438A).

Madrigali Guerrieri, et Amorosi

O gran Fernando, l'orgoglioso coro
Del tuo sommo valor canta e ragiona.[1]

The sonneteer sings, in his octave, first of the delights of love and then of the sounds of war; in the sestet (introduced musically by a magniloquent bass solo, supported by the unusually rich texture of six-part strings) he asks Ferdinand graciously to accept this new work filled with his praises. The phrase 'verde ancor novo lavoro' may be intended as a pun on the composer's name. But if Mars and Bellona together have woven the victor's laurel into an immortal crown, the implication is that Ferdinand enjoys success as a warrior besides wearing the regalia of a sovereign.

Certain marked dissimilarities in character between father and son may help to assign *Altri canti d'Amor* to a definite time and person. As is well known, Ferdinand II achieved with almost effortless ease a universally acknowledged notoriety for quarrelsomeness, bigotry and poor judgement. In the first few years of his reign he had charge of some part of the imperial forces, but after 1624 the command was left to Wallenstein and Tilly. When Tilly was defeated in 1632 at Leipzig, Ferdinand in desperation threatened to take command once more but was forcibly dissuaded by those among his ministers who not unreasonably feared the outcome. Ferdinand II was no warrior; and his two attempts at defending Vienna in 1619 and 1620 succeeded

[1] Many musicologists agree that in certain circumstances the notes and other information printed on record sleeves may prove valid reference material, inasmuch as this material is sometimes not easily available elsewhere. A warning should nevertheless be given to those readers who make use of texts and translations from this kind of source. The sonnet printed here appears, for example, in the American Decca album DL 79417 (Monteverdi: *Madrigali Guerrieri*) in such a form as to defy recognition. The rhyme-scheme is obscured by transposition of words and lines, and the sense by omission of words and punctuation. Little wonder that the first line — 'Let others sing of Cupid, the tender archer' — emerges as 'More songs of love does the archer sigh'. When a subjunctive is parsed as a substantive, trouble looms ahead; and the entire collection of texts and translations in this album presents countless examples of comparable nonsense. There are, of course, problems in dealing with texts of this period, and Monteverdi's printer was none too careful. He prints 'mentre Bellona', for instance, when the verb clearly demands a plural subject; and since the sonnet is about Mars (the brother or husband of Bellona) I have emended the passage to read 'Marte e Bellona', which fits the metrical scheme as well as the sense.

only because of unexpected last-minute military aid. Court flattery, and court poetry too, stop at nothing: a thanksgiving ceremony after a battle, calling for laudatory verses of the kind supplied to Monteverdi, could and did justify the musical and literary hyperbole perpetrated by both poet and composer.

Ferdinand III, at heart a peace-loving and artistic soul, showed considerable courage when he succeeded Wallenstein as generalissimo in 1634, and it was not long before his subjects recognized him as a man utterly different from his father. As King of Hungary and Bohemia, the young commander knew how to match the respect due to royalty with the obedience commonly accorded to a military leader, and he was certainly no weakling. Nominally responsible for the capture of Regensburg and Donauwörth, he was more directly involved in the battle of Nördlingen (5–6 September 1634), and his bravery together with that of his Spanish commander drew forth a warm tribute from a fellow-warrior: 'they won immortal glory in this battle; to the wonder of all men they were always amidst the musket shot yet devoid of fear, nor could they be drawn from thence by any representation, but replied "Let such princes as are afraid, keep themselves within their royal palaces" '.[1]

Monteverdi, although safely ensconced in Venice, had only to draw upon his personal recollections of a six-months' campaign with the Duke of Mantua in 1595 for the swords to clash and the air to be filled again with flame and thundering (see Ex. 1). Surely, then, *Altri canti d' Amor* presents a musical reflection of the verbal tribute to a dashing young king, rather than a sycophantic gesture towards his infinitely less talented father? *Ogni amante è guerrier* definitely refers to Ferdinand III, since his second name was Ernst, and the text gives both:

> *Carco di spoglie, O gran Fernando Ernesto,*
> *T'inchineranno alla tue invita spada*
> *Vinti cedendo le corone e i regni.*[2]

This lengthy, cantata-like text, with its vivid references to the

---

[1] Cf. William Coxe, *History of the House of Austria* (London, 1893), II, p. 287.
[2] Monteverdi, *Tutte le Opere*, VIII, p. 102.

Ex. I

brave Spaniards, the stubborn French and the tiresome Turks
and Scythians, contains one passage which indicates that the great
king *now* wears on his head the imperial diadem:

> *Seguir tra l' armi il chiaro e nobil sangue*
> *Di quel gran Re ch' or su la sacra testa*
> *Posa il splendor del diadema Augusto . . .*[1]

Ferdinand III, elected King of the Holy Roman Empire on 22
December 1636 at Regensburg, was crowned on 30 December
amidst general acclaim and rejoicing, and it is highly probable
that Monteverdi's musical offering had its first performance very

[1] Ibid., p. 99.

243

soon after the noble event. The intimate scale of the work, which requires only three singers and the usual continuo instruments, suggests that it may have been intended for a private occasion and an audience somewhat limited in numbers.

In complete contrast, the one remaining work connected with Ferdinand — the *Ballo: Movete al mio bel suon*[1] — conjures up a festive occasion enlivened by a chorus, a *corps de ballet*, a heroic tenor soloist, and an orchestra well supplied with all available continuo instruments of the plucked-string variety. Like the other Ferdinand pieces, this one is based on a text of unknown authorship. It consists of two cleverly interlinked sonnets, the last line of the first serving as the initial line of the second, with a musical overlap that is even more noticeable, for the tenor soloist ends the first section of the work by singing as far as the fourth line of the second sonnet, at which point the chorus enters with the words 'Movete al mio bel suon'. The poet's opening stanzas are unified by a similarity of bass line as well as a recurring ritornello with *corrente* overtones, but with the third stanza comes a change to triple time propelled by a rocking bass which later permeates the ballet proper. Before this change, however, the vocal line suddenly blossoms forth with stage directions, and it becomes clear that the tenor soloist personifies the poet himself, while the dance-like ritornellos introduce the Nymphs of the Danube. One of them hands the poet a lyre — the text uses the classical form *cetra*, while the more practical stage direction specifies *chitarrone* — but he does not begin to play it until she has placed a garland on his brow. The poet-image now being complete, he invites the nymphs to leave their river and dance to the sound of his music. The ballet, beginning with the usual *riverenza*, is sung as well as danced, its two main sections being separated by a 'canario, passamezzo, or other dance' without voices.

In spite of the reach-me-down verse and its often strained circumlocutions, Monteverdi's music exudes spontaneous charm

[1] A complete recording of this work by the Accademia Monteverdiana is being issued by Dover Publications. Other compositions from the eighth book, on this same disc, include *Hor che'l ciel e la terra* (with its second section *Così sol d'una chiara fonte*), *Ardo avvampo, Gira il nemico insidioso* and *Altri canti d'Amor*.

and brilliance which more than compensate for the unavoidable banalities of a command performance.[1] Yet the sonnets are not without historical interest. The poet's first invocation tells of 'a century of peace under the new King of the Roman Empire', expressing the hopes of his long-suffering subjects who had in fact to wait until the Peace of Westphalia in 1648 for even the beginnings of relief. Ferdinand wanted nothing better than to return to writing poetry and music, for he was an adept at both, and his brother the Archduke Leopold had described him epigrammatically as 'supporting his sceptre on the lyre and the sword'.[2] Not without reason does the text of the ballet refer to 'la nobil cetra' and 'il braccio armato'. It also refers to the union of Habsburg with Spain, when the poet asks to have brought to him 'the deep cup of great Ebro' — that Spanish river-valley famed for its excellent wine.

Once again the genuflection to a 'new king' prompts the suggestion that this work was written for the coronation festivities in 1636. It is known that on 30 December a ballet was indeed performed, following the recitation of a pastoral poem, *Vaticinio di Silvano*, by Valeriano Bonvicino.[3] The different lands of Ferdinand's empire, portrayed by appropriately costumed singers and musicians riding on a triumphal chariot, join in a chorus of praise and rejoicing. After descending from the chariot and offering a joint act of homage, they each contribute an individual tableau composed of music and dancing. Monteverdi's ballet might well have found a place of honour on such an occasion as this, and the agile Istrian nymphs undoubtedly reminded their new Emperor of the need to protect Vienna and keep alive its image as a gay and friendly city.

[1] Critical evaluation of this work has so far displayed little more than marked disagreement. Redlich, op. cit., p. 175, footnote 40, claims that it recalls *Il Ballo delle' Ingrate*; de'Paoli, op. cit., p. 309, opts for *Tirsi e Clori*; Guido Pannain, in his immense serial survey of Monteverdi's music, finds in it a return to madrigal style (*Rassegna Musicale*, XXXII (1962), p. 13). Perhaps a more useful and logical criterion might result from an attempt to discover in what ways a work is unique, rather than how it resembles other works which are patently dissimilar.

[2] Cf. Andreas Liess, *Wiener Barockmusik* (Vienna, 1946), p. 63.

[3] Cf. Wellesz, loc. cit.

Of the other *madrigali guerrieri*, few if any can be dated with any degree of accuracy. The duet for two tenors *Armato il cor* appeared in the *Scherzi musicali* of 1632, and must therefore have been composed before that date: perhaps its popularity led Monteverdi to add three similar duets (written between 1633 and 1637) in order to make a group of four, half of them warlike, the other half amorous, in readiness for the eighth book. The splendid Petrarch setting, *Hor che'l ciel e la terra* (often sadly and unaccountably shorn of its second section in performances and recordings[1]) probably belongs to the mid-1620's, when — as we have already seen — he was much in demand as a director of vocal and instrumental chamber music in the great houses of Venice. He set little of Petrarch, but since there are two examples in Book VI and none elsewhere, aside from the retrospective *Selva Morale* and eighth book, *Hor che'l ciel* may belong to an early phase of the *madrigali guerrieri*, to which category it certainly adheres. As Monteverdi admits, there were no warlike compositions prior to 1624, so that the boundary dates for this work as well as *Gira il nemico insidioso* and *Ardo avvampo* can be set at 1624–1637. Although the first is incredibly funny in its merciless guying of the *ballo a cavallo*, and the second unique as being the only secular work of Monteverdi for eight voices, they have nothing to compare with the fabulous unfolding of the final phrase in the Petrarch sonnet (see Ex. 2).

It cannot be considered an exaggeration to say that the *Combattimento* is as vital and moving a work today as ever it was; and like all true masterpieces, it proves itself capable of constant renewal, ever revealing seemingly fresh and unsuspected sources of its power to enchant the listener.[2] The white-hot inspiration which spurred Monteverdi to write a great work within a com-

[1] Pannain discusses the octave and sestet as if they were two separate and totally unrelated works in his 'Studi monteverdiani', in *Rassegna Musicale*, XXXII (1962), p. 12.

[2] If I might be allowed one personal reminiscence, it would be to acknowledge the deep impression this work made on me when, after giving many concert and studio performances, I had to conduct a stage presentation in Lisbon (Gulbenkian Festival, 1966). The perfect matching of mimed action to the music added a new dimension to the emotional impact of Monteverdi's score.

Ex. 2

paratively small framework must have come about as a fusion of more than two musico-literary elements. At least seven such elements demand our attention: art song as exemplified by the Italian monodists of the early seventeenth century, popular song as heard in the improvised musical declamation of poetry by Tasso and Ariosto, the power of scenic representation, the role of the orchestra, the abiding attraction of madrigalisms, antecedents in France, and — last but not least (for Monteverdi claimed its invention) — the third stream of music, neither *molle*, nor *temperato*, but *concitato*: excited and passionate and violent. By 1624 Monteverdi was a past master of monody in all its forms, yet he must have been conscious of its exclusively courtly and polite associations. He had travelled widely and had surely heard on countless occasions the improvisatory cantillations of lonely singers less conscious of an audience than of the power of poetry to evoke a musical phrase. Such singers still exist; and their flights of fancy have been captured by means of recording, their phrases and pauses neatly analyzed by the *Dämpfungsschreiber*:[1]

Ex. 3

El - la già sen - te mo - rir - si,   e'l___ piè le man-ca e - gro e lan - guen - te ____

(N.B. The notation is approximate, but the "bar-lines" are exactly equivalent to one second.)

Quite clearly there is no possibility of such a style deriving from Monteverdi's recitative, but a fairly strong case can be made out for the influence of popular upon art music. The composer strives for a free and natural declamation, implying a simple chordal structure of the kind that might be supplied by lute or guitar:

Ex. 4

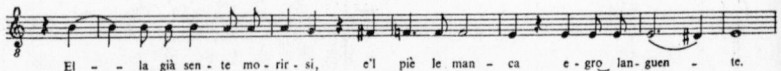

El - - la già sen - te mo - rir - si,   e'l piè le man - ca   e - gro lan - guen - te.

Another possible contributory source can be found in the French *air de cour*, which had already begun to re-shape Monteverdi's musical thought at the turn of the century. This time, however, it is not the elegant and suave type of melody that makes its impression, but a breathless and interrupted vocal line given by Guédron to Clorinda in the *Ballet de Tancrède* of 1619.[2] This is the dramatic moment of the discovery of Clorinda's true identity, when music should reflect the cruelty of the wounds, the tragic shock of recognition, the utter hopelessness of Tancred. Since Guédron's music was published by Boësset in 1620, it is at least

[1] Cf. Paul Collaer, 'Lyrisme baroque et tradition populaire', *Le 'Baroque' Musical* (Liège, 1964), p. 109.

[2] Cf. Margaret M. McGowan, *L'Art du Ballet de Cour en France, 1581–1643* (Paris, 1963), p. 125.

possible that a copy came to the notice of Monteverdi in Venice and that his previous experience of setting Tasso's epic (combined with the powerful influences mentioned above) resulted in the creation of a secular oratorio in which the quintessence of his musical and dramatic technique could raise emotional tension to a hitherto unparalleled degree.

It remains a matter for regret when this tension is slackened through disregard of the composer's instructions. Performances are still given, and recordings still appear, with Monteverdi's *martellato* semiquavers debased into a weak tremolando barely worthy even of a romantic tone-poem; the harpsichord continues to play when Clorinda sings her pathetic 'Amico, hai vinto', although the score states explicitly that we should hear only 'Clorinda in quattro viole', the jangling of armour being momentarily silenced. Worse still, the composer's hint to the narrator that he should ornament the stanza beginning 'Notte, che nel profondo e oscuro seno' seems rarely to reach its mark, even though the tenor part-book (as opposed to the short score in the *basso continuo* book) makes it clear that the *ribattuta della gola* and the *trillo* should play their part in enhancing this Orpheus-like invocation to Night:[1]

Ex. 5

If the *madrigali guerrieri* can be assigned to a relatively restricted period of time, the *amorosi* demand from a purely stylistic point of view considerably more space. The *Dichiaratione* printed in 1607 (*Scherzi musicali*) mentions that Monteverdi wrote not only

---

[1] Further details concerning performance are given in the preface to the Oxford University Press edition of the *Combattimento*. A recording based on this edition is available on Lyrichord, EA 72, where it is coupled with *Il Ballo delle Ingrate*.

secular but also sacred works in the French style,[1] and this is borne out by the third setting of the psalm *Confitebor tibi Domine*[2] in the *Selva morale e spirituale* of 1640. Some commentators state that the psalm resembles *Dolcissimo uscignolo*,[3] others affirm that it is a re-working of *Chi vol haver felice*,[4] both of which may have been composed between 1600 and 1607. The music of the psalm shows us that Monteverdi in fact drew on both of these Guarini settings:

Ex. 6

One other composition containing features and foibles of the French style may also belong to this early period: the unusual

[1] Cf. Strunk, op. cit., p. 411.
[2] Monteverdi, *Tutte le Opere*, XV, p. 352.
[3] Cf. Arnold, op. cit., p. 153.
[4] Cf. Leo Schrade, *Monteverdi* (repr. London, 1964), p. 176.

setting of the octave only from Petrarch's *Vago augelletto*, which makes use of six voices in the first quatrain and seven in the second. Possibly Monteverdi was less concerned at this stage in his career with the effects of 'laceramento della poesia'[1] than with the appearance of an unexpected solo voice which then proceeds to join in the tutti.

Mentre vaga Angioletta, an extremely difficult but highly effective duet for two tenors and continuo, has long been recognized as a musical treatise on the florid possibilities of baroque monody, seen in an added dimension because of the reflective inter-relationship of the two voices.[2] Every imaginable vocal figure is described in the poem by Guarini and simultaneously brought to life by Monteverdi's music, so much so that it seems almost impossible that such a collaboration could have been a mere accident. Guarini, who was no stranger to the courts of Ferrara, Mantua, Florence and Turin, gave throughout his life abundant proof of his love for music and admiration for virtuoso musicians. One of his poems is inscribed to 'Vittoria cantatrice'[3] — surely the famous Vittoria Archilei, who took part in the Florentine *intermezzi* of 1589 and achieved wide renown for the effortless charm of her vocal ornamentation.[4]

'Angioletta' could perhaps refer to some other singer whom he particularly admired, and although northern Italy (and especially Ferrara) was by no means lacking in lady singers of high quality, the one whose name began to radiate the greatest brilliance as Vittoria Archilei's sank into decline was Adriana Basile.[5] Her first visit to the court of Mantua lasted six years, from 1610 until 1616, coinciding with Monteverdi's last two years there. His admiration for her singing was unbounded, and even after hearing the finest

[1] Cf. Alfred Einstein, *The Italian Madrigal* (Princeton, 1949), II, p. 865.

[2] Monteverdi, *Tutte le Opere*, VIII, p. 246. There is a superb recording of this composition on Vanguard BG 579 (stereo: BGS 5007).

[3] *Opere* (Verona, 1737), II, p. 115.

[4] See the introductory chapter by Federico Ghisi, 'La Tradition Musicale des Fêtes Florentines et les Origines de l'Opéra', *Les Fêtes de Florence (1589)* (Paris, 1963), p. xviii.

[5] Cf. Alessandro Ademollo, *La bell'Adriana ed altre virtuose del suo tempo alla corte di Mantova* (Città di Castello, 1888).

singers that Rome and Florence could offer, he returns to the praise of 'la bell'Adriana' as singer, musician and actress: 'Before leaving Rome I heard Signora Hippolita sing very well; at Florence the daughter of Signor Giulio Romano, who sang very well and played the archlute and the harpsichord; but at Mantua I have heard Signora Adriana sing exceedingly well, play exceedingly well, and act exceedingly well'.[1]

In that same year, 1610, Monteverdi received a letter from Abbot Angelo Grillo thanking him for setting one of his sacred madrigals as a monody, and although the music is lost, the letter is preserved, complete with references to famous singers then in Mantua: 'I wish I had the tongue to praise it according to its merits, as I have the ear to appreciate it as it deserves, especially when it is sung by [Francesco] Campagnola [*sic*], or a comparable singer. For only a perfect singer with a heavenly voice, such as the Signora Adriana [Basile], should dare to approach such a composition. When Signora Adriana unites her voice with the instrument, and gives the strings life and speech with her direction, she wins our hearts with her sweet enchantment; we are carried to Heaven although our bodies remain on earth.'[2]

There is an almost uncanny similarity between Grillo's last sentence and the opening verse of Guarini's poem: 'While the beautiful Angioletta delights all sensitive spirits with her singing, my heart hastens to listen, and remains there magically entranced by the sound of her sweet song'. In a footnote to Grillo's tribute to Adriana Basile, Einstein cites yet another reference to the angelic voice ('Angioletta') in another of the Abbot's letters,[3] so that the poet would seem to be thinking of some particular diva when he wrote *Mentre vaga Angioletta*. Its laconic title, as given in

[1] 'Avanti mi partissi da Roma udì la Sig.ra Hippolita [Marotta] molto ben cantare, a Firenze la Sig.ra filiola del Sig.r Giulio Romano [Francesca Caccini] molto ben cantare et sonare di leutto chitaronato et clavicembano, ma a Mantova la Sig.ra Andriana benissimo cantare benissimo sonare et benissimo parlare ho udito . . .' (Letter dated 28 December 1610, in Malipiero, op. cit., p. 146.)

[2] Cf. Einstein, 'Abbot Angelo Grillo's Letters as Source Material for Music History', *Essays on Music* (London, 1956), pp. 175–6 (translation of an article which originally appeared in German in *Kirchenmusikalisches Jahrbuch*, 1911).

[3] Edition of 1616 (Giunti–Ciotti), I, p. 417. Ademollo mentions Guarini's poem, but does not relate it directly to Adriana Basile (op. cit., p. 154).

early editions of his works, reads 'Gorga di cantatrice', which leaves the choice rather wide. But even if Guarini (who died in 1612 and could therefore have heard Adriana Basile at the height of her powers) found his original inspiration in some other singer, Monteverdi's idea for such a virtuoso piece might well have been sparked off by the scintillating roulades of the one whom he heard 'benissimo cantare'.

His close collaboration with Ottavio Rinuccini during the festivities of 1608 remained with him throughout his life as a memory full of mixed emotions. On the one hand was the appalling stress of having to set to music an entire opera and a ballet, not to mention rehearsing and performing them within the space of only a few months; on the other hand the recollection of Rinuccini as a collaborator and friend (he spoke of him with piety in a letter of 1627[1]) must have moved him to believe that all in Mantua was not corrupt and evil. Apart from the Lament of Ariadne (1614), Monteverdi set only four of Rinuccini's poems: *Sfogava con le stelle* (Book IV, 1603) *Zefiro torna* (1632), *Bel pastor* (1651) and *Non havea Febo ancora*[2] — one of the four items *in genere rappresentativo* in the eighth book. This is undoubtedly a Mantuan work — the poem was already well known when Brunelli decked it forth in a colourful monodic garb in 1614.[3] Perhaps it was written for one of the lady singers who graced the Friday evening concerts of the Gonzagas — Settimia Caccini, Virginia Andreini or Adriana Basile. In Monteverdi's setting, its perennial freshness as a triptych with or without scenery has rarely been surpassed, and rarely has so brief an ostinato put forth such sinuous and superb melodic tendrils.

Of the remaining *madrigali amorosi*, there are three canzonets which in style and sentiment cleave close to the little-known charms of Book IX. Two of them, *Perchè t'en fugge, O Fillide?*

---

[1] Translated *supra*, p. 64.　　　[2] Monteverdi, *Tutte le Opere*, VIII, p. 286.
[3] Modern edition by Putnam Aldrich, *Rhythm in Seventeenth-century Italian Monody* (New York, 1966), p. 166. The number and order of verses differ somewhat between the two versions of Brunelli and Monteverdi. (We do not agree that Monteverdi's setting dates from his Mantuan years: its style, and the ground bass on which the major part of it is founded, seem to us to belong to the 1630's. — Eds.)

and *Non partir, ritrosetta*, call for the male-voice trio combination which dominates the posthumous publication, while the third, *Su, su, su, pastorelli vezzosi*, provides a fascinating comparison with another setting of the same poem.[1] The version in the eighth book is for high voices (S.S.A. or S.A.T.), while that of Book IX gives the darker timbre of an A.T.B. trio its opportunity to shine. *Ninfa che scalza il piede*, based (like the other canzonets) on poetry of unknown origin, makes use of a device that normally holds little interest for Monteverdi, although he achieves something very much like it in *Ogni amante è guerrier*. To begin with, a solo tenor sings a verse, and he is thereupon joined by a second tenor; only for the final verse do we hear the full trio by the addition of a bass voice. This kind of crescendo effect is nearer to the drama than to chamber music, yet it may well be that these light-hearted trios with continuo were written and performed by way of relaxation from heavier duties at the basilica and the confraternities of Venice.[2]

Any attempt to date such a variegated collection as appears in the eighth book invites disagreement and criticism, and the foregoing remarks are offered in the hope that further research will reveal new evidence and fresh ideas. Possibly some of the anonymous poetry will be traced in seventeenth-century anthologies; and some of the poems may even prove to be Grillo's, for we know from the Abbot's letters that Monteverdi set a fair amount of his verse, even though no detailed evidence of their collaboration can at present be provided. But, as Monteverdi himself said, 'Inventis facile est addere'.

[1] A third setting, this time by an unknown composer, is printed in facsimile and transcription in de'Paoli, op. cit., Appendix.
[2] A recording of Book IX is being issued by Dover Publications.

IV

The Operatic Composer

6 Figures of musicians by Agostino Tassi (*c.* 1580–1644)

ROBERT DONINGTON

Monteverdi's First Opera

Monteverdi's first opera, completed late in his fortieth year, was his *Orfeo* (1607) to a text by Alessandro Striggio.[1] It contains no element which was not based on precedent; but it reached complete maturity in that recently developed form. Everything that the pioneers of opera desired is here accomplished. Here are words as directly expressed in music as they wanted them expressed; here is music expressing them, as theirs did not, with the full inspiration of genius. It is all done with a deceptive air of simplicity: but that this air of simplicity *is* deceptive, we shall shortly see.

Orfeo opens with a short flourish called: 'Toccata which they play before the raising of the curtain three times with all the instruments, and they make it a tone higher wishing to play the trumpets with mutes'. If this had not been written, it would have been improvised: precedent required it, and continued to require it in seventeenth-century Italian operas whether or not music is written or trumpets are mentioned. Trumpets also imply drums, both being ordinarily supplied by the ducal or other local corps. Mutes raised baroque trumpets by a tone, so that the written

---

[1] Produced at Mantua in February 1607, and repeated there twice shortly afterwards; partially performed at Cremona in 1607; probably performed also in Turin, Florence and Milan around 1610. Libretto published at Mantua in 1607. Score published at Venice in 1609 and reprinted in 1615. Facsimile edited by Adolf Sandberger (Augsburg, 1927), now (1968) very scarce. First (partial) modern edition ed. Robert Eitner (Leipzig, 1881). In Malipiero's complete edition, XI, and separately (London, 1923) (these are not to be relied upon without reference to the sources). The best published edition is Denis Stevens's (London, 1967). Performing editions include J. A. Westrup's (Oxford, 1925), Hans F. Redlich's (Zürich, 1936) and Raymond Leppard's (London, 1967).

pitch of C major becomes concert D major,[1] leading to D minor
for the ensuing ritornello; and there, by inference, the trumpets
drop out as the Prologue opens into lyrical recitative to an unspecified accompaniment. 'All the instruments', as here pre-
scribed, is one of the instructions commonly scattered through
seventeenth-century Italian operas; but it was not common to list
at the beginning, as *Orfeo* lists, most of the instruments required.
Orfeo was so conspicuously successful that it was twice put into
print (in 1609 and 1615); most early Italian operas were printed
once, until the mid-century onwards, when few achieved even
one printing. The detail given in *Orfeo*, which seems so scanty
now, seemed lavish then. It was the normal expectation that most
of the orchestration and much of the music for the orchestral
instruments should be worked out at rehearsal and omitted from
the score.

The orchestra thus broadly indicated for *Orfeo* is again in
accordance with normal expectations at any such expensive court
entertainment of the late Renaissance — and more particularly
for the brilliant tradition of *intermezzi*, half dramatic and half
musical, between the acts of spoken dramas. And again, these
same expectations continued long into the baroque period. *Orfeo*
was neither unprecedented nor without sequel, but normal in
every respect but its abnormal greatness.[2] The list of instruments
mentions two harpsichords; two double basses (*contrabassi de
viola* or *de viola da gamba*, which may or may not mean the same
but probably do); ten standard members of the violin family
(*viole da brazzo*); a double harp; two small violins in the French
style (*alla Francese*, transposing an octave above the standard
violin[3] and in effect dancing-master's kits); two archlutes (as
listed, but three are later indicated); two (chamber) organs of

[1] Cf. *infra*, pp. 279–80, and Wolfgang Osthoff, 'Trombe sordine', *Archiv für
Musikwissenschaft*, XIII (1956), p. 77.

[2] For an excellent discussion of the *Orfeo* orchestra, see Westrup, 'Monteverdi and the Orchestra', *Music & Letters*, XXI (1940), p. 230. See also Paul
Collaer, 'L'Orchestra di Claudio Monteverdi', *Musica*, II (Florence, 1943), p. 86.

[3] This question has been well cleared up by David Boyden, 'Monteverdi's
Violini piccoli alla francese and *Viole da brazzo*', *Annales Musicologiques*, VI
(1958–63), p. 387.

wood (flue pipes); three bass viols (*bassi da gamba*); four trombones (as listed, but five seem to be required); a regal (portable organ with free-beating reeds, diminutive pipes and snarling tone); two cornetts (short wooden horns of narrow conical bore, capable, in skilled hands, of brilliantly silvery tone and prodigious agility); one little flute at the second octave (it doubles the sopranos of a chorus glitteringly two octaves above and seems to be a sopranino recorder). The trumpets are listed as one clarino (long trumpet played very high) with three (muted) trumpets (the same played lower); they certainly play muted in the opening Toccata. No drum part is written, but the lowest trumpet part (marked 'alto e basso') has the appropriate rhythms[1] (see Ex. 1a).

And all the *other* instruments? They should not necessarily double the written parts (certainly not at all points of the opera) but must often add to them. From 1607, the very year of *Orfeo*, we have Agazzari's astonishing instructions[2] for improvising orchestral 'divisions and counterpoints . . . florid passages both slow and fast . . . little replies, and fugal imitations' either as accompaniment or as instrumental interludes. The improvisation must have been controlled and directed at rehearsal by the musician in charge, whether he was the composer or not; it may well have been worked out on paper to some extent, but if so the orchestral parts which might have shown us the worked-out passages have disappeared.[3] We are left in any case with the same problem of reconstructing (which really means composing) music suitable and worthy to fill in the many gaps or incomplete passages in the surviving scores.[4]

---

[1] On trumpet parts in *Orfeo* and in a wider context cf. *infra*, pp. 279–80.

[2] Agostino Agazzari, *Del sonare sopra'l basso con tutti li stromenti e dell'uso loro nel conserto*, Siena, 1607 (the facsimile, Milan, 1933, is now (1968) scarce); text in Otto Kinkeldey, *Orgel und Klavier* . . . (Leipzig, 1910), pp. 216–21; English translation in Oliver Strunk, *Source Readings in Music History* (London, 1952), pp. 424–31.

[3] With exceptions which seem to be exceedingly rare: e.g. Barberini MSS. lat. 4213–17, 4225–6 and 4230 in the Biblioteca Apostolica Vaticana at Rome (but French material of this kind survives more extensively and is in course of investigation).

[4] Agazzari had anticipated his influential instructions in a letter dated 25 April 1606 at Rome, and he reprinted them in his *Sacrarum cantionum* . . . (Venice,

After the opening Toccata, the Prologue to *Orfeo* forms a compact little scene, in which the flexibility of the *stile recitativo* is combined with a formal structure of unexpected symmetry. We sense at once that quality not only of genius but of purely musical genius, which makes *Orfeo* a masterpiece of composition, as the earlier operas of Peri, Caccini and Cavalieri, interesting and historically important as they are, had none of them been. A small musical hint is picked up inconspicuously from the Toccata; so inconspicuously that it might seem unintentional if it did not recur subsequently throughout the opera — certainly with intention and probably with conscious intention. It is no more than a diatonic scale passage, up and down again at the start of the Toccata, and down but not up at the start of the ensuing ritornello: a mere musical commonplace, especially at this period; yet of such common materials are the finest strokes of art created, and the seeds of great ideas are frequently inconspicuous. The recurrence of this modest thematic material may be quite an important

1608). They were reproduced by Praetorius in his *Syntagma musicum*, III (Wolfenbüttel, 1618, and (most surviving copies) 1619), pp. 146–51; they were echoed by Giovani Battista Doni (*De' Trattati* . . . ed. Antonio Francesco Gori, Florence, 1763, II, pp. 110–13) in about 1635, and in 1640 by Pietro della Valle (*Della musica dell'età nostra*, printed in Angelo Solerti, *Le origini del melodramma*, Turin, 1903, pp. 159–60).

Further evidence for the more or less improvised addition of instruments and instrumental parts abounds in the many manuscript and few printed scores of seventeenth-century Italian operas. A recent article by my wife, Dr. Gloria Rose (*Journal of the American Musicological Society*, XVIII, 1965, p. 382), contains a provisional reappraisal of the situation. Further investigations were made by Dr. Rose and myself during the summer of 1966, but at the moment of writing (autumn, 1966) have not yet been sorted out or published. It does, however, seem to us (contrary to the current opinion) that Venetian opera accompaniments cannot have been reduced virtually to strings and continuo in the mid-seventeenth century, after the opening of the first public opera-houses. All kinds of orchestral instruments are mentioned in the Venetian scores: sporadically, it is true, but no more sporadically than elsewhere; and that goes on through the rest of the seventeenth century and longer. Thus the changes in idiom and orchestration between, let us say, Monteverdi's *Orfeo* at Mantua in 1607 and his *L'Incoronazione di Poppea* at Venice in 1642, are most misleadingly exaggerated by the different appearances of their surviving scores. This has been partly but not yet sufficiently recognized: the relevant evidence is still accumulating; and the question is one which we feel will need to come up for further consideration. (For a dissenting view cf. p. 285. — Eds.)

factor in giving *Orfeo* precisely what earlier extended works in monody lack: an effect of organic growth and uniformity. The freedom of the melody to follow every inflexion of the verbal text and every turn of the dramatic situation is in no way impaired: Monteverdi's music is at least as close to the expression of the words as Peri's or Caccini's; but there is a strength in his composition which theirs does not have, and it can partly be attributed to the taut design and closely braced structure underneath, which the felicitous movement on the surface so misleadingly conceals.

The form of the Prologue is recitative in strophic variation, spaced out by repetitions of the first ritornello. La Musica, the allegorical figure of music herself, is singing to us about the moving powers of music. Since this is recitative, the rhythm is fluid and should become quite free in performance; yet since the bass recurs substantially unchanged for each variation, the form is strict and sounds nicely balanced in performance. Very flexible in detail, very formal in construction: the combination is a surprising one, and it is the formal element which causes the surprise. For it was Monteverdi's intention (as it was Peri's and Caccini's) 'to make the words the mistress of the music and not the servant'.[1] We expect the music to follow the words, but we do not expect the music to follow its own laws as well, with as much independence as if it had no words to serve. That is where the genius of Monteverdi made such a difference. He could give the words their full expression with advantage, and not with disadvantage, to the expression of the music.

The downward scale of the Toccata already provides matter for the first ritornello and for the recitative, as a comparison of their first bars shows (see Ex. 1). Now the first act begins, with a shepherd rejoicing, in further recitative with strophic variation, at Orpheus' happiness in being newly accepted by Eurydice; and other nymphs and shepherds in chorus call on Hymen, as god of marriage, to come with his torch burning like the morning sun to drive the shadows away. This is a chordal dance, brilliantly con-

[1] Reported in the communication at the end of Claudio Monteverdi's *Scherzi Musicali* (Venice, 1607 — the year of *Orfeo*, once more) by his brother Giulio Cesare, as expressing Claudio Monteverdi's intentions.

trasting with the recitative before it; but flexible recitative and chordal chorus alike use the same descending scale and are as coherently united with the preceding Prologue as common thematic material can make them.

Ex. 1: Entries of ascending and descending scale-passages in Prologue and Act I (subsequent acts have similar entries). (Page-references here and in other examples are to the edition in *Tutte le Opere*, XI)

There is a poetic theme announced here, as well as a musical theme: it is the contrast between the happy light of the sun, and the dark clouds and shadows against which the chorus is already invoking protection — but as we perhaps already sense, invoking protection in vain. For indeed the opera is built around this poignant contrast, which unifies it dramatically as the scalewise resemblances and the formal devices unify it musically — all the more appropriately in that Orpheus's antagonist is Pluto the king of the dark underworld, but his father is Apollo the god of the bright sun. Soon Orpheus himself is praying to the sun, the 'life of the world', who 'sees all things'; and indeed the sun is traditionally a symbol both for the vital force of life and for the comprehending light of human consciousness. These archetypal truths are sung in timeless recitative: but as Orpheus voices the more personal query whether the sun has ever seen a more hapless lover more happily rewarded, the rhythm of both tune and bass pulses into time and motion to pass into arioso; then as Orpheus grows lyrical in praise of Eurydice, the music too grows lyrical and passes as easily into formal aria. It is a demonstration in miniature of musical structure responding effortlessly to dramatic development. In that effortless response lies the true art of *dramma per musica*, of music drama; and like so much true art, it is art of the kind that conceals art. We have to look quite closely to see just why the little passage is so convincing as opera.

But Eurydice answers with happy words just as convincingly *contradicted* by the music to which she sings them: a melodically outlined tritone (D descending to G sharp), which is the very interval (and on the very notes) subsequently most prominent in the sad scene of Act II where Eurydice's death is tragically announced. The tragedy is already implicit in the happiness. The contrast of light and shade colours the entire drama; and the moral of it is that very classical moral that extremes invite disaster, that any extremity of joy must swing over into an extremity of grief and that only in moderation lies safety or stability. Monteverdi may or may not have been conscious of introducing his Eurydice with that same poignant interval to which her death is later to be announced; but he was certainly conscious of her impending tragedy, and that would have been enough to tinge his feelings with a tragic undertone. Conscious craft or unconscious sureness — it does not matter which; both are attributes of genius, and both play their part in works of genius. We need only notice this small, typical detail as one more clue to the unmistakable artistic power and unity of the opera (see Ex. 2).

Act I ends with the chorus underlining the folly of extreme despair (to the same poetic metaphor of the sun displaying his shining rays all the more brightly after the storm clouds), since Orpheus was miserable in Eurydice's rejection but now is happy in her acceptance — 'so happy that there is nothing further which he can desire'. And again we may detect the implicit warning that this is going rather too far; that the pendulum is going to swing back; and that a stable reconciliation of these opposite extremes is not yet in sight.

Still working on the same theme-metaphor, Orpheus starts Act II by greeting once more the woods and slopes made happy by the sun which has turned his night to day. Then with the most simple yet poignant of modulations the tragedy breaks, announced in true classical manner by a messenger who tells of Eurydice's death by the fatal bite of a snake as she was gathering flowers in the grass (see Ex. 3).

What, in this charming but far from shallow myth, is the role of the snake in the grass? There was a snake in Eden, too, which brought disaster by tempting Eve, and through her Adam, to eat the apple of the tree of knowledge; but it was a fortunate disaster (theologically a *felix culpa* or fortunate sin) precisely because it was the tree of knowledge — because it drove them out of the unchanging bliss of Paradise into the beginnings of human consciousness, free will and moral responsibility. Unchanging bliss is an extreme which not only cannot but should not last; to be blunt, unchanging bliss is an infantile fantasy out of which we must grow in moving towards adult responsibility. As a symbol, the death of Eurydice by the bite of a snake suggests the painful death of an immature attitude which needs to be outgrown: a grief which may prove a blessing in disguise if Orpheus is capable of taking it in this way.

Ex. 2: entries of the tritone as a melodic interval at moments of grief in connection with the loss of Eurydice (others occur)

(O! sight too sweet, and too bitter. Thus for too much love do you lose me? And I, in my misery, do I lose......?)

Ex. 3: the turn of fortune and of harmony in the Messenger scene, Act II (p. 56)

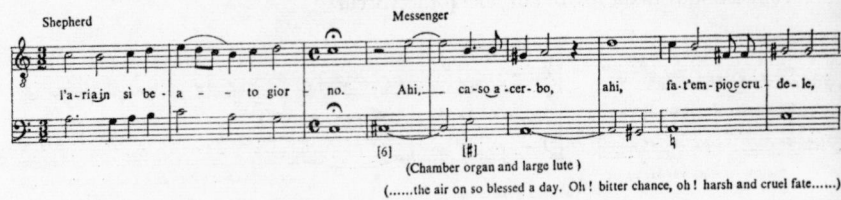

(Chamber organ and large lute)

(......the air on so blessed a day. Oh! bitter chance, oh! harsh and cruel fate......)

Orpheus *is* capable. He sets off at once for the underworld to fetch her back again. As literal reality, that is a mere impossibility; we are thereby warned, in effect, to take it as symbolical reality. The underworld is a traditional symbol for the unconscious, and it is there that Orpheus may recover, and in maturer form, not so much his outer bride, as the element of inner femininity within himself: what the ancients called his soul, his *anima*, and what Jung, following a Neoplatonic distinction between female *anima* and male *animus*, also recognized under this same name. It is this part of a man which, lying as it does on the unconscious side of him, can draw him down into himself in search of the self-knowledge he needs for the next stage in his growing up (for a woman it would be her inner masculinity or *animus*). Orpheus's arrival in the underworld, at the start of Act III, gets the accompaniment of 'Tromb. Corn. & Regali'. The abbreviation 'Tromb.' is probably for 'tromboni' (trombones) rather than for 'trombe' (trumpets) — or just possibly for both; 'Corn.' is for 'cornetti'. We expect trombones for scenes of the underworld, with which they were associated both before and after Monteverdi, through Mozart, and down at least to Weber. There is a natural impressiveness in the tone of the trombones which evokes awe and mystery without the need for any explanation. Charon, ferryman of the dead, now refuses passage to the living Orpheus in a bass voice of formidable depth, all the more so for being the first in the opera: the mere sound of him, when well sung, takes us right to the bottom of the world. He is followed by a Sinfonia for five low-lying instruments which makes the most of trombone sonority.

The aria in which Orpheus replies is 'Possente spirto', which is not only the most famous but the most elaborate in the opera. Music is given the fullest ascendancy here — but with the fullest dramatic justification; for Orpheus has only his supreme musicianship by which to charm his way past the stern guardian of the underworld. There are six long stanzas, in strophic variation. For the first four Monteverdi wrote out, as alternatives, both a plain version and an ornamented version. But I do not think that the plain version was intended to be sung plain: the choice intended here was, I think, between Monteverdi's ornamentation (as written out) and the singer's ornamentation (as more or less improvised in the customary manner of the time).

We have, among other parallels, two prefaces written within ten years of *Orfeo* which bear on this question.[1] They are not

[1] Bartolomeo Barbarino, *Il secondo Libro delli Motetti . . . a una voce sola . . .* (Venice, 1614), preface:

Because I have heard from many people that in my first book of motets . . . some of them are difficult to sing for those who do not have the inclination (*dispositione*) to add ornamental passages (*passaggiare*), therefore, in this second [book] I wanted to write the vocal part in two ways, simple and ornamented (*passaggiata*): the simple for those who do not have the inclination, and for those who have [a knowledge of] counterpoint and the inclination, who will be able by themselves to make up ornamental passages and the other refinements required for the good manner of singing; the ornamented, then, for those who, having the inclination, do not have counterpoint to be able to make up diminutions, as properly one must.

Enrico Radesca di Foggia, *Quinto Libro delle Canzonette, Madrigali et Arie, a tre, a una, et a due voci* (Venice, 1617), preface by the publisher:

[These compositions] are not given ornamental passages, in order that those who by nature are not endowed with the bent may not at all be deprived of the work; all the more in that it is clearly seen that, however skilful the singer may be, he will never extemporaneously perform that ornamental passage exactly as it is written down. . . . So those who do not have the bent may sing them as they are notated, for which I am sure they will not be ungrateful; and those who do have it [the bent] will be able to add the ornamental passages to their taste, according to their views. ('*Dispositione*' here translated 'bent'.)

See also Ern[e]st T. Ferand, *Die Improvisation in der Musik* (Zurich, 1938); *Die Improvisation in Beispielen . . .* (Cologne, 1956, English ed., Cologne, 1961) and other writings (especially 'Didactic Embellishment Literature in the Late Renaissance: A Survey of Sources', *Aspects of Medieval and Renaissance Music: A Birthday Offering to Gustave Reese*, ed. Jan LaRue, New York, 1966, p. 154). For some further discussion of the present question, see Robert Donington, *The Interpretation of Early Music*, 2nd ed., London, 1965, pp. 97–108, and 115–16 (not in 1st ed.).

completely clear; but they seem to suggest that whereas most singers want to ornament, not all are able. They seem to suggest that for those who do not want to ornament, and also for those who both want and are able to ornament for themselves, a simple text is best; while for those who want to ornament but are not able, an already ornamented text is best. It would, therefore, not be positively incorrect to sing Monteverdi's plain version as it stands; but still it would be far from what Monteverdi seems to have intended. The dramatic point of 'Possente spirto' is that Orpheus is exerting the utmost of his legendary vocal skill in order to persuade Charon to let him through; the role of Orpheus himself is a virtuoso role such as would only be entrusted to an outstanding singer who would certainly be able and might well be determined to ornament for himself; we have Doni's word for it about 1635[1] that ornamental passages 'are better adapted to theatrical music than to any other kind'.

Yet we know, too, from Caccini's famous preface to his *Nuove Musiche* (Florence, 1602) and elsewhere that ornamentation in early monody, elaborate as it might often be, was desired only in so far as it enhanced the dramatic impact and direct expressiveness of the words — not for its own sake, or where it might detract from the expression. Thus the last two stanzas of 'Possente spirto', which are given in only one, moderately ornamented version, seem intended to be sung more or less as they are written; for here the dramatic point is surely that Orpheus, having tried all his virtuoso arts, now adds to them this simpler appeal from the heart to the heart.

The accompaniment of 'Possente spirto' is for quiet chamber organ and lute, diversified by a succession of brilliant instruments whose parts are written out (very much as they would otherwise have been improvised) with ornamental figuration — also remarkable for its virtuosity. A pair of violins accompany the first stanza and follow it with a short ritornello; a pair of cornetts do the same for the second stanza, and a double harp of great depth and wide compass for the third; the fourth has simple written accompanying parts for two violins and *basso da*

[1] Cf. his *Trattato della Musica scenica* in op. cit., II, p. 69.

brazzo (cello), but no ritornello; the fifth shows only a continuo bass line; the sixth has a plain four-part accompaniment written out, with the instruction: 'the other parts [other than the voice] were played by three violins (*tre viole da braccio*), and a double bass (*contrabasso de viola*) touched very softly (*pian piano*)' (see Ex. 4).

For the first four stanzas, substantially the same sequence of

Ex. 4: ritornello for 'Arpa dopia' [*sic*], Act III (p. 94)

The second half of bar 2, top stave, according to Malipiero's emendation: original a tone higher. Most editorial accidentals are also in agreement with Malipiero. The augmented second appears, clearly printed, elsewhere in the opera (e.g. early in Act V: see Ex. 5). The four-note group on the treble stave on the third beat of bar 5 is printed a third lower in the original, but what is given here seems to have been intended.

bass notes recurs; for the fifth stanza, the bass is free and becomes grievously chromatic; for the sixth stanza, the strophic bass returns with a little coda formed from its last six notes. The three ritornellos have their own recurrent bass, each time with different melodies: a lesser strophic variation within the greater strophic variation. Charon then sings of his delight, to a variation of his first arioso, on substantially the same bass. He adds that pity would not become his stalwart heart; but even as Orpheus renews his appeal in a recitative conspicuous for its lamenting suspensions and leading to a melting arioso as the tension mounts and the bass grows more actively melodic, Charon is beginning to nod. Soon, to a very soft repetition of the low-lying sinfonia (but here on violins with chamber organ and double-bass viol), Charon falls asleep. (There are times when the best thing that can happen is for the stern guardian of the unconscious to fall asleep and let us make some new and healing contact with our deeper selves.) Another recitative for Orpheus leads to a return of the same arioso, over the same bass, but with the accompaniment reduced to organ alone. Orpheus gets into Charon's boat and pushes out for the farther shore, encouraged by a chorus of spirits more polyphonically elaborate than anything yet heard, and on new musical material, which, in an opera notable for its economy of musical material, well marks a new turn in the dramatic situation. This whole long scene is remarkable in many ways. It is consistently inspired, and the music is very beautiful. But also, it is very elaborate, and very elaborately organized. The construction is full of strict devices of form, whose presence we no more readily detect than we detect the formal devices in *Wozzeck*, of which Berg informed us that they helped him to give his music its tautness and unity, but were never intended to be noticed by the listener.

The listener to *Orfeo* is impressed throughout by its evident freedom, and by the easy grace with which it is obviously following every refinement of its verbal text. The music sounds, as it was meant to sound, spontaneous in the service of the words. But it is a spontaneity supported by the most masterly and self-conscious craftsmanship. We may not, perhaps, be aware of the craftsmanship; but we are very much aware of the authority behind the freedom, the real conviction behind the seeming casualness, the sense of inevitability behind the appearance of inconsequence. All this superb craftsmanship was quite new in the young art of opera, and it remained unusual. The rambling impression made on first acquaintance with all too many of the unpublished Italian operas of the seventeenth century is not, unfortunately, dispelled by closer study. But *Orfeo* yields new secrets of its cunning at each fresh examination. Its forms are of an almost academic strictness. Its thematic material, which seems to derive at every moment newly from the words, or from uncalculated instrumental inspiration, proves to be largely based on the ascending and descending scales first introduced in the opening Toccata and later developed both in the monody and in the ritornellos and sinfonias, which are themselves reiterated with great architectural skill and telling effect. The more careful the analysis we make, the closer the links we keep uncovering; and it is this unsuspected closeness of construction, combined with sheer musical inventiveness, which underlies our sense not merely of inspiration, but of mastery.

At the start of Act IV the dramatic continuity is brought out by that same sinfonia which opened the third act and returned just before its concluding chorus. We are in the palace of Pluto, king of the underworld; and his wife Proserpina is pleading with him, like a true woman, to remember his own impetuous love for her, and restore Eurydice to impetuous Orpheus. Pluto, both touched and oddly disturbed (his fear is of losing Proserpina again), agrees, on the famous condition that Orpheus must not look round at Eurydice on the upward journey. The chorus of spirits praises briefly this triumph of love in the very underworld; and Orpheus gives the honour to his all-powerful lyre (he persists in calling it anachronistically a cittern, *cetra*, but the poetic licence in no way disturbs us): the lyre by virtue of which he will this day be gathered to the white breast of his beloved. It is a little threefold aria in strophic variations, with an enchanting threefold ritornello for two violins moving cheerfully in thirds (momentarily but delightfully varied to sixths) above a bass which is also recurrent: again strophic variation form, though the variation in the middle is slight, and the last is the same as the first. The familiar scalewise thematic material is not here conspicuous: yet it is included, both upwards and downwards, and in both melody and bass. It never does emerge as a conscious motive in the Wagnerian manner; but it is, however modestly, part of what makes the opera cohere.

But now, using the same sinister tritone which Eurydice first sang in the days of their happiness, and which showed its true meaning when the Messenger repeated it in announcing Eurydice's death, Orpheus voices his sudden doubt: is she really following him? Is it perhaps all a trick? 'Here they make a noise behind the curtain', we read in the score. More likely it is really in his imagination; but on the plausible argument that 'what Pluto forbids Love commands' he turns round; he looks at the sweet light of her eyes (a chamber organ accompanies him); they are veiled in darkness (harpsichord, cello, big lute); a spirit sternly rebukes him; she spans her original tritone most poignantly with the descending scale, to lament the 'vision too sweet, and too bitter'; she asks 'by too much love have you lost me? And I wretched one lose the power to rejoice in light and sight' — and with that the spirit orders her back, and she is gone for ever. Crushed as he now is, Orpheus adds the diminished third, the augmented second and the major seventh, besides the tritone, to the assortment of harsh vocal intervals such as in the early seventeenth century were not only harsh in themselves, but all the harsher from unfamiliarity. They afterwards became part of a style. In the famous lament from Monteverdi's otherwise lost *Arianna*, they passed into the widest circulation, became much imitated, and may be heard resounding even so far afield as the wonderful lament of Dido, in Purcell's masterpiece, where the tritone is the most poignant interval (see Ex. 5, p. 274).

We have now reached the most touching moment of all this touching, naïve but enduring love story. It is enduring because it has depths underlying the naïve story that we enjoy so much; and indeed we find parallels to it in many other mythologies. There is, for example, a Japanese parallel in which a husband

7 Part of the ritornello for double harp in 'Possente spirto' in Act III of *Orfeo*
(1609 edition)

recovers his wife from the land of the shadows on condition of never seeing her face; he breaks the condition by taking a lighted torch to look at her but sees instead her horribly decaying corpse, which pursues him in vampire form to the entrance of the underworld. Delaying her by dropping fruit, he is just in time to block the entrance with a rock and stop the spirits from coming out and getting him. As in so many tales, the prohibition was meant to be broken; he was meant to see for himself that something on the feminine side of him was waiting to decay away and be outgrown; he was meant to be pursued by agonizing regret, and to win his difficult victory over the retrogressive forces which would have pulled him back into unconsciousness if he had not made a supreme effort to prevent them. The lighted torch reminds us of Psyche, who was visited every night by Cupid, but on condition of never trying to see him; she, too, broke the prohibition, brought a lamp to him, and was immediately plunged into desperate adventures the outcome of which was nevertheless her ultimate reunion with Cupid, not in childlike and unseeing innocence, but in maturer consciousness. Prometheus was punished by gnawing agony for stealing the light as well as the warmth of fire from the gods. Adam and Eve were punished by being thrust out of Paradise — into human consciousness and responsibility. The punishment is also the reward. It is painful to grow out of childlike unconsciousness and irresponsibility. But we are meant to grow up, and these myths of prohibitions broken and difficulties overcome have helped humanity in growing up all over the world. Even so far away as the North American Indians, tales have been collected with all the main features of the myth of Orpheus and Eurydice.

So it seems that Orpheus, too, was meant to look. He was meant to look back; but he was not meant to slide back. He wants to, and tells us so in a brief recitative grinding downwards (as he would like to slide downwards after his Eurydice) scalewise (in echo of her last downwards scale) from D, through the painfully diminished third B flat to G sharp, to complete once again the obsessive tritone. 'But who denies me now?', sings Orpheus; 'what hidden power', he complains, 'draws me against my will to the hateful light?' Hateful, yes, but healing and maturing, as the music already hints by growing both richer and more coherent. The orchestra glides smoothly from A major to D minor, through G minor and C major; on to F major; back through A minor and E major to A major. Nothing very memorable or remote; but these are healing modulations after the violent sideslips and harshly juxtaposed tonalities which have gone before.

In Act V the reconciliation is effected to which these extremes of joy and grief have been painfully but valuably leading up. Apollo, father of Orpheus and a divine representative of that light of the sun which is also a symbol for the light of human consciousness, 'descends in a cloud singing'. He offers Orpheus the crucial choice of clinging unprofitably to his misery, or of moving forward into a maturer state. 'Too much you rejoiced in your happy fortune; now you lament too much your bitter and hard destiny. Do you still not know that no joy down here endures? Therefore if you wish to enjoy immortal life, come with me to heaven which invites you.' Orpheus asks: 'Shall I never again see

Ex. 5: harsh melodic intervals and harmonic juxtapositions in *Orfeo*, other than the tritone

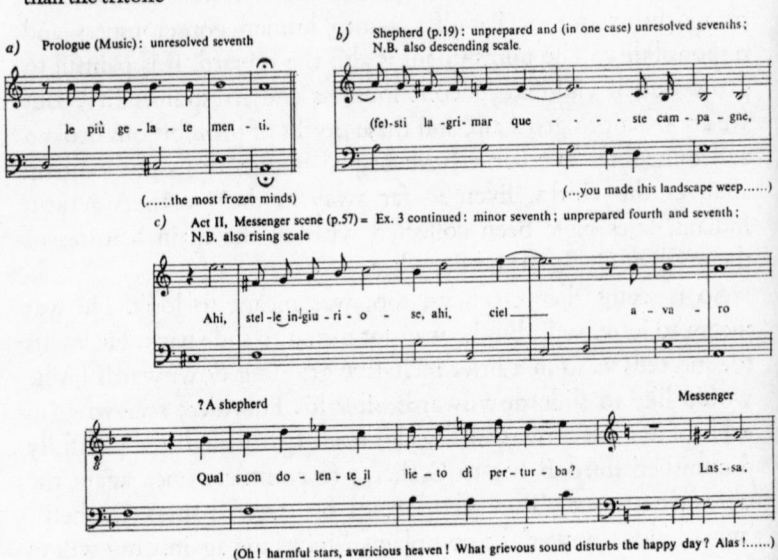

a) Prologue (Music): unresolved seventh

le più ge - la - te men - ti.

(......the most frozen minds)

b) Shepherd (p.19): unprepared and (in one case) unresolved sevenths; N.B. also descending scale.

(fe)-sti la-gri-mar que - - - - ste cam - pa - gne,

(...you made this landscape weep......)

c) Act II, Messenger scene (p.57) = Ex. 3 continued: minor seventh; unprepared fourth and seventh; N.B. also rising scale

Ahi, stel-le in-giu-ri-o - se, ahi, ciel____ a - va - ro

?A shepherd

Qual suon do - len-te il lie-to dì per-tur-ba?

Messenger

Las - sa.

(Oh! harmful stars, avaricious heaven! What grievous sound disturbs the happy day? Alas!......)

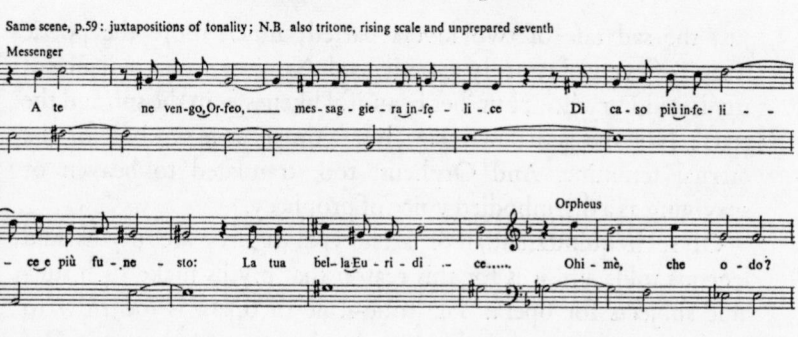

Same scene, p.59: juxtapositions of tonality; N.B. also tritone, rising scale and unprepared seventh

(M. I come to you, Orpheus, a messenger of grief, telling of a most unhappy, tragic event. Your fair Eurydice...... O. O! what do I hear? M. Your beloved wife is dead. O. Alas!)

In the second edition (1615) the second note in the vocal part is D, not C.

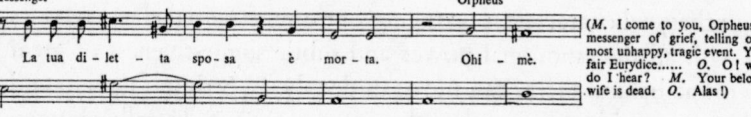

Orpheus (p.139): augmented second; N.B. also unresolved seventh and descending scale

(And I shall weep with you for ever.)

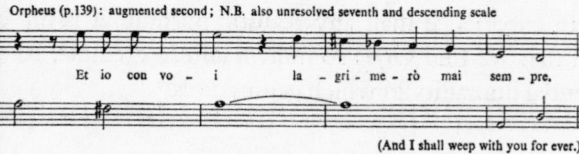

Orpheus (p.141): diminished third, diminished fourth; N.B. also rising and falling scale and augmented second in bass

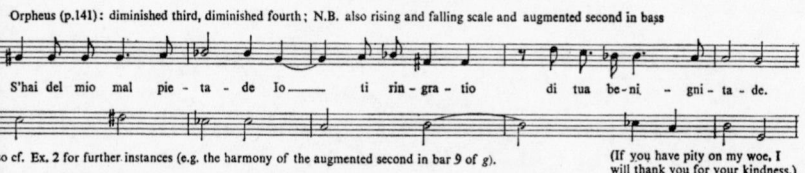

also cf. Ex. 2 for further instances (e.g. the harmony of the augmented second in bar 9 of g).

(If you have pity on my woe, I will thank you for your kindness.)

the sweet radiance of my loved Eurydice?' Apollo answers: 'You will look lovingly upon her beautiful likenesses in the sun and the stars'. At that, Orpheus accepts, and the two join in a duet almost as ornamented though not as long as Orpheus's 'Possente spirto' in Act III, to which this is artistically the counterpoise. That is not, of course, the ending most familiar from classical antiquity, which has Orpheus torn to pieces by infuriated Maenads (their fury being variously explained), while his head survives to sing prophecies of wisdom, like other speaking heads of myth and legend. But the symbolism is basically the same. Not just the sad tale of two lovers parted; much more the poetic image of events inwardly experienced. Not 'the sweet radiance of my loved Eurydice'; but 'her beautiful likenesses in the sun and the stars'. Not the actual woman; but woman as a symbol for the eternal feminine. And Orpheus, too, translated to heaven or surviving as a disembodied voice of prophecy.

Of such quintessential or archetypal figures are myths and legends told; and it is for this reason that myths make such suitable subjects for opera. The time-scale of opera is too slow to leave room for much individual development of character. But archetypal characters, portraying our quintessential characteristics with all the emotional power and subtle suggestiveness of great music behind them, can move us deeply. In Striggio's poem and Monteverdi's music, the characters are not literally human beings in whose doings we can literally believe; they are symbolically human and convey in that way more of the concentrated essence of human experience than any realistic portrait. It is on this deeper level that we find *Orfeo* so human and so credible. It has the quintessential humanity in which genius deals.

JANET E. BEAT

Monteverdi and the Opera Orchestra
of his time

Of the seven full-length operas that Monteverdi seems to have written between 1607 and 1642 the music of only three has survived. The score of the earliest work, *Orfeo* (1607), was published two years after the first performance. At this time such scores were not printed as performing copies but probably as tributes to patrons recording great occasions. This accounts for the fact that most of the directions for the instruments in *Orfeo*[1] are given in the past tense. The score names a vast number of instruments, most of which are listed in the previous chapter.[2]

In the Renaissance orchestra, which is the *ad hoc* type to which Monteverdi's large orchestra in *Orfeo* belongs, the instrumental timbres were used dramatically and had great symbolical significance for the audiences. Trombones and the bass members of the viol family were associated with infernal scenes; gods and allegorical or noble figures were accompanied by lutes, viols, cornetts, recorders and harpsichords; pastoral scenes always included parts for wind instruments; and many other comparable effects were constantly used. For instance, both celestial and infernal spirits appear in the same scene during the sixth *intermezzo* to *La Pellegrina* (1589), so they are musically defined by each having a separate group of accompanying instruments: the celestial spirits are accompanied by harps, citterns and viols, the infernal spirits by viols, a *lira* and trombones.[3]

[1] *Tutte le Opere*, XI. [2] Cf. *supra*, pp. 258–9.

[3] Cf. D. P. Walker, ed., *Musique des intermèdes de 'La Pellegrina'* (Paris, 1963), pp. li–lii, and R. L. Weaver, 'Sixteenth century instrumentation', *Musical Quarterly*, XLVII (1961), p. 363.

On examining the score of *Orfeo*, it will be seen that the instrumentation is heavily influenced by these traditions. This is particularly true of Act III, where fortunately a great many details concerning the orchestration are given. As the scene is set on the shores of the Styx, it is not surprising to find references to the regals and trombones. The act is built up in the following way:

(*i*) a dialogue between Orpheus and Hope which is accompanied by the *basso continuo* — no instruments specified.

(*ii*) Charon challenges Orpheus, to the sound of a regal.

(*iii*) a sinfonia in five parts — no instruments specified.

(*iv*) Orpheus sings his entreaty, 'Possente spirto', whose first four verses are each accompanied by a continuo group of a chitarrone and an organ with wooden pipes but with differing obbligato instruments: two violins, two cornetts, a double harp, and two violins and a cello (*basso da brazzo*), respectively.

(*v*) Orpheus continues his song for two more verses in arioso accompanied by three violins and a double-bass viol.

(*vi*) a dialogue between Charon and Orpheus — continuo instruments not specified.

(*vii*) Charon falls asleep to the sounds of sinfonia *iii* repeated 'very softly' by an organ with wooden pipes, violins and a double-bass viol.

(*viii*) Orpheus crosses the Styx to the sounds of the organ with wooden pipes.

(*ix*) a seven-part sinfonia — no instruments specified.

(*x*) a chorus of spirits accompanied by a regal, an organ with wooden pipes, five trombones, two bass *viole da gamba* and a double-bass viol.

(*xi*) sinfonia *ix* is repeated — no instruments specified.

As well as this typical chthonian instrumentation, the opera also includes passages scored in the pastoral tradition. On two occasions Monteverdi gives us details. The chorus 'Lasciate i monti' in Act I is accompanied by a string ensemble, three chitarroni, a double harp, two harpsichords and a sopranino recorder; and a ritornello which is played behind the scenes during the shepherds' duet 'In questo prato' in Act II is scored for two chitarroni and two recorders.

There are other links with the *intermezzo* too. The fact that instruments played behind the scenes is important. This was the usual practice in the Renaissance, but in the later public operas the orchestra was moved to a position in front of the stage. There is also the toccata to be considered. It is the first of the 26 orchestral pieces in *Orfeo*. (The number of such pieces was drastically reduced in his later works.) All the instruments play a conventional flourish three times on a chord of C major. The names given to the four upper parts — *clarino, quinta, alto e basso, vulgano* — are similar to those in general use during the seventeenth century to denote the register of the trumpet parts, as the players specialized in expertly controlling only certain areas of the complete range of the instrument. The *clarino* trumpeter always played the highest part; thus the other three *trombe* mentioned in the list at the beginning of the score must have played the lower ones.[1] Which instrument played the lowest part of all, marked *basso*? Caldwell Titcomb has provided an answer. 'This *basso* part was clearly designed for kettledrums; the drums were so much taken for granted where trumpets were involved that they did not even have to be included in the list of instruments. The kettledrummer may have rolled throughout on the note c; but if he was any good, he enlivened his part rhythmically, as did probably the fourth trumpeter too.'[2] How can we interpret *trombe con sordini*? It can only mean muted trumpets. This particular tone-colour was popular, as Wolfgang Osthoff has pointed out.[3] He has also drawn attention to the fact that the reduced volume of sound produced by muted trumpets was most appropriate for *Orfeo*: the room used for it by the Accademia degli Invaghiti was small, since the performance was a private one.[4]

[1] The word *clarino* properly refers to the top of the trumpet's range and not to the instrument itself, although it is often used in this context.

[2] Caldwell Titcomb, 'Baroque court and military Trumpets and Kettledrums: technique and music', *Galpin Society Journal*, IX (1956), p. 69.

[3] Wolfgang Osthoff, 'Trombe sordine', *Archiv für Musikwissenschaft*, XIII (1956), p. 77.

[4] Ibid., p. 80.

When mutes were used the pitch of the instruments was raised a tone.[1] Presumably the *clarino* was pitched a tone higher than the *trombe*, as it was apparently unmuted. The court and military trumpet was at this time usually pitched in D, though sometimes with a crook it was lowered to C.[2] It appears, therefore, that all the instruments had to play the toccata in D major to accommodate the muted trumpets. Finally, it was the custom to play fanfares three times. A contemporary description of Guarini's comedy *L'Idropica* (1608) says that, after the trumpets had sounded a fanfare for the third time, the curtain opened.[3]

The harpsichords, organs, lutes and harp in *Orfeo* are all continuo instruments. Agostino Agazzari's *Del sonare sopra'l basso con tutti li stromenti e dell'uso loro nel conserto* (1607) is one of the more important of the early instrumental methods to be printed. In it he divides instruments into two classes: those which interpret the *basso continuo* as a foundation, and those which interpret it in an ornamental manner. He writes: 'As foundation there are those which guide and sustain the entire body of the voices and instruments . . ., such as the Organ, Gravicembalo, etc., and similarly, in the case of a few or single voices, the Lute, Theorbo, Harp. etc.'[4] Later on he adds: 'As ornamentation are those which disport themselves (*scherzando*), and play counterpoints (*contrapontegiando*), and thus make the harmony more agreeable and sonorous; such are the Lute, Theorbo, Harp, Lirone, Cither, Spinet, Chitarrina, Violin, Pandora, and the like'.[5]

He also gives the players the following advice: 'when one plays an instrument which serves as foundation, one must play with great judgement . . . playing the work as simply and correctly as possible, and not with many florid passages or runs'.[6] About an 'ornament' instrument he says: 'therefore, whoever plays the

[1] Cf. J. E. Altenburg, *Versuch einer Anleitung zur heroisch-musikalischen Trompeter-und Pauker-Kunst* (Halle, 1795), p. 86.

[2] Cf. Titcomb, op. cit., p. 66.

[3] Cf. J. A. Westrup, 'Monteverdi and the orchestra', *Music & Letters*, XXI (1940), p. 238.

[4] Translated in F. T. Arnold, *The Art of Accompaniment from a Thorough-Bass as practised in the XVIIth and XVIIIth centuries*, 2nd ed. (London, 1965), p. 68.

[5] Loc. cit.   [6] Ibid., p. 70.

Lute, . . . must play nobly, with much invention and variety, and not as some do who, because they have a facile hand, do nothing but play runs and diminutions from beginning to end, especially in the company of other instruments which do the same, when nothing is heard but chaos (*zuppa*) and confusion, displeasing and offensive to the listener'.[1]

The instrumentation was changed to suit the mood of the words, so a variety of tone-colours was heard during passages written for the continuo. In the preface to Cavalieri's *Rappresentazione di Anima e di Corpo* (1600) is written 'Signor Emilio [Cavalieri] would commend a change of instruments in conformity with the sentiment of the person reciting'.[2] This often happens in *Orfeo* when certain instruments are specified during passages of *basso continuo* accompaniment.

Unfortunately a gap of over 30 years separates *Orfeo* from the next two Monteverdi operas which have survived — *Il Ritorno d'Ulisse in Patria* (1640) and *L'Incoronazione di Poppea* (1642).[3] The manuscripts contain little orchestral music and bear no instrumental specifications. Obviously we cannot apply the instrumentation used in the earlier work to the later ones written at the end of his life: we must also remember that the one was written for a Renaissance academy and the others for a public opera-house.

As the years passed Monteverdi seemed to rely more and more upon the violin family. The *Ballo delle Ingrate* (1608) is scored for a string ensemble (*cinque viole da brazzo*), as is *Il Combattimento di Tancredi e Clorinda* (1624) for which he specifies an ensemble of violin, viola, cello, a double-bass viol and a harpsichord (*quattro viole da brazzo, Soprano, Alto, Tenore et Basso, et contrabasso da Gamba, che continuerà con il Clavicembano.*)[4] There are also the madrigals in Books VII (1619) and VIII (1638) which have instrumental accompaniments, mainly for two violins. However, there are more elaborate exceptions. For example, '*A quest'olmo*' (Book VII) uses violins and recorders or transverse flutes (*flauti o*

[1] Ibid., p. 72.   [2] Ibid., p. 47.

[3] *Tutte le Opere*, XII and XIII. On the date 1640 cf. Osthoff, 'Zur Bologneser Aufführung von Monteverdis "Ritorno d'Ulisse" in Jahre 1640', *Oesterreichische Akademie der Wissenschaften: Anzeiger der Phil.-hist. Klasse*, XCV (1958).

[4] *Tutte le Opere*, VIII, pp. 314 and 132, respectively.

fifare).[1] *Con che soavità* from the same book is accompanied by three instrumental groups: the first consists of continuo instruments only — two chitarroni, a harpsichord and a spinet; the second of two violins, a viola and a harpsichord; the third of a viola and a cello (or two viols) and a *contrabasso* with an unspecified continuo instrument.[2] *Altri canti d'amor* (Book VIII) uses a group of violins and viols.[3] Such scoring is in keeping with the obviously increasing vogue for string orchestras. For instance, Francesca Caccini's *La Liberazione di Ruggiero dall'isola d'Alcina* (1625) has a chorus accompanied by five viols, an *archiviolata lira*, an organ with wooden pipes, and harpsichords; Michelangelo Rossi's *Erminia sul Giordano* (1637) specifies four violins and *basso continuo*; and a serenata by Cesti for the birth of Cosimo de'Medici (1642) has an orchestra of six violins, four alto, four tenor and four bass viols, a double-bass viol, a large harpsichord and a small one, a theorbo and a chitarrone.[4]

The few directions to the string players that Monteverdi had printed in his scores must be mentioned, too. No doubt the techniques he demands were well-known before they were published: they are exceptional only in that they were printed at all. In *Altri canti d'amor* he asks that the violins play with 'long and sweet bows' (*Viole sole toccate con arcate lunghe e soavi*), but it is the *Combattimento* which is in this respect most famous, for its requests for pizzicato and a measured 'tremolando'. Monteverdi directs his string players to lay down their bows and pluck the strings with two fingers (*Qui si lascia l'arco, e si strappano le corde con duoi diti*). The tremolando is quite different from the one we use today. In the preface to the complete madrigal book he explains that he considered one semibreve to equal a spondaic beat (used for slow, stately dances) and that sixteen semiquavers struck rapidly in succession equalled a pyrrhic measure (used for lively and warlike dances). It appears that the musicians in 1624

---

[1] *Tutte le Opere*, VII, p. 14; '*fifara*' in the score, but two were intended.

[2] Ibid., p. 137; cf. *supra*, pp. 196–7.

[3] *Tutte le Opere*, VIII, p. 2; cf. *supra*, pp. 240–3.

[4] Cf. Weaver, 'The Orchestra in early Italian Opera', *Journal of the American Musicological Society*, XVII (1964), p. 83.

misunderstood his novel textures and did not care for his pyrrhic measures, for he adds that particularly those who played the *basso continuo* reduced his string of repeated semiquavers to a single semibreve, thus destroying the intended resemblance to agitated speech.[1]

To be able to interpret the instrumentation of Monteverdi's last operas it is not sufficient merely to study these shorter works: we must examine the wider Venetian scene in more detail. The evidence contained in various paybooks suggests that the orchestra at St. Mark's followed the general trend towards the use of string and brass instruments. Two significant facts can be adduced, though the exact sequence of this trend cannot be traced, since unfortunately the ensemble was put on the general payroll shortly after Monteverdi's arrival in Venice and the names of the instruments played by the various musicians disappear from the documents. In the first place, eleven years before Monteverdi's induction as *maestro di cappella*, we learn that St. Mark's was using the typical Renaissance ensemble, with a predominance of trombones, *cornetti* and woodwind.[2] Secondly, of the seventeen players listed in the paybook in December 1642, those whose instruments also can be identified were string players.[3] This general tendency is borne out by the instructions for performing Monteverdi's church music given in his *Selva morale* of 1640; but there can be no doubt that the versatility of the strings was the most useful asset for the kind of concertato music he was writing.

The size and constitution of the Venetian opera orchestra in the seventeenth century is a more controversial topic. This is not surprising, as the sources of information that have come down to us are tantalizingly sketchy. The scores themselves contain very little orchestral detail. Nevertheless, by studying the 112 manuscripts contained in the Contarini Codices,[4] some useful con-

---

[1] Cf. also *supra*, pp. 237 and 249.

[2] Cf. Denis Arnold, 'Towards a Biography of Giovanni Gabrieli', *Musica Disciplina*, XV (1961), pp. 204–5.

[3] Cf. Archivio di Stato, Venice: Procuratia de Supra, Registro 12 (Cassier Chiesa 1639–45), entry for 23 December 1642.

[4] These manuscripts, in the Biblioteca Nazionale Marciana, Venice, contain the music of operas produced between 1639 and 1692.

clusions can be drawn, in conjunction with facts that can be deduced from archival records.

Henry Prunières mentions that there was an orchestra of sixteen for the 1637 Venetian operatic season presented by the Manelli-Ferrari troupe (twelve string players, two trumpeters and two harpsichordists),[1] and an illustration of the Grimano Theatre in the middle of the century shows an orchestra of twelve.[2] This latter example may not be an accurate record of the instrumentalists, as the drawing is executed in a rather mannered style. The instruments depicted are a chitarrone, a harpsichord, various members of the violin family and possibly two trumpets.

Further evidence has been found in the Venetian State Archives by Denis Arnold.[3] A small account-book belonging to the impresario Marco Faustini which covers the 1658-9 operatic season at the S. Cassiano Theatre, contains an entry dealing with the fees of the instrumentalists. Only nine payments — including one to the tuner — are recorded for each of the 24 performances:

Violin	17 lire
D.Gio: Battista	18 lire, 12 soldi
Secondo Violin	12 lire
Tomini	12 lire
D.Lorenzo Violin	10 lire
Violetta	4 lire, 13 soldi
Theorbo from Padua	14 lire
The Priest who plays the Theorbo	13 lire
The Tuner	4 lire, 13 soldi

Total 105 lire, 15 soldi ($= c.$ 15 ducats)

Another list, dated 1665, is also printed by Arnold. It records ten payments:

[1] Cf. Henry Prunières, *Cavalli et l'Opéra Vénitien au XVIIe siècle* (Paris, 1931), p. 17.

[2] *Musica*, II (Florence, 1943), pl. XXII.

[3] Cf. Denis Arnold, ' "L'Incoronazione di Poppea" and its orchestral requirements', *Musical Times*, CIV (1963), p. 176.

To Sig. Antonio first keyboard instrument	24 lire, 16 soldi
To the second keyboard instrument	10 lire
To Sigra Prudenza third keyboard instrument	10 lire
Sig. Carlo Savion	15 lire
To the first violin, Sig. Rimondo	18 lire, 12 soldi
Sig. Domenico, second violin	14 lire
To Sig. Marco, Viola da brazzo	12 lire
To Ruzzier, Violetta	4 lire
To the first theorbo	18 lire, 12 soldi
To the second theorbo	11 lire

Total   138 lire

This entry also includes payments made to some soldiers. Why they were engaged is not entered. Could they have been musicians too? Perhaps they were used to provide brass and percussion fanfares, as the scores often contain directions such as *Chiamata de la magica tromba* in Cavalli's *La Rosinda* (1651) and *Tocco di tamburri* in his *Veramonda, l'Amazzone di Aragona* (1652).[1]

The orchestras represented in these lists are small, and the second one in particular is heavily weighted with continuo instruments. As Arnold points out, the fees mentioned may be only the payments due to the principals in the orchestra, and further expenditure on instrumentalists may be hidden among other items, such as the entry for the soldiers.[2] References to larger orchestras are known, such as the one described in the *Mercure galant* which played during a performance of Carlo Pallavicino's *Il Nerone* in 1679. It is reported that 40 instruments were present: recorders (*flûtes douces*), trumpets, drums, viols and violins.[3]

Nevertheless, it seems from this evidence that in the mid-seventeenth century a small rather than a large orchestra was employed. This theory is upheld by remarks passed by visitors to Venice. 'The Symphony (i.e. the orchestra) is much smaller than

[1] *Veramonda* is entered under the wrong title, *Il Delio*, in the old Marciana catalogue.
[2] Cf. Denis Arnold, op. cit., p. 177.
[3] *Le nouveau mercure galant, contenant tout ce qui s'est passé de curieux au mois de avril de l'année 1679* (Paris, 1679), pp. 66–7 and 71.

at Paris; but it is never the worse for that . . .'[1] 'The symphony
(i.e. orchestra) is of little importance, inspiring melancholy rather
than gaiety. It is composed of lutes, theorbos and harpsichords
which accompany the voices with marvellous exactness.'[2] The
dimensions of the orchestra pit must also have influenced the
number of instrumentalists employed. Was that of the S. Giovanni
Crisostomo Theatre, where *Il Nerone* was performed, larger than
those of the S. Cassiano and SS. Giovanni e Paolo theatres, where
many of the most splendid operatic ventures were staged?
Giovanni Battista Doni in his *Trattato della musica scenica* (written
about 1635) complains that in rehearsal 'the pains, the disgusts,
the anxieties and the griefs that the poor musicians feel in arranging together so many players and sounds in so narrow a place,
would scarcely be believed. For, with much loss of time and
[much] confusion, they must arrange the instruments, distribute
the lamps, order the seats, erect the music stands, and tune the
instruments. And God knows if, after tuning them well, they
don't often have to do the whole thing again from the beginning,
because of the multiplicity of the strings and their slackening on
account of [the heat of] the lamps . . .'[3] It appears also that the
instrumentalists' fees were much smaller than those of the singers.
For instance, the total expenditure on the orchestra for the season
of 24 performances mentioned earlier was about 360 ducats,
whereas a prima donna received nearly 350 ducats. This evidence,
added to the fact that the early scores, on the whole, make few
demands, supports the idea that a small orchestra was normally
required.

The orchestration of the operas presents us with a problem too.
Besides the instruments mentioned in the previous paragraphs,
others are specified in the manuscripts themselves. The scores in
the Contarini Codices name violins, viols, organs, a harpsichord,
trumpets, flutes (or recorders), bassoons, drums and other percussion instruments. Composers and copyists do not seem to

[1] Maximilien Misson, *A New Voyage to Italy* (London, 1714), pp. 269–70.

[2] Limojon de St. Didier, *La Ville et la République de Venise* (Paris, 1680),
quoted from Prunières, op. cit., p. 61.

[3] Translated in Gloria Rose, 'Agazzari and the improvising orchestra',
Journal of the American Musicological Society, XVIII (1965), p. 390.

have followed many conventions when writing out the scores. While the solo vocal parts are given in full, the instrumental ones lack numerous details. A few scores do include certain pieces with the instrumental parts written out in full and specified: for example, the ritornello in Act I, scene 5 of the anonymous opera *Il Pio Enea* (1641) is marked *fagotti, regali*. Unfortunately the majority of the scores are not so generous with their information. The following details are to be found from time to time:

(*i*) instrumental parts written out, but no specifications given, e.g. the sinfonia to Act I of Cavalli's *Ormindo* (1644).

(*ii*) instrumental staves left either entirely or partially blank, e.g. the Venetian manuscript of Monteverdi's *L'Incoronazione di Poppea* and the manuscripts of operas by Pietro Andrea Ziani.

(*iii*) nothing except the *basso continuo* given, but with orchestral parts implied or at the most highly probable, e.g. Cavalli's *La Didone* (1641) bears the cryptic message 'Aria with all the instruments', but only the bass line is given.

(*iv*) instruments named but no music written for them, e.g. Giovanni Maria Pagliardi's *Numa Pompilio* (1674) asks for 'trumpets which sound'.

(*v*) *balli* named, but once again only the *basso continuo* or no music at all is given, e.g. Monteverdi's *Il Ritorno d'Ulisse* contains a *ballo* for eight Moors who perform a Greek dance while they sing, but no music is given.

The manuscripts mainly offer the last three methods listed.

The most frequently named instruments are the violins. Directions such as 'Aria with violins' and 'Lament with violins', which appear in Cavalli's *Giasone* (1649) and *La Statira* (1655) respectively, are not uncommon. Occasionally other members of the violin family are mentioned too. The manuscript of Cavalli's *Veramonda* has '*viola*' written against two staves in the final scene of Act III, and there is even a cello solo marked in Legrenzi's *Eteocle e Polinice* (1675). An aria in Act II, scene 5 is headed 'Aria with instruments and violoncello obbligato'. The score is written in four instrumental parts; the upper two staves are both marked 'violoncello' and the lowest one '*contrabasso*'; the third part, being figured, must be for the continuo.

The word '*viole*' occurs frequently too. It was used in the 1600's as a generic term for all members of the bowed-string family, and so it cannot be translated with any certainty when it appears in the scores. The only instrumental specification to be given in the manuscript of Cavalli's *Le Nozze de Teti e di Peleo* (1639) is the *Sinfonia di viole* in Act II. Peleus has asked for some sublime music to assuage the pangs of love, and this sinfonia is played in answer to his request. Was this piece played by an ensemble of viols or by one dominated by violas? Both answers are possible, particularly as the gentle sounds of the viols and the rich, dark tones of the violas are equally suited to the occasion:

Ex. I

* There are some partially and wholly blank bars in this piece.

Viols were kept in the Venetian opera orchestra for many years. Although they were ousted from the treble regions of the ensemble by the violins, they were retained as tenor and bass instruments. References to viols still occur in scores written in the 1670's. For example, they were used in Petronio Franceschini's *Arsinoe* (1677) and in Pallavicino's *Il Nerone* (1679). The *violone* (bass viol) was used for many years as the bass of the string ensemble. A single reference to *violoni* can be found in the manuscript of Giovanni Antonio Boretti's *Eliogabalo* (1668),[1] but it appears, from a letter written by Thomas Hill in 1657, that the double-bass was a more popular orchestral instrument: 'the organ and violin they are masters of, but the bass viol they have not at all in use and to supply its place they have the bass violin with four strings, and use it as we do the viol'.[2]

Trumpets appear to have been popular too, judging from the many references made to them. This is not surprising, as the librettos provide many opportunities for battle and ceremonial scenes. The ringing, brilliant sounds of the trumpets are the traditional musical symbol for the passions and sentiments expressed in such situations. A few examples will suffice to show the fashion for fanfare-like pieces. Act III of Giovanni Domenico Partenio's *Genserico* (1669) is opened by a 'sinfonia with trumpets'; Cavalli's *Ercole Amante* (Paris, 1662) has trumpets named three times for instrumental pieces, and, as already mentioned, there is the part for the 'magic trumpet' in his *La Rosinda*. This last piece has only the bass line written in the manuscript.

Woodwind instruments are very rarely mentioned in the manuscripts dating from the middle of the century. In fact, most of the instrumental specifications occur in the later scores, which tend to be more detailed in every respect. The bassoons and regals in *Il Pio Enea* are only mentioned once for a passage following a *recitativo secco* in which the fury of the underworld spirits is described. Thus it can be seen that the symbolical scoring of the *intermezzi* was still regarded, by composers and audiences, as a valid mode of expression.

It is quite possible that extra instrumentalists were hired as the occasion demanded. The score of Cesti's *Il Pomo d'oro*, written for production in Vienna in 1667, names an impressive array of instruments — flutes, cornetts, trumpets, trombones, a bassoon, violins and viols (of every size), a harpsichord, a theorbo, an organ and a *graviorgano*.[3] Again the scoring is executed in the

---

[1] *Eliogabalo* is attributed to Cavalli in the old Marciana catalogue.

[2] W. H., A. F., and A. E. Hill, *A. Stradivari. His life and work (1644–1737)* (London, 1902), p. 110.

[3] Cesti, *Il Pomo d'oro*, ed. Guido Adler, *Denkmäler der Tonkunst in Österreich*, III², IV² (Vienna, 1896–7). '*Graviorgano*' could mean a positive organ.

intermezzo tradition. Act I, scene 1 is set in Pluto's kingdom, and so Proserpina's aria is accompanied by two cornetts, two trombones, and a continuo section of a trombone, a bassoon and a regal. This combination of instruments is similar to that used by Monteverdi in Acts III and IV of *Orfeo*. In scene 13 of the same act Cesti uses a *graviorgano* and a theorbo as Juno appears to Paris. This is surely a deliberate attempt to use the traditional instrumentation associated with the deities and the nobility. The whole scene is archaic in manner so as to produce a very solemn atmosphere. Two other examples also bear an affinity with Monteverdi's opera. The trumpet fanfares which herald the arrival of Pallas Athene in Act II, scene 13 are reminiscent of the toccata in *Orfeo*, and the gentle music played by the viols and *graviorgano* as Oenone falls asleep in Act IV, scene 1 is akin to that played for Charon as he too falls asleep in Act III of the earlier work.

Scoring in this fashion could also be applied to Cavalli's *Le Nozze di Teti*. The manuscript contains eleven independent pieces for the orchestra, including the *balli*, although during the arias and choruses only the *basso continuo* is given for the most part. Nevertheless, the orchestra plays an important descriptive role in this work. How many extra musicians were employed for its performance? Hugo Goldschmidt goes so far as to claim that horns as well as trumpets and drums were played during the horsemen's chorus in Act I, scene 4;[1] there are no positive specifications given in the Venetian manuscript, though the nature of the instrumental parts suggests that these instruments could well have been used. If this were so, then surely horns would have been used for the *Chiamata alla Caccia* in Act I, scene 2 as well. (Only helical horns could have performed this piece in 1639, as R. Morley-Pegge has explained.)[2] All this is purely supposition. Two important points must be borne in mind: that as the years passed, the number of descriptive sinfonias declined, their place being taken by elaborate scenic effects; that these two particular operas were both especially festive pieces and that therefore it is reason-

---

[1] Cf. Hugo Goldschmidt, 'Das Orchester der italienischen Oper im 17. Jahrhundert', *Sammelbände der Internationalen Musikgesellschaft*, II (1900), p. 16.

[2] Cf. R. Morley-Pegge, *The French Horn* (London, 1960), pp. 82–4.

able to assume that funds more substantial than usual were allocated to them.

Less extravagant orchestras, indeed, seem to have been the norm, with possibly a few extra wind players hired for crowd scenes. Perhaps Faustini's soldiers come into this category. It is highly probable that musicians appeared on the stage, or at least performed in the wings. For example, in Pagliardi's *Numa Pompilio* there is a three-part ritornello marked 'trombe'. Underneath the music is written 'people with trumpets'; it is feasible, therefore, to suppose that this piece was actually performed by musicians on the stage. The same could be said of Act I, scene 1 in Cesti's *Argia* (1667), where the following direction appears: 'the boat fires three times, and trumpets and drums sound'. The instruments play before and after the chorus 'A terra', and so the trumpeters and drummers could have been on the stage mingling with the singers. Giovanni Domenico Freschi's *Berenice Vendicata* (1680) furnishes us with a most tantalizing description of a processional scene. Unfortunately, only the bass line, or else no music at all, is given for the instruments. This triumphal procession takes place near the beginning of Act I, and it is headed 'Chorus of trumpets'. As some simple percussion instruments are named, I feel that the singers could have played them. The instruments, mentioned in the following list from the manuscript, could have been played on the stage, thus making this a most spectacular scene:

- (*i*) Chorus of trumpets while the procession passes: only the bass line is given.
- (*ii*) Six drums: the rhythm ♩ ♫♫ ♫ | ♫♫ ♫♫ ♫, etc. is given.
- (*iii*) When the procession passes: no music is given.
- (*iv*) Chorus of the Long Trumpets: no music is given.
- (*v*) Chorus of the Tenor and/or Bass Recorders (*flauti grandi*): no music is given.
- (*vi*) Six sticks (*bastoni*), probably similar to claves: no music is given.
- (*vii*) Chorus of the Sopranino Recorders (*flautini*): no music is given.

(*viii*) Chorus of the Cymbals (*cembali*): no music is given.

Finally, music was sometimes played behind the scenes, as is suggested by the direction 'Chorus of the Huntsmen within' in Cavalli's *Il Ciro* (1665). Many of the frequent trumpet fanfares in these operas could have been played in the wings too.

The only remaining section of the orchestra to be discussed is that which constituted the *basso continuo*. The number of players in the continuo section seems to have been fairly large, as the orchestral and orchestration lists show. It seems to be significant that St. Didier named only the continuo instruments. They must have made a great impression on him, especially as he comments upon their disciplined playing. On the other hand, he could have been a little bored by the lack of a good, solid violin texture such as he would have heard in his native France. There seem to have been at least two keyboard instruments used in every orchestra: one for the recitatives, and the other for the orchestral items. The second of the Faustini lists quoted above records payments to three keyboard players. Perhaps the third musician was an organist. Organs are sometimes mentioned in the manuscripts: an *organo* played in the prologue to the anonymous opera *Il Germondo* (1666) and in that to Freschi's *Olimpia Vendicata* (1682) as well. We must not forget the regals in *Il Pio Enea*, nor the *graviorgano*, regal and organ in *Il Pomo d'oro*.

The various members of the lute family were still retained in the orchestra. Of these, the theorbo appears to have been the most popular. Two manuscripts, those of Boretti's *Eliogabalo* and Legrenzi's *Eteocle e Polinice*, specify a *tiorba*. In the latter work the theorbo part is written out in full: it is in the nature of an obbligato and has imitative passages with a cello. This instrument was not always so popular with the audiences 'because the necks of the orchestral theorbos always hide many things from sight' (*parceque . . . le Manche des Theorbes de l'orchestre cache toujours quelques chose de la veüe*).[1]

The harp is the only instrument which is mentioned neither in

[1] *Le nouveau mercure galant*, etc. (Paris, 1683), quoted in Simon Towneley Worsthorne, *Venetian Opera in the seventeenth century* (Oxford, 1954), p. 98.

the manuscripts nor in contemporary writings in connection with the public operas. It was an expensive instrument and was usually to be found in association with private music-making. Writing about the use of the double harp earlier in the century, Nigel Fortune has speculated that it 'was an expensive, aristocratic instrument, the favourite of the cultured few'. It appears on the title-pages of more than a dozen monody-books written by aristocratic dilettanti, and the professional composers, such as Monteverdi and Lorenzo Allegri, who recommended its use in other music worked in these aristocratic circles.[1]

During rehearsal the co-ordination of so many improvising musicians must have created a considerable problem. One wonders if all the orchestras played with such finesse as the one that St. Didier heard. Monteverdi remarks that it took five months of intensive rehearsal to present his *Arianna* (1608),[2] but I doubt whether the opera-house managers would have allowed such an extravagant use of time. Of course, if the same players were employed regularly the problem of ensemble would not have been so acute. The composer usually directed the rehearsals, and so presumably he would have indicated the most suitable places for ornamentation and would also have assigned specified roles to each of the continuo players.

Besides working from figured and unfigured basses, *intavolature* were used. These were short scores made by the players themselves. Doni grumbles: '... to say nothing of the trouble and time it takes to make so many copies of the tablature of the bass...'[3] Knowing this, we may suppose that the curious passages in Luigi Rossi's *Il Palazzo incantato* (1642) which interrupt Prasildo's recitative in Act I, scene 12 must be *intavolature*.[4] The first passage is marked 'Here all the instruments play' (see Ex. 2). Surely these cannot be merely chordal interruptions by the *basso continuo* alone, as the players would not have needed fully-realized harmonies to be written out. The chords must represent a sequence

[1] Cf. Nigel Fortune, 'Continuo Instruments in Italian Monodies', *Galpin Society Journal*, VI (1953), pp. 12–13.

[2] Cf. *supra*, pp. 47 and 49–50.

[3] Translated in Rose, loc. cit.

[4] Luigi Rossi, *Il Palazzo incantato*, Royal College of Music, London, MS. 546.

of harmonies upon which the players of Agazzari's 'instruments of ornament' improvised melodies. Similar passages, though with just the bass line given, are to be found in Monteverdi's *Il Ritorno d'Ulisse*. The first passage, in Act I, scene 1, is preceded by the in-

Ex. 2

structions: 'you repeat this sinfonia many times until Penelope arrives on the stage' (*Questa sinfonia si replica tante volte insino che Penelope arriva in scena*). The second one follows in scene 4; it is headed 'Here departs the boat of the Phaeacians, who escort the sleeping Ulysses, and in order not to wake him you play the following sinfonia gently always upon one chord' (*Qui esce la Barca de'Feaci chi conduce Ulisse che dorme e perchè non si desti si fa la seguente sinfonia toccata soavamente sempre su una corda*) (see Ex. 4*b*).

A study of the scores written during the 1640's and 1650's shows that the composers demanded little from their orchestras. Even the small number of descriptive sinfonias needed only a string band to perform them. Composers tended to rely upon descriptive phrases rather than upon a multi-coloured orchestra to achieve their effects. The most popular orchestral pieces were those which accompanied battle-scenes. Monteverdi's novel textures in the *Combattimento* had many imitators. Two good examples can be found in Cavalli's *La Didone*. They are called '*Combattimento*' and '*Passata dell'Armata*'. Nevertheless, Monteverdi provides us with the most effective fight scene in the operatic field. In Act II, scene 12 of *Il Ritorno d'Ulisse*, Ulysses puts the smarmy Irus to flight. The duel is accompanied by sturdy violin parts which stride up and down, mainly on the chord of G major. During the final bars Irus's voice enters whining 'Son vinto' ('I am vanquished'), and the episode dramatically fades away into *recitativo secco*. This is in Monteverdi's best *stile concitato* vein (see Ex. 3).

Maritime scenes were popular too. Cavalli wrote a *Sinfonia*

Ex. 3

Navale in Act II, scene 5 of *La Didone*. This provides us with a
clue to the way in which we may interpret the improvised sinfonia
in Act I, scene 4, of Monteverdi's *Il Ritorno d'Ulisse* mentioned
above. The *Sinfonia Navale* is in an undulating barcarolle rhythm

which is played by the strings over a pedal E in the bass. The other sinfonia was probably performed in a similar manner, particularly as the composer directed that only one chord was to be used:

Exx. 4*a* and 4*b*

Qui esce la barca de' Feaci che conduce Ulisse che dorme, e perchè non si desti si fa la seguente sinfonia toccata soavemente sempre su una corda.

* Sinfonia

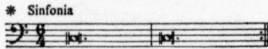

* The time signature is given as **C** in *Tutte le opere*, XII, p. 36.

Conversely we may look to Monteverdi for a solution to the instrumentation for the *Concilio Infernale* in Act I of Cavalli's *Le Nozze di Teti*. The G minor sinfonia which follows Orpheus's plea 'Rendetemi il mio ben, tartarei numi' in Act III of *Orfeo* is written for strings and an organ with wooden pipes. Identical instrumentation would be effective in the *Concilio Infernale* too, particularly as in both examples only the middle and lowest registers of the instruments are used, thus producing a rich, dark sound. It would also be possible to use a regal instead of the organ with wooden pipes, as in the underworld ritornello in *Il Pio Enea*:

Exx. *5a* and *5b*

Concilio Infernale

Sinfonia

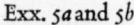

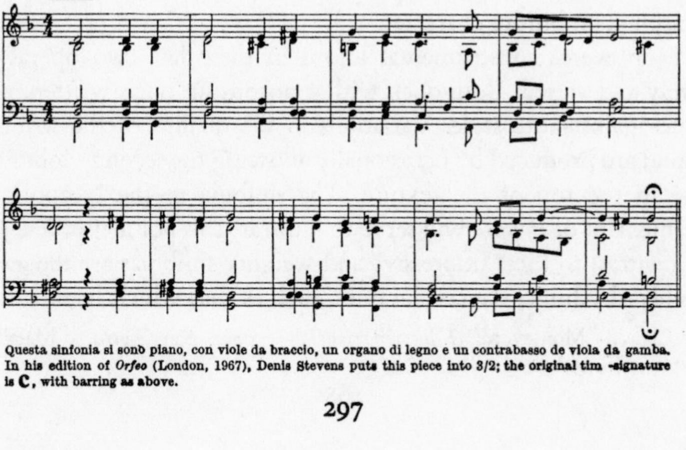

Questa sinfonia si sonò piano, con viole da braccio, un organo di legno e un contrabasso de viola da gamba. In his edition of *Orfeo* (London, 1967), Denis Stevens puts this piece into 3/2; the original tim -signature is C, with barring as above.

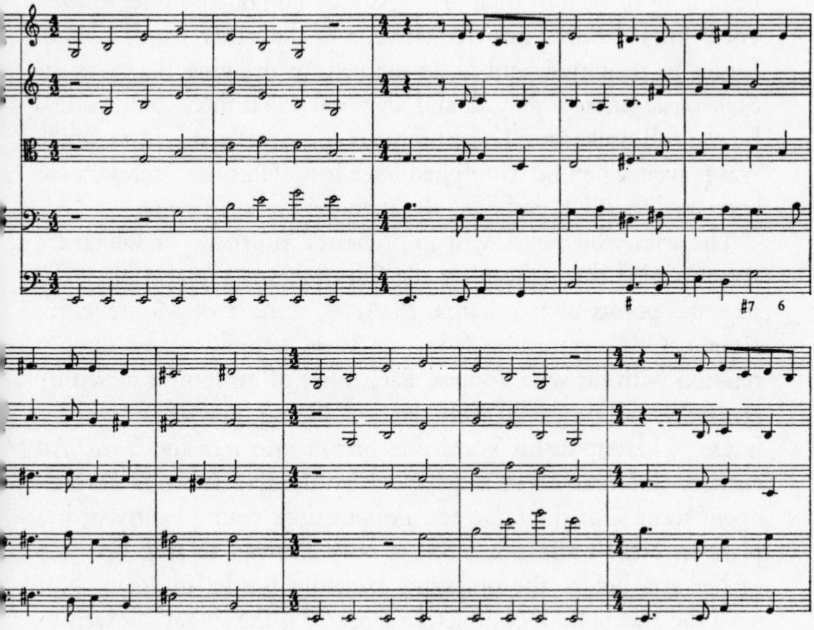

As the orchestra was used so little, this tended to increase the dramatic tension in the scenes in which it did play. Monteverdi handled his orchestra with great skill in Act II, scene 12 in *Il Ritorno d'Ulisse*. It is in this scene that Penelope tests the suitors with her husband's bow. All the suitors start with great confidence. This is expressed musically by the sinfonia which is played at the beginning of each of their arias. As they fail, one by one, so their vocal lines dissolve into recitative. On the other hand, Ulysses begins in recitative, and as he succeeds in drawing the bow the *Sinfonia da guerra* is played, and his vocal line is then accompanied by the full orchestra. This sinfonia is the same as the *Lotta* which was played when he triumphed over Irus. Thus the orchestra has been used to link together all the action in this long scene.

The arias which end with an orchestral ritornello or which are accompanied throughout by the full orchestra are also placed at strategic points in the drama. In Act I, scene 1 of Monteverdi's *Poppea*, Otho, returning from the wars, happily muses upon a reunion with his wife Poppea. Each verse of his song is closed by an orchestral ritornello until he sees Nero's guards outside his house, whereupon his vocal line breaks into *recitativo secco*. An entirely different effect is achieved by the gay ritornello which opens scene 4 of the same act. Poppea sings triumphantly of her place in Nero's affections. She is only allowed to sing one line of her aria before the orchestra excitedly bustles in again. Not until the ritornello is completely repeated is the singer allowed to continue. This simple technique brilliantly sums up Poppea's grasping, ambitious character.

Monteverdi's instrumental idiom in these last two operas is lively and varied. Both open with sonorous sinfonias written in a note-against-note style. Variations in the quality of the strings' sound are produced by occasionally allowing the second violins to rise to the top of the texture. The sinfonia in the Neapolitan manuscript of *Poppea* will serve to illustrate this point[1] (see Ex. 6). In contrast to these impressive and weighty sinfonias are the gay, highly rhythmic, dance-like ones, such as that which heralds the

[1] Claudio Monteverdi, *L'Incoronazione di Poppea*, San Pietro a Maiella, Naples, MS. 49A.2.7.

Ex. 6

arrival of Minerva dressed as a shepherdess, in Act I, scene 8 in *Il Ritorno d' Ulisse*. Yet another is to be found in Poppea's coronation scene (Ex. 7). It would not be out of place to introduce

Ex. 7

trumpets here. Most of the music written on the upper two staves can be played on the open notes of trumpets in B flat. The other notes involved — the submediant and the leading-note — do not belong to the harmonic series of the natural instrument, though they were sometimes included in trumpet music. The baroque trumpeter could have played them, but the intonation would have been slightly suspect. Praetorius states that the trumpeter should learn to 'tame and rule' his instrument 'well and through artifice'.[1] All the notes could have been played quite easily on *trombe da tirarsi* (slide trumpets). C. S. Terry mentions that a specimen of a slide trumpet dated 1651 is to be found at the Berlin Hochschule für Musik.[2] There may be other places where it would be possible to introduce trumpets too. Osthoff suggests that some of Otho's sinfonias in Act I should be played on muted trumpets.[3]

Monteverdi also uses the orchestra to help with the formal structure of the acts. As in *Orfeo*, so in these later works some of the sinfonias and ritornellos recur. I have already drawn attention to the repetition of sinfonias in Act II of *Il Ritorno d'Ulisse*, and there are other examples in this work. The opening sinfonia is played three times: twice during the prologue and once in Act I; and the ritornello which ends Penelope's aria 'Torna il tranquillo mare' in Act I, scene 1 re-appears in the following scene. Similar examples can be seen in *Poppea*: for instance, the ritornello at the end of the prologue is repeated in the opening scene of Act I. But the most important role given to the orchestra occurs in Act I, scene 11. Here, in an impassioned duologue, Otho reproaches Poppea for her infidelity, and she replies with an announcement of her intention to leave him. The scene is opened by a sinfonia which is repeated between each verse. It is transposed for Poppea's verses and for its final appearance too, after which the singers end angrily in *recitativo secco*. The recitative makes an even more dramatic effect than usual due to the extended part for the orchestra throughout this episode.

Even though the orchestra's role in the mid-seventeenth century was small, it was nevertheless an important one. Out of the 37 scenes which were set to music and are contained in Malipiero's edition of *Poppea*, the orchestra plays in only fourteen. The Venetian manuscript of this work shows signs of being a much used copy. There are many directions and remarks written in Monteverdi's own hand, and so we may assume that this

[1] Michael Praetorius, *Syntagma Musicum*, II (Wolfenbüttel, 1619), p. 32.
[2] Cf. C. S. Terry, *Bach's Orchestra*, rev. ed. (London, 1958), p. 31.
[3] Cf. Osthoff, op. cit., pp. 77–9 and 82.

manuscript is not a sketch which needs amplification but the real score which was used for performance. The many pages of *basso continuo* would have been divided among a varied group of instruments to produce a beguiling and delicate web of sound. This improvised accompaniment was admirably suited for following the intensely emotional and flexible declamation of the singers. A greater use of the full orchestra for accompaniments would have forced the vocal line into more rigid rhythmic patterns for the sake of gaining unanimity of performance from such a large body of musicians. This would have been against the very nature of music written according to the *seconda prattica*. Therefore it is not surprising to find that a small string orchestra sufficed to meet the majority of the needs of the composers. The few scores that demand large, multi-coloured orchestras are the exception rather than the rule and tend to belong to the years after Monteverdi's death. So powerful and subtle was his musical invention that he had no need for all the trappings of such a band.

V

Bibliography

BIBLIOGRAPHY

Compiled by Denis Arnold and Nigel Fortune

A complete bibliography of works dealing with Monteverdi would include virtually every history of music, most books on the various genres in which he composed and a great number of articles on many subsidiary themes. To reduce this vast literature to manageable proportions we have included only writings which add something new to Monteverdi's music, life or ambience, or are in some way significant for the historiography of the subject. Similarly in compiling the list of editions, no attempt has been made to include every individual edition of each madrigal or motet, or those included in anthologies; but important landmarks in the rehabilitation of his music have been mentioned, as have editions which are readily available. Arrangements of the music which falsify the original text have been omitted, except those of interest to the student of taste. Reprintings without substantial changes have also been ignored, as have manuscript versions of the various dramatic works.

SECTION A — EDITIONS

I. COLLECTED EDITIONS

Tutte le Opere di Claudio Monteverdi, ed. Gian Francesco Malipiero, I–XVI (Asolo, 1926–42); 2nd edition with revisions only in VIII, XV and XVI (Vienna, 1954 ff.); supplementary volume (Venice, 1966).

12 Composizioni vocali profane e sacre (inedite), ed. W. Osthoff (Milan, 1958).

II. Dramatic Music

L'Orfeo, ed. R. Eitner (Berlin, 1881).

—— ed. V. d'Indy (Paris, 1905).

—— ed. G. Orefice (Milan, 1910).

—— ed. G. F. Malipiero (London, 1923).

—— ed. C. Orff (Munich, 1923): 'freier deutscher Neugestaltung'; revised versions (Mainz, 1929, 1931 and 1940).

—— ed. A. Sandberger (Augsburg, 1927): a facsimile of the original edition of 1609.

—— ed. O. Respighi (Milan, 1935): 'realizzazione orchestrale'.

—— ed. G. Benvenuti (Milan, 1935): 'trascrizione ritmica, realizzazione e strumentazione'.

—— ed. G. Benvenuti (Milan, 1942).

—— ed. P. Hindemith (Vienna, 1954).

—— ed. A. Wenzinger (Kassel, 1955).

—— ed. D. Stevens (London, 1967).

—— ed. B. Maderna (Milan, 1967).

L'Arianna (the surviving Lament in its solo version).

—— ed. F. A. Gevaert (Paris, 1868).

—— ed. A. Solerti in *Gli Albori del Melodramma* (Milan, 1904).

—— ed. O. Respighi (Leipzig, 1910), 'armonizzato e orchestrato'.

—— ed. C. Orff (Mainz, 1931): 'in freier deutscher Neugestaltung'.

—— ed. C. Orff (Mainz, 1952): 'trascrizione libera'.

—— ed. H. J. Moser (Kassel, 1961): 'für Alt Solo, fünfstimmigen gemischten Chor, Cembalo und Basso continuo'.

—— ed. H. Bornefeld (Kassel, 1962).

Il Ballo delle Ingrate, ed. L. Torchi (Milan, 1907) in *L'Arte Musicale in Italia*, VI.

—— ed. C. Orff (Mainz, 1931): as *'Tanz der Spröden'*.

—— ed. A. Toni (Milan, 1932).

—— ed. D. Stevens (London, 1960).

Il Combattimento di Tancredi e Clorinda, ed. L. Torchi (Milan, 1907) in *L'Arte Musicale in Italia*, VI.

—— ed. A. Toni (Milan, 1921).

Bibliography

Il Combattimento di Tancredi e Clorinda, ed. G. F. Malipiero (London, 1931).

—— ed. G. F. Malipiero (London, 1954); translation by P. Pears.

—— ed. D. Stevens (London, 1962).

Ballo: Movete al mio bel suon, ed. D. Stevens (London, 1967).

Il Ritorno d'Ulisse in Patria, ed. R. Haas (Vienna, 1922) in *Denkmäler der Tonkunst in Österreich*, XXIX. Jahrg., 57 Bd.

—— ed. V. d'Indy (Paris, 1926): 'adaptation musicale'.

—— ed. L. Dallapiccola (Milan, 1942): 'trascrizione e riduzione per le scene moderne'.

—— extracts ed. J. A. Westrup (London, 1929).

L'Incoronazione di Poppea, ed. H. Goldschmidt (Leipzig, 1904) in *Studien zur Geschichte der italienischen Oper im 17. Jahrhundert*, II.

—— ed. V. d'Indy (Paris, 1908).

—— ed. C. van den Borren (Brussels, 1914).

—— ed. E. Krenek (Vienna, 1937).

—— ed. G. Benvenuti (Milan, 1937).

—— ed. G. Benvenuti (Milan, 1938): a facsimile of the Venetian manuscript.

—— ed. G. F. Ghedini (Milan, 1953).

—— ed. H. F. Redlich (Kassel, 1958).

—— ed. W. Goehr (Vienna, 1960).

—— extracts ed. J. A. Westrup (London, 1929).

III. Secular Chamber Music

1. Collections

12 fünfstimmige Madrigale, ed. H. Leichtentritt (Leipzig, 1909).

12 fünfstimmige Madrigale, ed. A. Mendelssohn (Leipzig, 1911).

15 madrigals, ed. H. F. Redlich (London, 1954 ff.).

Collected madrigals in practical editions, ed. G. F. Malipiero (Vienna, 1967).

6 duets, ed. L. Landshoff (Leipzig, 1927).

Canzonette a tre voci, ed. G. Cesari (Milan, 1939) in *Istituzioni e Monumenti dell' Arte Musicale Italiana*, VI.

—— ed. H. Trede (Basle, 1951).

Scherzi musicali, ed. H. Trede (Kassel, n.d.).

Arie, canzonette e recitativi, ed. G. F. Malipiero (Milan, 1953).

Scherzi musicali [a una voce], ed. M. Flothuis (Amsterdam, 1958).

5 songs, ed. G. Hunter and C. Palisca (Bryn Mawr, 1963).

2. Individual Madrigals

A quest'olmo, ed. G. F. Malipiero (Milan, 1958).

Ardo, e scoprir, ed. R. Manning (New York, 1955).

Ardo, sì, ma non t'amo, ed. G. F. Malipiero (Venice, n.d.) in *Adriano Willaert e i suoi discendenti*.

Chiome d'oro, ed. R. Manning (New York, 1955).

Ecco mormorar l'onde, ed. H. Müller (Leipzig, 1924).

—— ed. L. Castellazzi (Buenos Aires, 1955).

Lamento d'Arianna [complete], ed. G. Wolters (Wolfenbüttel, 1961).

—— ed. C. Perinello (Milan, 1919) in *Raccolta Nazionale delle Musiche Italiane*.

Lasciatemi morire, ed. J. A. Parkinson (Llangollen, 1954).

—— ed. L. Castellazzi (New York, 1955).

Non più guerra, ed. H. and E. Ross (New York, 1955).

Ohimè, se tanto amate, ed. H. and E. Ross (New York, 1955).

Poichè del mio dolore, ed. A. Payson (New York, 1964).

Sestina, ed. D. Randolph (New York, 1956).

—— ed. G. Wolters (Wolfenbüttel, 1961).

Stracciami pur il core, ed. C. Burney (London, 1789) in *A General History of Music*.

Su, su, su, ed. L. Castellazzi (New York, 1951).

T'amo, mia vita, ed.? (London, 1883).

Tu dormi, ed. D. Smithers (New York, 1964).

IV. Church Music

1. Collections

Sacrae Cantiunculae, ed. G. Terrabugio (Milan, 1910).

—— ed. G. Cesari (Milan, 1939) in *Istituzioni e Monumenti dell'Arte Musicale Italiana*, VI.

Bibliography

Sacrae Cantiunculae, ed. Janos Gabor (Budapest, 1943).
Vespro della Beata Vergine, ed. H. F. Redlich (Vienna, 1949).
—— ed. G. F. Ghedini (Milan, 1952).
—— ed. G. Wolters (excerpts, Wolfenbüttel, 1954 ff; complete in one vol., Wolfenbüttel & Zürich, 1966).
—— ed. W. Goehr (Vienna, 1957).
—— ed. H. F. Redlich (Kassel, 1958): revised edition.
—— ed. D. Stevens (London, 1961).

2. Individual Works
Angelus ad pastores, ed. K. G. Fellerer (Mainz, 1936).
—— ed. R. Field (New York, 1964).
Ave Maria, ed. H. Hucke (Regensburg, 1962).
Ave Maris Stella, ed. G. Biella (Milan, 1964) in *Musica Sacra, rivista bimestrale*.
Beatus Vir, ed. J. Steele (London, 1965).
Christe, adoramus te, ed. R. Jesson (London, 1967); supplement to *Musical Times*, May 1967.
Crucifixus a 4, ed. E. Gross (Sydney, n.d.).
—— ed.? (Düsseldorf, n.d.).
Currite populi, ed. C. Pineau (Paris, 1914).
Exultant caeli, ed.? (Milan, 1963) in *Musica Sacra, rivista bimestrale*.
Exulta filia, ed. D. Arnold (London, 1960).
Hodie Christus natus est, ed. R. Field (New York, 1964).
In tua patientia, ed.? (Milan, n.d.) in *Musica Sacra* series.
Lauda Sion, ed. R. Venè (New York, 1960).
—— ed. H. Hucke (Regensburg, n.d.).
Laudate Dominum, ed. D. Arnold (London, 1966).
Magnificat a sei voci, ed. K. Matthaei (Kassel, 1942).
—— ed. D. Arnold (London, 1967).
Messa a quattro voci (1640), ed. A. Tirabassi (Brussels, 1914).
—— ed. D. Arnold (London, 1962).
Messa a quattro voci (1651), ed. B. Somma (Rome, 1948).
—— ed. H. F. Redlich (London, 1952).
Messa a sei voci (1610), ed. H. F. Redlich (London, 1962).

O beatae viae, ed. W. Goehr (London, 1960).

O bone Jesu, ed. L. Castellazzi (Llangollen, 1947).

O Domine Jesu Christe, ed. G. F. Spinelli (Milan, 1963) in *Musica Sacra* series.

O quam pulchra, ed. F. Vatielli (Turin, 1922) in *Antiche Cantate Spirituali*.

Quam pulchra es, ed.? (Milan, n.d.) in *Musica Sacra* series.

Salve, O Regina, ed. R. Ewerhart (Cologne, 1957).

Salve Regina a una voce, ed. C. Pineau (Paris, 1914).

Salve Regina a due voci, ed.? (Milan, 1966) in *Musica Sacra, rivista bimestrale*.

Sonata sopra Sancta Maria, ed. L. Torchi (Milan, 1907) in *L'Arte Musicale in Italia*, VI.

——— ed. B. Molinari (Milan, 1919): 'versione ritmica e strumentale'.

Surgens Jesus Dominus, ed.? (Milan, n.d.) in *Musica Sacra* series.

Veni sponsa Christi, ed. R. Venè (New York, 1960).

SECTION B — BOOKS

Abert, Anna Amalie, *Claudio Monteverdi und das musikalische Drama* (Lippstadt, 1954).

Ademollo, Alessandro, *La bell'Adriana ed altre virtuose del suo tempo alla corte di Mantova* (Città di Castello, 1888).

Adrio, Adam, *Die Anfänge des geistlichen Konzerts* (Berlin, 1935).

Arnold, Denis, *Monteverdi* (London, 1963).

——— *Monteverdi Madrigals* (London, 1967).

Artusi, Giovanni Maria, *L'Artusi ovvero delle imperfettioni della moderna musica*, I (Venice, 1600); II (Venice, 1603).

——— *Discorso secondo musicale di Antonio Braccino da Todi* (Venice, 1608); facsimile edition (Milan, 1924).

Banchieri, Adriano, *Lettere armoniche* (Bologna, 1628).

Bertolotti, Antonio, *Musici alla Corte dei Gonzaga in Mantova dal secolo XV al XVIII* (Milan, 1891).

Caffi, Francesco, *Storia della musica sacra nella già cappella ducale di San Marco in Venezia dal 1318 al 1797* (Venice, 1854); facsimile edition (Milan, 1931).

Bibliography

Canal, Pietro, *Della musica in Mantova* (Venice, 1881).

Davari, Stefano, *Notizie biografiche del distinto maestro di musica Claudio Monteverdi* (Mantua, 1884).

Einstein, Alfred, *The Italian Madrigal*, 3 vols. (Princeton, 1949).

Goldschmidt, Hugo, *Studien zur Geschichte der italienischen Oper*, 2 vols. (Leipzig, 1901–4).

Kreidler, Walter, *Heinrich Schütz und der Stile Concitato von Claudio Monteverdi* (Stuttgart, 1934).

Malipiero, G. Francesco, *Claudio Monteverdi* (Milan, 1929).

Martini, Giambattista, *Esemplare o sia Saggio fondamentale di Contrappunto* (Bologna, 1774–5; facsimile edition (Farnborough 1965)).

Müller, Karl Friedrich, *Die Technik der Ausdrucksdarstellung in Monteverdis monodischen Frühwerken* (Berlin, 1931).

Osthoff, Wolfgang, *Das dramatische Spätwerk Claudio Monteverdis* (Tutzing, 1960).

de'Paoli, Domenico, *Claudio Monteverdi* (Milan, 1945).

Passuth, L., *A mantuai herceg muzsikusa, Claudio Monteverdi korának regényes törtenete* (Budapest, 1959); German trans. as *Monteverdi: Der Roman eines grossen Musikers* (Vienna, etc., 1959).

Prunières, Henry, *La vie et l'œuvre de C. Monteverdi* (Paris, 1924, 2nd ed., 1931); English translation (London, 1926).

Redlich, Hans Ferdinand, *Claudio Monteverdi. Ein formgeschichtlicher Versuch* (Berlin, 1932).

—— *Claudio Monteverdi. Leben und Werk* (Olten, 1949); a revised English version appeared as *Claudio Monteverdi. Life and Works* (London, 1952).

Le Roux, Maurice, *Claudio Monteverdi* (Paris, 1951).

Santoro, Elia, *La famiglia e la formazione di Claudio Monteverdi; note biografiche con documenti inediti* (Cremona, 1967).

Sartori, Claudio, *Monteverdi* (Brescia, 1953).

Schneider, Louis, *Un précurseur de la musique italienne aux XVIe et XVIIe siècles. Claudio Monteverdi* (Paris, 1921).

Schrade, Leo, *Monteverdi, Creator of modern music* (London, 1950; repr. 1964).

Tellart, R., *Claudio Monteverdi, l'homme et son œuvre* (Paris, 1964).

Tiby, Ottavio, '*L'Incoronazione di Poppea*' *di Claudio Monteverdi* (Florence, 1937).

—— *C. Monteverdi* (Turin, 1944).

SECTION C — ARTICLES

Ademollo, Alessandro, 'I Basile alla corte di Mantova', *Giornale Ligustico*, XI (1895).

Adrio, Adam, 'Ambrosius Profe (1589–1661) als Herausgeber italienischer Musik seiner Zeit', *Festschrift Karl Gustav Fellerer zum sechzigsten Geburtstag*, ed. Heinrich Hüschen (Regensburg, 1962).

Anon., 'Preziose scoperte di autografi di Claudio Monteverdi', *La Bibliofilia*, XXXVIII (1937).

Apel, Willi, 'Anent a ritornello in Monteverdi's Orfeo', *Musica Disciplina*, V (1951).

Arkwright, G. E. P., 'An English pupil of Monteverdi [Walter Porter]', *The Musical Antiquary*, IV (1912–13).

Arnold, Denis, 'Alessandro Grandi, a disciple of Monteverdi', *Musical Quarterly*, XLIII (1957).

—— ' "Il Ritorno d'Ulisse" and the chamber duet', *Musical Times*, CVI (1965).

—— ' "L'Incoronazione di Poppea" and its orchestral requirements', *Musical Times*, CIV (1963).

—— 'Monteverdi and the art of war', *Musical Times*, CVIII (1967).

—— 'Monteverdi the instrumentalist', *Recorder & Music Magazine*, II (1967).

—— 'Monteverdi's church music: some Venetian traits', *Monthly Musical Record*, LXXXVIII (1958).

—— 'Music at a Venetian confraternity in the Renaissance', *Acta Musicologica*, XXXVII (1965).

—— 'Notes on two movements of the Monteverdi "Vespers" ', *Monthly Musical Record*, LXXXIV (1954).

—— ' "Seconda pratica": a background to Monteverdi's madrigals', *Music & Letters*, XXXVIII (1957).

—— 'The influence of ornamentation on the structure of early

17th century church music', *Bericht über den siebenten Internationalen Musikwissenschaftlichen Kongress, Köln 1958* (Kassel, etc., 1959).

—— 'The Monteverdi Vespers — a postscript', *Musical Times*, CIV (1963).

—— 'The Monteverdian succession at St. Mark's', *Music & Letters*, XLII (1961).

—— 'The significance of "Cori spezzati" ', *Music & Letters*, XL (1959).

Benvenuti, Giacomo, 'Il manoscritto veneziano della Incoronazione di Poppea', *Rivista Musicale Italiana*, XLI (1937).

—— 'Il Ritorno d'Ulisse in Patria non è di Monteverdi' [*sic*!], *Il Gazzettino* (Venice, 17 May 1942).

Biella, Giuseppe, 'I "Vespri dei Santi" di Claudio Monteverdi', *Musica Sacra*, serie seconda, XI (1966).

—— 'La Messa, il Vespro e i sacri concenti di Claudio Monteverdi nella stampa Amadino del 1610', *Musica Sacra*, serie seconda, IX (1964).

Bonta, Stephen, 'Liturgical problems in Monteverdi's Marian Vespers', *Journal of the American Musicological Society*, XX (1967).

Borren, Charles van den, ' "Il Ritorno d'Ulisse in Patria" de Claudio Monteverdi', *Revue de l'Université de Bruxelles*, III (1925).

Boyden, David D., 'Monteverdi's *violini piccoli alla francese* and *viole da brazzo*', *Annales Musicologiques*, VI (1958–63).

Carse, Adam, 'Monteverde and the orchestra', *The Sackbut*, II (1921).

Castéra, R. de, 'L'Orfeo de Monteverdi', *Guide Musical*, L (1904).

Castiglione, Niccolò, 'Significato storico del melodramma nella prima metà del seicento', *Rassegna Musicale*, XXVI (1956).

Cesari, Gaetano, 'Die Entwicklung der Monteverdischen Kammermusik', *III. Kongress der IMG, Haydn-Zentenarfeier* (1909).

—— 'L' "Orfeo" di Claudio Monteverdi all' "Associazione di Amici della Musica" di Milano', *Rivista Musicale Italiana*, XVII (1910).

Chevaillier, Lucien, 'Le récit chez Monteverdi', *Revue d'Histoire et de Critique Musicales*, X (1910).

Chiereghin, Salvino, 'Claudio Monteverdi', *Rivista Musicale Italiana*, XLVII (1943).

Cimbro, Attilio, 'I Madrigali di Claudio Monteverdi', *Musica*, II (Florence, 1943).

Collaer, Paul, 'L'orchestra di Claudio Monteverdi', *Musica*, II (Florence, 1943).

Courville, Xavier de, 'L'Ariane de Monteverdi', *Revue Musicale*, III (1922).

Cucchetti, Gino, 'La tomba di Claudio Monteverdi finalmente identificata', *La Carovana* (1959).

Dallapiccola, Luigi, 'Per una rappresentazione di "Il Ritorno di Ulisse in Patria" di Claudio Monteverdi', *Musica*, II (Florence, 1943).

Damerini, Adelmo, 'Il senso religioso nelle musiche sacre di Claudio Monteverdi', *Collectanea Historiae Musicae*, IV (1966).

Damerini, Gino, 'Venezia al tempo di Monteverdi', *Musica*, II (Florence, 1943).

Davari, Stefano, 'La Musica a Mantova: notizie biografiche di maestri di musica, cantori e suonatori presso la corte di Mantova nei secoli XV, XVI, XVII, tratte dai documenti dell'Archivio Storico Gonzaga', *Rivista Storica Mantovana*, I (1884).

Einstein, Alfred, 'Abbot Angelo Grillo's letters as a source material for music history', *Essays on Music* (London, 1956). Originally published in German in *Kirchenmusikalisches Jahrbuch*, XXIV (1911).

Einstein, Alfred, 'Italian madrigal verse', *Proceedings of the Musical Association*, LXIII (1936–7).

—— '*Orlando Furioso* and *La Gerusalemme Liberata* as set to music during the 16th and 17th centuries', *Notes*, VIII (1951).

Epstein, Peter, 'Dichtung und Musik in Monteverdis *Lamento d'Arianna*', *Zeitschrift für Musikwissenschaft*, X (1927–8).

—— 'Monteverdi in unserer Zeit', *Die Musik*, XXII (1929–30).

—— 'Zur Rhythmisierung eines Ritornells von Monteverdi', *Archiv für Musikwissenschaft*, VIII (1926).

Fletcher, Iain, 'From Tasso to Marino', *Nine*, VII (1951).

Fortune, Nigel, 'A Handlist of printed Italian secular monody books, 1602–1635', *R.M.A. Research Chronicle*, III (1963).

Fortune, Nigel, 'Duet and trio in Monteverdi', *Musical Times*, CVIII (1967).

—— 'Italian secular monody from 1600 to 1635: an introductory survey', *Musical Quarterly*, XXXIX (1953).

—— 'Italian 17th-century singing', *Music & Letters*, XXXV (1954).

Gallico, Claudio, 'Emblemi strumentali negli "Scherzi" di Monteverdi', *Rivista Italiana di Musicologia*, II (1967).

—— 'La "Lettera amorosa" di Monteverdi e lo stile rappresentativo', *Nuova Rivista Musicale Italiana*, I (1967).

—— 'Monteverdi e i dazi di Viadana', *Rivista Italiana di Musicologia*, I (1966).

—— 'Newly discovered documents concerning Monteverdi', *Musical Quarterly*, XLVIII (1962).

Ghisi, Federico, 'L'orchestra in Monteverdi', *Festschrift Karl Gustav Fellerer zum sechzigsten Geburtstag*, ed. Heinrich Hüschen (Regensburg, 1962).

Goldschmidt, Hugo, 'Claudio Monteverdis Oper: Il Ritorno d'Ulisse in Patria', *Sammelbände der Internationalen Musikgesellschaft*, IX (1907–8).

—— 'Das Orchester der italienischen Oper im 17. Jahrhundert', *Sammelbände der Internationalen Musikgesellschaft*, II (1900–1).

—— 'Die Instrumentalbegleitung der italienischen Musikdramen in der ersten Hälfte des XVII. Jahrhunderts', *Monatshefte für Musikgeschichte*, XXVII (1895).

—— 'Monteverdis Ritorno d'Ulisse', *Sammelbände der Internationalen Musikgesellschaft*, IV (1902–3).

Grout, Donald J., 'The Chorus in early opera', *Festschrift Friedrich Blume zum 70. Geburtstag*, ed. Anna Amalie Abert and Wilhelm Pfannkuch (Kassel, etc., 1963).

Haas, Robert, 'Zur Neuausgabe von Claudio Monteverdis "Il Ritorno d'Ulisse in Patria"', *Studien zur Musikwissenschaft*, IX (1922).

Heuss, Alfred, 'Die Instrumental-Stücke des "Orfeo"', *Sammelbände der Internationalen Musikgesellschaft*, IV (1902–3).

—— 'Die venetianischen Opern-Sinfonien', *Sammelbände der Internationalen Musikgesellschaft*, IV (1902–3).

Heuss, Alfred, 'Ein Beitrag zu den Thema: Monteverdi als Charakteristiker in seinen Madrigalen', *Festschrift zum 90. Geburtstage Sr. Excellenz des Wirklichen Geheimen Rates Rochus Freiherrn von Liliencron* (Leipzig, 1910).

Howes, Frank, 'Notes on Monteverde's Orfeo', *Musical Times*, LXV (1924).

Hughes, Charles W., 'Porter, pupil of Monteverdi', *Musical Quarterly*, XX (1934).

Krenek, Ernst, 'Meine Textbearbeitung von Monteverdis "Poppea" ', *Anbruch*, XVIII (1936).

—— 'Zur dramaturgischen Bearbeitung von Monteverdis "Poppea" ', *23, eine Wiener Musikzeitschrift*, XXXI–XXXIII (1937).

—— 'Zur musikalischen Bearbeitung von Monteverdis "Poppea" ', *Schweizerische Musikzeitung*, LXXVI (1936).

Kretzschmar, Hermann, 'Die venetianische Oper und die Werke Cavallis und Cestis', *Vierteljahrsschrift für Musikwissenschaft*, VIII (1892).

—— 'Monteverdis "Incoronazione di Poppea" ', *Vierteljahrsschrift für Musikwissenschaft*, X (1894).

Laloy, Louis, 'Un précurseur du drame lyrique: Claudio Monteverdi', *Revue de Paris*, XXVIII (1921).

Leichtentritt, Hugo, 'Claudio Monteverdi als Madrigalkomponist', *Sammelbände der Internationalen Musikgesellschaft*, XI (1909–10).

—— 'On the prologue in early opera', *Proceedings of the Music Teachers' National Association*, XXXI (1936).

de Logu, Giuseppe, 'An unknown portrait of Monteverdi by Domenico Feti', *The Burlington Magazine*, CIX (1967).

Lunelli, Riccardo, 'Iconografia monteverdiana', *Rivista Musicale Italiana*, XLVII (1943).

Lupo, Bettina, 'Sacre monodie monteverdiane', *Musica*, II (Florence, 1943).

Maione, Italo, 'Tasso-Monteverdi: *Il Combattimento di Tancredi e Clorinda*', *Rassegna Musicale*, III (1930).

Malipiero, G. Francesco, 'Claudio Monteverdi', *Musica*, II (Florence, 1943).

Malipiero, G. Francesco, 'Claudio Monteverdi da Cremona', *Rassegna Musicale*, II (1929).

—— 'Claudio Monteverdi da Cremona', *Illustrazione* (1937).

—— 'Claudio Monteverdi of Cremona', *Musical Quarterly*, XVIII (1932).

Maragliano Mori, Rachele, 'Claudio Monteverdi, maestro di canto', *Rassegna Musicale,* XXI (1951).

Mitjana, Rafael, 'Claudio Monteverdi och det lyriska dramats uppkomst', *Ord och Bild*, XX (1911).

Noble, Jeremy, 'Monteverdi: methods and misconceptions', *Musical Times*, CIII (1962).

Ortolani, Giuseppe, 'Venezia al tempo di Monteverdi', *Rassegna Musicale*, II (1929).

Osthoff, Helmuth, 'Gedichte von Tomaso Stigliani auf Giulio Caccini, Claudio Monteverdi, Santino Garsi da Parma und Claudio Merulo', *Miscelánea en homenaje a Monseñor Higinio Anglès*, II (Barcelona, 1961).

Osthoff, Wolfgang, 'Die venezianische und neapolitanische Fassung von Monteverdis "Incoronazione di Poppea"', *Acta Musicologica*, XXVI (1954).

—— 'Monteverdi-Funde', *Archiv für Musikwissenschaft*, XIV (1957).

—— 'Monteverdis Combattimento in deutscher Sprache und Heinrich Schütz', *Festschrift Helmuth Osthoff zum 65. Geburtstage*, ed. Lothar Hoffmann-Erbrecht and Helmuth Hucke (Tutzing, 1961).

—— 'Neue Beobachtungen zu Quellen und Geschichte von Monteverdis "Incoronazione di Poppea"', *Die Musikforschung*, XI (1958).

—— 'Per la notazione originale nelle pubblicazioni di musiche antiche e specialmente nella nuova edizione Monteverdi', *Acta Musicologica*, XXXIV (1962).

—— 'Trombe sordine', *Archiv für Musikwissenschaft*, XIII (1956).

—— 'Zu den Quellen von Monteverdis Ritorno d'Ulisse in Patria', *Studien zur Musikwissenschaft*, XXIII (1956).

—— 'Zur Bologneser Aufführung von Monteverdis "Ritorno

d'Ulisse" im Jahre 1640', *Oesterreichische Akademie der Wissenschaften: Anzeiger der Phil.-hist. Klasse*, XCV (1958).

Palisca, Claude V., 'Vincenzo Galilei's counterpoint treatise: a code for the "Seconda Pratica"', *Journal of the American Musicological Society*, IX (1956).

Pannain, Guido, 'Claudio Monteverdi nell' "opera in musica"', *Musica*, II (Florence, 1943).

—— 'Studi monteverdiani', *Rassegna Musicale*, XXVIII–XXXI (1958–61), and *Quaderni della Rassegna Musicale*, III (1965).

de'Paoli, Domenico, 'A few remarks on "Orfeo" by Claudio Monteverdi', *The Chesterian*, XX (1939).

—— 'Claudio Monteverdi', *Bolletino Bibliografico Musicale*, IV (1929).

—— ' "Orfeo" and "Pelléas"', *Music & Letters*, XX (1939).

Parry, C. Hubert H., 'The significance of Monteverde', *Proceedings of the Musical Association*, XLII (1915–16).

Picenardi, Guido Sommi, 'D'alcuni documenti concernenti Claudio Monteverde', *Archivio Storico Lombardo,* serie terza, IV (1895).

Prunières, Henry, 'L'Orfeo de Monteverdi', *Revue Musicale*, IV (1923).

—— 'Monteverdi à la chapelle de Saint-Marc', *Revue Musicale*, VII (1926).

—— 'Monteverdi and French music', *The Sackbut*, III (1922).

—— 'Monteverdi e la musica francese del suo tempo', *Rassegna Musicale*, II (1929).

—— 'Monteverdi's Venetian operas', *Musical Quarterly*, X (1924).

—— 'The Italian cantata of the XVIIth century', *Music & Letters*, VII (1926).

Pulver, Jeffrey, 'Claudio Monteverdi', *The Strad*, XXV–XXVI (1915–16).

Quittard, Henri, 'L'Orchestre de l'*Orfeo*', *Revue d'Histoire et de Critique Musicales*, VII (1907).

Redlich, Hans F., 'Aufgaben und Ziele der Monteverdi-Forschung', *Die Musikforschung*, IV (1951).

—— 'Claudio Monteverdi: some problems of textual interpretation', *Musical Quarterly*, XLI (1955).

Bibliography

Redlich, Hans F., 'Claudio Monteverdi: zum Problem der praktischen Ausgabe seiner Werke', *Schweizerische Musikzeitung*, XIX–XX (1934). Translated into Italian as: 'Sull'edizione moderna delle opere di Claudio Monteverdi', *Rassegna Musicale*, VIII (1935).

—— 'Das Orchester Claudio Monteverdis, i: Instrumentalpraxis in Monteverdis Madrigalwerk', *Musica Viva*, I (1936).

—— 'Monteverdi', *Die Musik in Geschichte und Gegenwart*, IX (Kassel, etc., 1961).

—— 'Monteverdi', *Grove's Dictionary of Music and Musicians*, 5th ed. (London, 1954), and supplementary volume (London, 1961).

—— 'Monteverdi e l'orchestra', *L'Orchestra* [in onore Gino Marinuzzi, 1882–1945] (Florence, 1954).

—— 'Monteverdi-Gesamtausgabe', *Anbruch*, X (1928).

—— 'Monteverdi-Renaissance', *Atlantis*, VIII (1936).

—— 'Monteverdis "Incoronazione di Poppea"', *Schweizerische Musikzeitung*, LXXVII (1937).

—— 'Monteverdis Kirchenmusik', *Anbruch*, XVII (1935).

—— 'Monteverdi's religious music', *Music & Letters*, XXVII (1946).

—— 'Neue Monteverdiana', *Anbruch*, XIII (1931).

—— 'Notationsprobleme in Cl. Monteverdis "Incoronazione di Poppea"', *Acta Musicologica*, X (1938).

—— 'Notes to a new edition of Monteverdi's Mass of 1651', *Monthly Musical Record*, LXXXIII (1953).

—— 'The Editing of Monteverdi', *Renaissance News*, VII (1954).

—— 'The Re-Discovery of Monteverdi, on the occasion of a new edition of *L'Incoronazione di Poppea*', *Music Review*, XXIII (1962).

—— 'Zu Monteverdis letzte Oper', *Anbruch*, XIX (1937).

—— 'Zur Bearbeitung von Monteverdis "Orfeo"', *Schweizerische Musikzeitung*, LXXVI (1936).

Reiner, Stuart, 'Preparations in Parma — 1618, 1627–28', *Music Review*, XXV (1964).

Riemann, Hugo, 'Eine siebensätzige Tanzsuite von Monteverdi

Bibliography

v. J. 1607', *Sammelbände der Internationalen Musikgesellschaft*, XIV (1912–13).

Ronga, Luigi, 'La vocalità nella musica italiana da Palestrina a Monteverdi', *Letterature Moderne*, I (1950).

—— 'Su Monteverdi e sull'opera italiana del seicento', *Rivista Musicale Italiana*, LVII (1955).

—— 'Tasso e Monteverdi', *Poesia*, I (1945).

Rose, Gloria, 'Agazzari and the improvising orchestra', *Journal of the American Musicological Society*, XVIII (1965).

Rosenthal, Albi, 'A hitherto unpublished letter of Claudio Monteverdi', *Essays presented to Egon Wellesz*, ed. Jack Westrup (Oxford, 1966).

Sartori, Claudio, 'Monteverdiana', *Musical Quarterly*, XXXVIII (1952).

Schmitz, Eugen, 'Zur Geschichte des italienischen Continuo-Madrigals im 17. Jahrhundert', *Sammelbände der Internationalen Musikgesellschaft*, XI (1909–10).

—— 'Zur Geschichte des italienischen Kammerduetts im 17. Jahrhundert', *Jahrbuch der Musikbibliothek Peters*, XXIII (1916).

Schrade, Leo, 'Claudio Monteverdi — ein Revolutionär der Musikgeschichte', *Neue Zeitschrift der Musik*, CXXIII (1962). Reprinted in Leo Schrade, *De Scientia Musicae Studia atque Orationes*, ed. Ernst Liechtenhahn (Stuttgart, 1967).

—— 'Monteverdi's *Il Ritorno d'Ulisse*', *Musical Quarterly*, XXXVI (1950). An extract from Schrade's book listed in Section B.

—— 'Sulla natura del ritmo barocco', *Rivista Musicale Italiana*, LVI (1954).

Schwartz, Rudolf, 'Zu den Texten der ersten fünf Bücher der Madrigale Monteverdis', *Festschrift: Hermann Kretzschmar zum siebzigsten Geburtstage* (Leipzig, 1918).

Solerti, Angelo, 'Un balletto musicato da Claudio Monteverde sconosciuto a' suoi biografi', *Rivista Musicale Italiana*, VII (1904).

Sonneck, O. G., 'Italienische Opernlibretti des 17. Jahrhunderts in der Library of Congress', *Sammelbände der Internationalen Musikgesellschaft*, XIII (1911–12).

Stevens, Denis, '*Madrigali Guerrieri, et Amorosi*: a reappraisal for the quatercentenary', *Musical Quarterly*, LIII (1967).

—— 'Monteverdi's Venetian church music', *Musical Times*, CVIII (1967).

—— 'Ornamentation in Monteverdi's shorter dramatic works', *Bericht über den siebenten Internationalen Musikwissenschaftlichen Kongress, Köln 1958* (Kassel, etc., 1959).

—— 'Where are the Vespers of yesteryear?', *Musical Quarterly*, XLVII (1961).

Stuart, Robert Louis, 'Busenello's libretto to Monteverde's "L'Incoronazione di Poppea": its place in the history of the drama and the opera', *Musical Times*, LXVIII (1927).

—— 'Busenello's "L'Incoronazione di Poppea"', *Musical Opinion*, LI (1928).

Tessier, André, 'Les deux styles de Monteverde', *Revue Musicale*, III (1922).

—— 'Monteverdi e la filosofia dell'arte', *Rassegna Musicale*, II (1929).

Tiersot, Julien, 'L'Orfeo de Monteverde', *Le Ménéstrel*, LXX (1904).

Torrefranca, Fausto, 'Il Lamento di Erminia di Claudio Monteverdi [*sic*!]', *Inedito*, II (1944).

Vogel, Emil, 'Claudio Monteverdi', *Vierteljahrsschrift für Musikwissenschaft*, III (1887).

Weaver, Robert L., 'The Orchestra in early Italian opera', *Journal of the American Musicological Society*, XVII (1964).

Weismann, Wilhelm, 'Ein verkannter Madrigal-Zyklus Monteverdis [*Ecco Silvio*]', *Deutsches Jahrbuch der Musikwissenschaft für 1957* (1958).

Wellesz, Egon, 'Cavalli und der Stil der venetianischen Oper vom 1640–1660', *Studien zur Musikwissenschaft*, I (1913).

—— 'Die Aussetzung des Basso Continuo in der italienischen Oper', *International Musical Society. Fourth Congress Report* (London, 1912).

Westrup, J. A., 'Claudio Monteverdi', *The Heritage of Music*, III (London, 1951).

—— 'Monteverde's "Il Ritorno d'Ulisse in Patria"', *Monthly Musical Record*, LVIII (1928).

Bibliography

Westrup, J.A., 'Monteverde's Orfeo', *Musical Times*, LXVI (1925).

—— 'Monteverde's "Poppea" ', *Musical Times*, LXVIII (1927).

—— 'Monteverdi and the madrigal', *The Score*, I (1949).

—— 'Monteverdi and the orchestra', *Music & Letters,* XXI (1940).

—— 'Monteverdi's "Lamento d'Arianna" ', *Music Review*, I (1940).

—— 'Stages in the history of opera, i: Claudio Monteverde', *Musical Times*, LXX (1929).

—— 'The Originality of Monteverde', *Proceedings of the Musical Association*, LX (1933–4).

—— 'Two first performances: Monteverdi's "Orfeo" and Mozart's "Clemenza di Tito" ', *Music & Letters*, XXXIX (1958).

Willetts, Pamela J., 'A neglected source of monody and madrigal', *Music & Letters*, XLIII (1962).

Worsthorne, Simon Towneley, 'Venetian theatres: 1637–1700', *Music & Letters*, XXIX (1948).

Zimmerman, Franklin B., 'Purcell and Monteverdi', *Musical Times*, XCIX (1958).

Index

Index

Capello, Giovanni Francesco, 123
Carissimi, Giacomo, 119, 191
Casa, Girolamo dalla, 137-8
Casola, Don Bassano, 205 n
Cavalieri, Emilio de', 91, 160 n, 260, 281
Cavalli, Francesco, 123, 129, 285-90 *passim*, 292, 294, 296
Cesti, Marc'Antonio, 282, 289-92 *passim*
Chiabrera, Gabriello, 200
Chieppo, Annibale, 26-9
Cifra, Antonio, 222
Clemens non Papa, 91, 167
Collaer, Paul, 248 n, 258 n
Contarini Codices, 283, 286
Costa, Francesco, 203
Cotta, Padre Ansaldo, 232
Coussemaker, Edmond de, 139 n
Coxe, William, 242 n
Crequillon, 91, 167
Crotti, Francesco, 123

Davison, Archibald T., 214 n
Diruta, Girolamo, 164, 166
Donati, Ignazio, 169
Donato, Baldissare, 116
Donfrid, Johannes, 230 n
Doni, Giovanni Battista, 83, 194, 204, 260 n, 268, 286, 293
Donington, Robert, 267 n

Earle, John, 234
Einstein, Alfred, 96, 155 n, 209 n, 251 n, 252
Eitner, Robert, 257 n
d'Este, Alfonso, 108

Farnese, Odoardo, 61, 73, 74, 76, 80, 81
Faustini, Marco, 284, 291, 292
Federhofer, Hellmut, 233 n
Ferdinand II (Emperor), 70, 231, 233, 234, 238, 240-2 *passim*
Ferdinand III (Emperor), 231, 233, 238, 240-5 *passim*

Ferand, Ern[e]st T., 140 n, 267 n
Ferrari, Benedetto, 234
Ficino, Marsilio, 162
Fiorino, Ippolito, 26, 28
Foerster, Kaspar, 166
Fogliani, Alfonso, 145
Follino, Federico, 26, 27, 29, 235 n
Fontanella, Alfonso, 91, 145, 160 n
Fortune, Nigel, 121 n, 193 n, 195 n, 199 n, 204 n, 293
Foscarini, Giovanni Battista, 66
Franceschini, Petronio, 288
Franzoni, Amante, 117, 118, 123
Freschi, Giovanni Domenico, 291, 292
Frescobaldi, Girolamo, 109, 119, 190 n

Gabrieli, Andrea, 93, 168
Gabrieli, Giovanni, 123, 178, 196, 283 n
Gabussi, Giulo Cesare, 232
Gaffurio, Franchino, 154
Gagliano, Marco da, 26, 28, 68, 108, 144, 194, 204, 222
Galilei, Vincenzo, 86, 141-2, 148 n, 152-3, 154, 159 n, 163, 164 n
Gaspari, Gaetano, 142 n, 169 n
Gastoldi, Giovanni, 31, 115-8 *passim*, 122
Gesualdo, Carlo, 91, 107, 108, 111, 114, 160 n, 194, 220, 238
Ghisi, Federico, 251 n
Ghizzolo, Giovanni, 169
Girelli, Santino, 187
Giustiniani, Vincenzo, 228 n
Glareanus, 152
Goldschmidt, Hugo, 128 n, 290
Gombert, Nicolas, 91, 92, 167, 170, 173, 174-6, 177
Gonzaga, Eleonora, 232
Gonzaga, Ferdinando II, 34-6, 38, 39-47 *passim*, 52-9 *passim*, 110, 115, 205 n, 232
Gonzaga, Francesco II, 25, 38, 115
Gonzaga, Francesco, 40, 42
Gonzaga, Guglielmo, 99
Gonzaga, Scipione, 144

Index

A *carro* forming part of the wedding celebrations in Mantua in 1608, dep
Città di Ma